THE *THINKING CL*
Series editor: C

The *Thinking Clearly* series sets out the main issues in a variety of important subjects. Written from a mainstream Christian stand-point, the series combines clear biblical teaching with up-to-date scholarship. Each of the contributors is an authority in his or her field. The series is written in straightforward everyday language, and each volume includes a range of practical applications and guidance for further reading.

The series has two main aims:
1. To help Christians understand their faith better.
2. To show how Christian truths can illuminate matters of crucial importance in our society.

Also in the *Thinking Clearly* series:

THE *THINKING CLEARLY* SERIES

Series editor: Clive Calver

Angels

JOHN WOOLMER

MONARCH
BOOKS

Mill Hill, London and Grand Rapids, Michigan

First published by Monarch Books in the UK 2003,
Concorde House, Grenville Place,
Mill Hill, London, NW7 3SA.

Distributed by:
UK: STL, PO Box 300, Kingstown Broadway, Carlisle,
Cumbria CA3 0QS;
USA: Kregel Publications, PO Box 2607, Grand Rapids,
Michigan 49501.

ISBN 1 85424 606 2 (UK)
ISBN 0 8254 6216 9 (USA)

British Library Cataloguing Data
A catalogue record for this book is available
from the British Library.

Book design and production for the publishers by
Bookprint Creative Services
P.O. Box 827, BN21 3YJ, England.
Printed in Great Britain.

Contents

Dedication:

For Joyce (with Cyril and Lis),
Parish Secretary extraordinary, decipherer of hieroglyphics,
typist, sub-editor, encourager and friend.

Acknowledgements

With grateful thanks to all who have shared their experiences which have made the writing of this book possible: to Michael Green for invaluable theological advice, to Alison Morgan for much help with Chapter 7, to Deborah Wearing for contributing her testimony in Chapter 10, to Peter S Williams author of *The Case for Angels* for helpful criticism, and above all to Jane for the gift of a fountain pen and for her immense patience in helping me to understand a few of the mysteries of the word processor. Finally, to Joyce Martin, for as ever, wrestling with her former rector's manuscript, and to Monarch Books for much editorial critique, kindness, availability and encouragement.

Foreword

I have never, I believe, seen an angel for myself. I am beginning to revise that view for all sorts of reasons; but I can certainly say I have never seen the orthodox sort of angel, all in white with shining wings and an other-worldly smile. I think I have always known they exist, though I wouldn't have been able to tell you why.

I began to take a proper interest in angels when I shook myself out of some of my early, simplistic understandings of my Christian faith and asked myself what it was I really did believe. At one stage in the journey I listened awestruck to Bishop Michael Marshall talking about Mary and her meeting with Gabriel (Luke 1:26ff), the messenger who carried the most precious news the world had ever known so that Mary might do the same. Bishop Michael called her the first evangelist, "receiving Jesus into herself in order to bring Him to others". And there, awesome and quiet, stood the Angel; one who also "stands in the presence of God". I had reason years later to remember those words, when Kate described the towering golden figures filling the corners of the room where we were praying for a tormented and violent man (see p. 24).

I started properly to read the Bible, and found angels arriving from every direction and in the most unexpected ways. They flew into my life in other forms, too. When David Wynne's magnificent "Majestas" was completed and unveiled high up on the West front of Wells Cathedral in 1986, the figure of

Christ was flanked by two angels, looking wild and dangerous. I spent hours looking up at them. I came across a painting by Caravaggio dated 1598 in which the "youthful angel" so delicately guiding the hand of St Matthew as he writes his Gospel "seems just to have arrived from on high", in the words of the art historian E. H. Gombrich (p. 12, *The Story of Art*, 15th Edn., Phaidon). I could swear that I heard the rush of wind. Angels were real. They came to people, and they carried with them the fragrance of Jesus. They came with greetings, with peace in their wings; and so often with words like Gabriel's, "do not be afraid". But they also came to do business. My mother could certainly testify to that, from her experience of answered prayer, crying out in anguish for my ailing father in a Spanish hotel room late in her life. So could many of those people we met in Rwanda, just after the genocide.

I am very grateful for this book and for the clarity of John Woolmer's blending of scholarship and experience. Word and Spirit come together in an earthed understanding of life which comes only from a heart and mind which long to know God. That doesn't surprise me, from years of knowing the author. I am glad to read straightforward statements about angels both of light and of darkness, and that angels intervene, and can deceive: to read the words of the early Fathers, to see the Koran quoted as well as the Bible, to receive the most remarkable testimonies (and among them not least the words of Deborah in Chapter 10), and to find the whole built on foundations of exploration and clarity in theology which tally closely with my own experience in the church and the world. It is good to have it stated that "unusual spiritual experience can make for light heads, and poor theological judgment". On the other hand John's sentence, "as a mathematician, I would maintain that the simplest explanation, the literal one, is most likely to be correct" also rings true, especially in a church which often – in a very worldly way – longs to rationalise matters of faith, applying ever more cerebral entanglements in order to make the facts fit the ideology, until casuistry reigns. This book resonates with the good sense of those words of C. S. Lewis, "Reality is usually something you could not have guessed. That is one of the reasons I believe Christianity. It is a religion you could not have guessed. If it offered up just the kind of Universe we had always expected, I should feel we were making it up. It has just that queer taste about it that real things have."

There is crucial truth in all this – not in some propositional, doctrinal way; but rather following that dictum of James Fowler in *Stages of Faith* (Harper 1995), "Truth is lived; it is a pattern of being in relation to others and to God." This book has been written out of passion and with intellectual clout; clear-thinking, clear-seeing, straight-speaking. It is eloquent of faith in God. I am very glad of it.

Perhaps the last word should rest with a card which is pinned above the desk in a friend's office in London and reads simply, "Angels can fly because they take themselves lightly." How I long for an understanding in me and in the church I love which allows us, indeed draws us to take ourselves lightly: and which, like those who stand in His presence, compels us to take God very seriously indeed.

Martin Cavender, Abingdon
February 2003

Introduction

Dear Reverend Woolmer,

I remember when you told us about people who had seen angels. It was very exciting. Imagine seeing an angel! Thank you for all the interesting assemblies you have done for us. Good luck!

Love from Arminel

I remember when you told us that some people you knew had seen an angel. I never knew that angels were real.

From Lewis

These letters were two of many from the pupils of St Paul's Junior School, Shepton Mallet, written after my final weekly assembly. I don't think that I had talked about angels very often, but they featured in a surprising number of the charming farewell letters.

Modern people, especially the theologically erudite, often dismiss angels as part of an outdated spiritual culture, which we neither need nor should believe in. By contrast, a significant minority seem to display an inordinate interest in both angels and "spirit guides". There has been a huge proliferation of books about angels, both from Christian and New Age writers. The latter often have a dangerous veneer of Christianity in their early pages, but invariably end up commending practices which are clearly forbidden in Scripture. "Rent an Angel" would seem to be a rather irreverent summary of some of them. There seems to be a considerable need for the gift of discernment. St Paul's words about prophecy: "Test everything" (1 Thessalonians 5:21) apply equally powerfully to experiences with angelic powers.

Angels have often been the subject of theological debate and controversy. The magnificent medieval wagon roof of St Peter & St Paul's Church, in my former parish of Shepton Mallet, bears witness to ancient battles. The angel guarding the north west corner of the roof is well peppered with grapeshot, fired in 1645 by Cromwell's soldiers in the Civil War. Godly Puritans regarded the carved images of angels as highly offensive.

Much earlier, the Fathers of the church wrote and preached much about angels. Great men like Anthony of Egypt, who died in 356, were familiar with spiritual beings – both good and evil. Augustine of Hippo, who died in 430, even baptised a man who previously had had an after-death experience with angels in Paradise.

This book is an attempt to write something that is biblical, experiential and critical. I am increasingly conscious of the difficulty of the task, and of the vast amount of material available. In Scripture, there are over 300 specific references to angels, without including texts which mention archangels, seraphim, and principalities.

People often ask me in what forms angels appear. There seem to be three main categories of experiences. Some people have seen visions of "traditional angels", dressed in white, accompanied by very bright light; others have experienced help and protection from apparently "real people" who have come and gone so quickly, and acted so efficiently, that often an angelic explanation seems by far the most likely; a third group of experiences involve unexpected protection from serious danger. In these cases, like the servant of Elisha in 2 Kings 6, those protected have been unaware of angelic help until after the event.

Inevitably, in the book, there are many contemporary stories. I have only included those which seemed theologically important, and whose integrity I feel confident about. Not all are in the strictest sense about angels, because there is a *considerable overlap* between supernatural experiences and angelic ones. Luke (see Acts 16:9, 18:9, 22:17, 23:11 and 27:23) gives five similar examples of

God communicating with Paul, but only the incident in the storm at
sea includes an angel. Paul, himself, in his great vision of Paradise,
described in 2 Corinthians 12, does not mention angels, but this
experience is highly relevant to our subject.

This is not a book about spiritual warfare, and hence the Book of
Revelation has been touched on very lightly. It is, I hope, a book
that may help people's faith and discernment. Strange things do
happen, strange experiences do occur. How are these to be tested in
the clear light of Scripture? What is the relevance of angels to our
post-modern culture? Can angels deceive? Far more importantly,
what did Jesus, and the rest of Scripture, teach about such experiences?

My belief is that angels are a wonderful part of God's creation.
We must neither exaggerate their significance, nor ignore them.
Usually, in Scripture, angels appear to help and instruct people,
acting by the sovereign command of God, but we are also warned
that "Satan himself masquerades as an angel of light" (2 Corinthians 11:14). In today's world, angels still appear to people, and we
need to know whether they are God's messengers or part of Satan's
fallen army. For the most part, the ministry of angels is invisible,
unnoticed except by a few discerning people. This book is written
for those who, like me, don't have that sort of spiritual experience,
and yet are willing to believe in, and wish to understand a little
better, this largely hidden world. We will face the inevitable question – Why do some people have these experiences while others are
denied them? Jesus' famous response to Thomas, "Because you
have seen me, you have believed; blessed are those who have not
seen me and yet have believed" (John 20:29) seems to answer this
frequently-asked question.

My hope is that this book, with all its omissions and inadequa-
cies, may help the reader to develop a spiritual sensibility to wend
his way through the theological minefield of scepticism and disbelief on the one hand, and naïve credulity on the other.

John Woolmer
June 2003

1

Postcards from Heaven?

The opening chapter is a personal account of eight experiences of some of the writer's closest friends. Eight jewels of varying intensity are strung together on the simple chain of friendship and trust. At the end of the chapter theological questions begin to be posed.

Postcards from Heaven?

Winchester Cathedral seems a beautifully safe place. Impeccable singing, marvellous architecture, and sensible orthodox Anglican worship, combine with a deep sense of history and beauty, to soothe rather than to challenge.

Jane Austen lies buried on the northern side of the nave. St Swithun, of rain-making fame lies, finally undisturbed, just outside the walls. Izaak Walton, theologian and fisherman extraordinary, is commemorated in a magnificent stained glass window. A 19th century diver who rescued the Cathedral from sinking into the mire of the water meadows of the Itchen has a generous statue. Somewhat less peacefully, the rather gruesome cadaver, or death mask, of the last Catholic bishop – the fearsome Stephen Gardiner of Queen Mary's unhappy reign – is there for all to see. Worshippers and tourists normally flock in.

It was a beautiful June afternoon. The ancient Cathedral seemed strangely still. The tourists were quiet, a small congregation prepared for an unusual event – unusual in the 1970s – a service of healing in an Anglican Cathedral.

Guidance in China (my first postcard)

The speaker was a small, seemingly elderly, man. He was in his sixties, but the ravages of wartime imprisonment by the Japanese made him look older. His high-pitched voice was quite difficult to hear. After the normal pleasantries, he launched into his talk with a personal reminiscence. Before the Second World War, Ken McAll[1] and his wife Frances had been missionaries in China. It was a threatening time, with constant danger both from the Red Army which was trying to wrest control from the Nationalistic government, and from the Japanese who were also invading parts of China. Ken, Eric Liddell,[2] and other mission workers were increasingly aware of God's direction, and protection.

Ken explained that one day, he was returning to Siaochang along the rough road through the fields and heading towards the village, when he was aware of someone walking behind him. He was told not go to that village, but to go instead to a different village, where he was needed. Ken took it to be the voice of a local farmer who knew what was going on. It was best not to show any fear by looking round. When he reached the village, the gate was opened, and he was pulled inside. The villagers asked him what had made him change direction (some of them had watched him from afar). Ken said "That man out there told me to come," but when he, and the locals, looked out there was no one else to be seen. Then Ken realised that his unseen companion had spoken in English – unlikely for a Chinese farmer! The villagers then told him that if he had continued in the direction that he was heading, he would have landed in a Japanese trap, as the village to which he had been walking was occupied by Japanese troops. Moreover, a local skirmish had left several wounded, some of whom had been brought into the village, and several people needed his medical attention. One of the wounded became a Christian, and eventually joined the staff of the teacher training college where Eric Liddell had taught.

Ken realised that his life had been saved by the direct intervention of the Lord. His world-view had changed. Writing about the incident,[3] he commented, "My mocking intolerance of the implicit belief of the Chinese in ghosts and the spirit world was gone. I understood, too, that the spirit world holds both good and evil influences, and I realised that my daily prayer for protection had been dramatically answered."

This was the highly unusual beginning to a very challenging talk. Ken continued with an account of his wartime captivity, shared with his wife, during which they had discovered that the power of prayer could replace unavailable medicines. As prisoners, they had been crammed into a freezing cold factory, into which some 1,200 prisoners had been herded by the Japanese. The talk then moved on to tell of his more recent experiences of healing, including new insights into psychiatry which he had gained during post-war studies. He spoke as though the sort of experiences that he was relating should be part of our normal Christian life.

I listened spellbound. I had attended the meeting reluctantly (and how often are the most important meetings and services the ones to which we go with the greatest reluctance?). I should have been umpiring on the nearby school cricket field, or driving my car to help a natural history expedition. Instead, at the bidding of a saintly colleague, who had a seemingly eccentric interest in places and people of healing, I had persuaded Jane, my newly-wed wife, to join me in the Cathedral.

For me, as an inexperienced young priest, that afternoon was another of God's turning points. A reluctant ordinand, and an uncertain school chaplain, I was still in a spiritual wilderness. Once or twice I had received very clear guidance. A previous period at a liberal theological college had almost convinced me that if God was only interested in creating dog-collared social workers, then there was no God. I was rescued from scepticism by the strange combination of a double family tragedy and the thoughtful direction of Faulkner Allison, the Bishop of Winchester. He sent me off to an evangelical college which restored my faith in the God of Scripture. A few strange students even seemed to believe that prayer really changed situations; and, even more alarmingly, that the God portrayed in the Acts of the Apostles could be encountered today. I had read about these sorts of experiences, but that afternoon in Winchester Cathedral was the first time I had ever heard someone speak directly about these sorts of things. A living testimony seemed worth a hundred books!

Eventually the speaker was done. A time of prayer followed including the laying-on of hands. My colleague, Philip, invited me to join him in the sanctuary. It would be nice to record that I witnessed instant answers to our prayers – I am not aware that we did, but I do know that I left the Cathedral with a rather different world-view. For the first time in my life, I had met someone who had experienced the Living Lord not only through conversion, and in prayer and worship; but also in power, in His presence, and in miracles.

A vision and a mission

After Kenneth McAll's testimony in Winchester Cathedral, I began to expect that God could, and would, intervene in everyday situations. I was able to organise a short mission in Winchester College, where I was the junior chaplain, in October 1974 with a well-known speaker. The time of mission was preceded by intense prayer. The previous August, Jane and I had been on holiday in the Tyrol, in Austria. Early one morning, I was praying outside our tent, and the Lord seemed to direct my eyes to a field of newly cut corn. The field sloped upwards, and at the base of the field there were about 30 corn stooks. Then I noticed a thin line of stooks stretching up the right hand side of the field over the horizon. God seemed to say to me, "Those nearest will be converted in next term's mission, and the work will continue for many years."

At the beginning of the autumn term Peter, a younger colleague and fellow mathematician, and I had a powerful and lengthy time of prayer, when I think we prayed for the whole school by name. The mission was unexpectedly and extraordinarily successful. About 30 boys seemed to be genuinely brought to faith, and when Jane and I left the college soon afterwards, for normal parish ministry, Peter took up the baton, and the work grew dramatically for about five years.[4]

In the midst of the growth period, Mark Stibbe, aged 16, became aware of the presence of committed Christians in his boarding house. He described his feelings:

> Another maths teacher, Peter, courageously continued to promote the work, encouraging the boys to meet in groups to read the Word, get right with God and pray for unsaved friends.
>
> In 1976, aged 16, I became aware of the presence of Christians in my boarding house. I was severely aggravated by this, and from time to time would disrupt the prayer meetings and bully those I knew were committed Christians. However, on 17th January 1977, I was walking down the High Street in the town late at night. I remember distinctly looking up at the stars and asking "Is there anybody out there?" Straight away, my heart started to beat very fast as I listened to an inner voice asking the question, "If you died tonight, where would you stand before the judgment seat of Christ?" As I considered that question, I realised that I would have absolutely no grounds for going to heaven. I had led a very rebellious and sinful life. I had never accepted the call to follow Jesus Christ, though I had heard it several times before that night. So I ran. I ran as fast as I could to the maths teacher's house. He kindly let me in even though I knew he found me a very difficult pupil. That night, however, I knelt and asked Jesus Christ to forgive me for my sins and to come into my life as my Lord, my Saviour and my friend.[5]

Mark was truly converted, but like many young disciples, a few years later, he went through a period of uncertainty, which was settled in an unusually dramatic way. Mark described it, to me, as follows:

A visitor in the cathedral close (the second postcard)

> In the Christmas holidays of 1980, I was struggling with my faith. I was enjoying my new-found freedom as an undergraduate, while

at the same time trying to live the Christian life. As a result, I was wrestling with the issues of commitment and compromise.

At the height of my inner turmoil, I remember going to bed one night feeling very restless. At the time, I was staying at my parents' house in Norwich Cathedral Close. I remember shutting the door, and then retiring. I always shut my bedroom door as a matter of routine; my mother kept a rather large Siamese cat that used to come into my room uninvited.

I woke up at six minutes past one in the morning. My digital alarm clock revealed the time. I was definitely awake not sleeping. The next moment the bedroom door flew open very quickly. Strangely, it did not crash against the wardrobe next to it, but came very suddenly to a halt, a very few centimetres away from it.

What happened next will remain with me for the rest of my life.

In walked a tall, white, radiant, figure, about seven or eight feet in height. I looked towards the face but there were no definable features. The light was simply too bright for me to make out any discernible features. But I knew it was a face.

For a few seconds, the angelic being stood before me. I was not at all frightened. A hand reached out to me, beckoning. I heard the words, "Follow me." Then the figure left. Needless to say, I was greatly impacted by the event. I told my parents the next morning. They could see that I was in a state of shock. They were unusually receptive. As a result of what I took to be a visit from the angel of the Lord, I decided that day to live the rest of my life completely for Jesus Christ. Though I have had times of weakness and wilderness since then, my heart has been wholly for the Lord. The days of divided loyalties ended there and then.

Ken remained a friend until his death, at the age of over 90, in 2002. Mark, now Vicar of St Andrew's Chorleywood in Hertfordshire, remains a friend and an inspiration. For me, the meeting in Winchester Cathedral, followed by the mission, were more than postcards, they were like divine telegrams (or e-mails in today's world) which transformed my expectations of what God could and would do.

His face shone like an angel (the third postcard)

Years later in 1990, I had settled down in parish ministry. In the intervening years, I had learnt a certain amount about healing and deliverance with Michael Green at St Aldate's Church in Oxford. I had moved to Somerset, where I had been parish priest in a small Somerset town for eight years. My health wasn't good, and I was awaiting a hip operation. It was rather embarrassing to be the chairman of the Diocesan Healing Group and to be limping like Jacob!

On St Luke's Day, 18th October 1990, I was taking our normal weekday Communion service. It was a small service, attended by about fifteen people. An elderly retired priest, Canon Theo Weatherall, and his wife were part of the regular congregation. During the service, I noticed that Theo's face was shining in an extraordinary way. It reminded me of the account of Moses descending the mountain referred to by St Paul in 2 Corinthians 3:7–15. Perhaps, Stephen's face shining in the Sanhedrin, (Acts 6:15) would have been a more appropriate text. Theo was quite new to our town and he had had a very long and distinguished ministry. He had been most kind to me and, at the age of 80, and despite coming from a very different theological tradition, had enthusiastically taken part in some mission house groups a month earlier.

Under a sort of divine compulsion, and feeling rather foolish, as he left the church, I mentioned to Theo what I had seen. Not unnaturally he looked a little embarrassed. He smiled in his normal kindly way, and he and his wife walked back to their nearby home.

Next afternoon while I was trying to persuade the local hospital that I did need to know when they were going to operate on my hip, the parish phone rang. Caroline Weatherall spoke, "I think Theo's just died – could you come round?"

When I arrived a few minutes later, Theo was sitting in his chair, looking incredibly peaceful, but clearly dead. I thought of the previous day's service, and was deeply moved by what I had seen, and glad that I had spoken to both of them at the end of the service.

White clothes in Zambia (the fourth postcard)

About 19 months later, a young Zambian grandmother was walking with a friend to her village along a narrow track. It was very early, and the light was just breaking over the trees. It had been a strange couple of days. A small group of white people, including myself, and some high-up Zambian church officials, had descended on her village. On the first evening the villagers had given the visitors a great welcome, including a traditional bonfire, with dancing, singing and acting. The next day there had been worship, dancing and preaching in the open air, under some tall trees, in front of their little thatched church. Many people had turned out and, at the end of the morning, there had been a time of prayer in the little church. This had been a strange event, with many people screaming and much confusion. There was a definite sense of a dark conflict raging within many people and perhaps within the wider community.

Her village, called Muto Wan Koko (The Severed Chicken's Head) had quite a reputation as a place of darkness, and it seemed to have lived up to its reputation. In the previous afternoon, the visiting preacher, supported by a Zambian church leader, had addressed the people and challenged the local spiritual powers in no uncertain manner. The calm pleasantries of the morning had been replaced by a harsh decisive challenge to her and the villagers to renounce all things concerned with witchcraft, to throw away all tainted objects, and above all "to choose that day whom they would serve" (cf Joshua 24:15). The local spiritual powers – a water spirit and a snake spirit – had been openly challenged. The people had laughed – not with pleasure as in the morning – but with disapproval, and hollow derisive mockery. They were displeased that an arrogant Westerner was telling them how to live, and what to do, and worse still, what not to do. The day had ended in some confusion and uncertainty.

As she walked towards the church, the woman wondered how the new day would turn out. Then she and her friend noticed a figure dressed in white walking along the path in front of them. This seemed very strange – Zambian people do not wear pure white clothes. The figure went to the right of the little church, she went to the left. She then felt that she should go round the far end of the church, and meet whoever it was that she had seen. The atmosphere seemed quite strange. When she walked around the church, there was no sign of the person dressed in white, whom she had seen so clearly. The ground was quite open, just a few trees, a few huts and a well. Her spirit soared – surely she had seen an angel coming to cleanse the church after yesterday's terrible spiritual battle?

A few hours later, she was in the back of the overcrowded little church. The Westerners still seemed confused, but the visiting Zambian leader was speaking with great eloquence about how the Holy Spirit had overwhelmed him and transformed him two years earlier at a clergy conference. As he stopped speaking, she felt impelled to come forward. She certainly wasn't a leader, not even a member of the Mothers' Union (the only leadership group for women in her church), but she must speak. She glided forward, and her face glowed with an unearthly spiritual certainty as she told her story.

The atmosphere was beautiful. An amazing morning followed, of evangelism and healing (with very little need for deliverance). The local priest, Father James, was equally astonished. Two years later he welcomed another team back to his village, and the work continued. Seven years later, he cycled over 50 km with a flat tyre to give his testimony and join some of the original team in another village. He knew the power of the Spirit, and he knew that what the young grandmother had testified was true.

For me, although the outcome of the sign of Theo's shining face and the Zambian lady's glowing countenance were so very different – they were identical spiritual experiences. There was a real sense, and I write cautiously, of transfiguration. There was a deep supernatural beauty that simply wasn't the work of man.

There were many positive outcomes of this encounter. Confirmation of the spiritual reputation of Muto came two years later. I met an 80-year-old Zambian priest, still church planting and evangelising. In conversation, I mentioned Muto. He said that he had been there 30 years earlier, and that it was the darkest village that he had ever visited! Father James became a powerful, spirit-led, man of prayer, and a great friend. We've met up several times since that first encounter. On one occasion, he prayed for one of my team, who, when she came home, testified to the extraordinary grace and power of his prayers. She hadn't understood a word (James had prayed in the local dialect), but had sensed the transforming presence of God. Amongst other things, she now leads the prayer ministry team in her local church.

For myself, it was another unforgettable experience. It was as though God had *sovereignly* calmed a violent storm, and then had instilled deeper faith into many of his servants.

The Diocesan Registrar (the fifth postcard)

I had three English companions on that Zambian trip: my wife Jane, Martin Cavender, who had just given up a safe job as Diocesan Registrar (the legal adviser to the Diocese of Bath and Wells) to become the organiser of the then embryonic Springboard team (the Archbishop of Canterbury's special evangelistic team headed initially by Michael Green and Bishop Michael Marshall, and later to be greatly expanded), and his son Henry. We also had wonderful support from Archdeacon Tobias Kaoma, a member of Bishop Bernard Malango's staff.

Not long afterwards, Martin found himself in a difficult pastoral situation in England. After a long Sunday of ministry, the husband of a very committed local Christian asked for prayer. He was on the fringes of the church and had a violent temperament. He was an ex-guardsman, very large, and his wife showed signs of physical battering. Martin and two others engaged in a time of prayer, which became quite difficult, violent and dangerous. Eventually the man was "clothed and in his right mind", and a considerable healing process seemed to have begun. After Martin debriefed with other members of his prayer team, one lady, quite new to this sort of ministry, remarked innocently, "Didn't you see the four golden angels in each corner of the room as we were praying?" After the experiences in Zambia, Martin was rather less surprised than he would have been a few years earlier, when his ministry had been confined to the relative safety of his diocesan office.

Hesitant Henry (the sixth postcard)

Martin's son Henry came as a late addition to our team to Zambia. A priest dropped out at very short notice, and Martin suggested that his son Henry came, mainly to make a film of the trip. Henry, not yet a Christian, was both intrigued and scared by what he was required to film. It wasn't difficult to film his father giving radio and TV interviews even if it was surprising to see the church taken so seriously by the national media. It wasn't hard to shoot the exuberant Zambian worship, so refreshingly different from what he was used to at home. It was rather harder to watch people being prayed for – and apparently benefiting from the experience. It seemed both intrusive and frightening to film the people who seemed troubled by malevolent spirits. These people were mainly young women, often with babies on their backs.[6]

When Henry returned he spent his pre-university gap year living in Bath, and frequently found his friends asking him about things that he had seen in Africa. When he reported what he had seen and heard, the usual reaction was, "You must be joking", followed by a turned back and a walking away. The strange thing was that the next day the same people used to come back and say, "Tell me again what you saw in Africa."

For eight years, Henry remained on a spiritual knife-edge – believing and yet not quite committed. He married, and he and his wife started attending an Assemblies of God Church. But still he remained just beyond the fringe, convinced yet strangely unmoved.

Then one night, Henry dreamed that, with his wife, he was walking along a dusty road in a hot country. The signposts they had been following led them, suitcases in hand, to their destination. Reaching the brow of a hill, there before them lay the most perfect beach, brilliant blue sky, clean sand and glorious sea. Excited, they rushed past the huge hotel which beckoned their immediate check-in and went straight onto the beach, baggage and all; where they sat in the shade of a grass shack and chatted to friends about their journey. Then quite suddenly the sky turned black, the sea boiled up, the waves crashed, and bolts of fire began to rain down on the beach, which was now covered with screaming, running people. As they raced for cover, trying to get back to the hotel to register, Henry felt a lump of brimstone hit his leg. All he knew was that he must get back to register at the hotel, which previously they had ignored. People were dying around them – and then Henry woke up.

He was baptised, by immersion, the very next Sunday. God's postcard had woken him up! His mother arrived for the service. She was a little late, having driven 200 miles. Henry was just about to be immersed, and was explaining to the congregation all that he had seen in Zambia, but that he had delayed making a real profession of faith until now. In his testimony, he described himself as "Hesitant Henry".

A wet night in November (the seventh postcard)

Meanwhile, I was trying (unsuccessfully) to write a book on the beauty of butterflies and their theological significance. It was to have the nice title of *The Angel and the Blue Charaxes*.

Blue Charaxes butterflies had distracted my preaching as they flew around the trees in the Zambian village which I have just described. I went to Compton House near Sherborne with a request to photograph a Blue Charaxes butterfly. Robert Gooden[7] had some flying in his tropical garden. I hadn't met Robert but we'd spoken, pleasantly, on the phone. When he greeted me, I remember saying "I expect you'll think I'm a little strange, but I want to photograph a Blue Charaxes as I noticed some flying high up in the trees when I was preaching in a Zambian village the day before a local lady saw an angel."

He smiled, and said, "My wife had her life saved by an angel on the A303!" Later Rosemary Gooden wrote to me about the incident:

In November 1992, our eldest son John came home for a surprise weekend visit. He was training to be a doctor at St George's Hospital in London, and I remember the great excitement and pleasure that we all felt when he walked through the front door – totally unexpectedly.

On Sunday evening Michael, another son, and I took him to catch the 17.34 train back to Waterloo. It was dull wet evening as we drove home down the dual carriageway, through the darkness and the rain. The traffic was going slowly, and I pulled into the outer lane to overtake a line of cars driving nose to tail. Suddenly over the brow came a car at high speed, directly towards us (completely on the wrong side of the dual carriageway! on the A303). A fatal accident seemed inevitable. I could not pull out of the way because of the solid line of traffic on my left.

Then we were pushed – a gap appeared in the block of traffic on my left, and my car was firmly pushed into the space. The oncoming vehicle hit my car at the only point where it could bounce off unharmed.

I didn't mention this to Michael – in case he thought that I was in a state of shock – but the first thing he said to me was, "We were pushed, weren't we? There was nowhere to go, then suddenly there was a space and we were pushed into it." We both knew that this was the act of a guardian angel!

My editor asks, pertinently, "Why didn't the angel get the car completely clear?" I think we could equally ask why Paul's angel (Acts 27:23) waited until the ship was nearly wrecked to intervene. It is clear that the sailors wouldn't have listened to Paul (cf Acts 27:10, Acts 27:21 and Acts 27:33) until the situation was desperate. The saving of all the men, even with the loss of the ship, was somehow even more remarkable than if the sea had calmed, and everything had been well. In the same way, if there had been no impact on the A303, Rosemary and Michael would probably have doubted the reality of their experience. In our imperfect world, a slightly flawed diamond seems more likely to be genuine. Twice recently, in important pastoral situations, I have been given an African-sounding word. In each situation, the people concerned corrected one letter of my word, and then responded dramatically to the power and clarity of the revelation. In one case a powerful curse, from some 30 years earlier, was broken (see p 238f); in the other, a clear insight into a serious parish problem emerged. The slight inaccuracy of my two words enhanced the situation. The people I was praying with felt involved and their faith was strengthened.

Emma's angels (the last postcard)

Just before the new millennium began, Don Latham, a well-known author and speaker, led a parish weekend for us. His powerful theme "See that you fulfil your potential" (see Colossians 4:17) left many of us very challenged. It confirmed to me that I should seek a change of direction for the last few years of my active ministry. He, too, spoke of angels and protection. One of our parishioners, Clare, had never really thought about this aspect of Christianity. Angels were in the pages of the Bible, not in today's church. Soon afterwards, an incident during a family holiday in Majorca changed her mind. Here is her story:

We had just arrived in Majorca, and had decided to take the children straight down to the beach. Hannah (7), Tim (5) and Emma (3) were making sandcastles and we were sitting close by watching and talking. We suddenly realised that we could not see Emma. The others had been so absorbed in making their castle that they hadn't noticed her go.

We started rushing along the beach looking for her, not leaving Hannah and Tim out of our sight. I described her to lots of people in case they had seen her. The beach was very crowded and Emma was very small, and she didn't seem to be anywhere. The sea was in front of us, a busy road behind, and a yachting marina about half a mile away, so there were lots of dangers. I panicked and called the police and then waited and prayed with Hannah and Tim while Simon continued to search up and down the beach.

I prayed so hard and so intensely for Emma to be returned to us safely. I knew the only thing I could do was to put the situation in God's hands. Suddenly, a man ran up to me (at this point Emma had been missing for nearly 40 minutes) and told me that his wife had Emma and was carrying her back to us along the beach. I ran with him towards his wife, and Emma was safely in her arms. We all cried, and Emma was very relieved to be back with us.

The couple were very fair and somehow glowed with an inner light which made them seem radiant. They shook our hands and we thanked them again and again, and then they left. When we turned round to look for them they had disappeared.

Emma has always told us that the angels came and found her and brought her back to us. She had reached the marina when they found her and picked her up – at the very point when she was in most danger.

We know that God sent his angels to protect her and bring her back safely to us.

Questions to ponder

I have offered eight "postcards from heaven" – the missionary in China, the young convert whose faith was strengthened by a visit from an angel, the ancient Canon's shining face the day before he died, the young Zambian grandmother in a spiritually dangerous village, angels apparently present when difficult prayer ministry was taking place, a dream which led to salvation, incredible protection from a road accident, and the surprising rescue of a little girl.

Obviously, very different interpretations of each of these incidents could be made. Ultimately, I want to answer six simple questions. (1) Are the accounts true? (2) Has the Bible got any similar stories or relevant texts? (3) What fruit came from these events and did they glorify the name of Jesus? (4) What are the dangers of these sorts of experiences? (5) What are the theological issues raised by them? (6) Why is it important to have a theology of angels in today's world? These questions also need to be asked of all such experiences. I would also add a seventh general question. Why do angelic experiences seem so much more common in today's world?

The first question we will look at immediately. The biblical evidence is discussed in Chapters 2 and 3; the fruit of these experiences is an ever-present issue by which each incident should be tested; the dangers are discussed in Chapters 8 and 9, and by means of a testimony in Chapter 10. The final chapter will look again at all the questions. For the moment, we ask:

Are the accounts true?

When faced with these sorts of stories, we, inevitably, will react in a number of different ways: (i) they are unbelievable and can't be true; (ii) the events occurred as recorded, but there is a simple rational explanation; (iii) the events occurred, but there has been considerable spiritual deception; (iv) they may be true – but so what?

Of these four reactions, the first is the easiest to deal with. We are, I believe, dealing with reliable witnesses who have nothing to gain and no reason for inventing, exaggerating, or embroidering these simple stories (see 2 Timothy 2:2). Many similar stories are recorded and we shall look at others later in this short book. It is a natural reaction to doubt things that we haven't seen (viz. Thomas, John 20:24ff). I have never seen an angel, but that doesn't cause me to doubt the veracity of my friends. An African may not have seen people walking across a frozen river, but if the witnesses are reliable he will believe them.

The second is the most likely reaction. Obviously, stories about faces lighting up, dreams, miraculous deliverance from accidents, and strangers finding children could easily have a rational explanation (that doesn't stop God being involved, but in the context of *this study* it reduces their significance). However, several of the stories won't fit those kinds of explanations. Kenneth McAll in the desert in China, the lady in Zambia, Mark's experience in his bedroom, and Martin's praying partner seeing angels protecting the room, demand a higher level of interpretation.

Spiritual deception is a possibility (see 2 Corinthians 11:14 and other texts which we will discuss later). Spiritual deception does occur. It has happened to me more than once, and on each occasion, it was a very unpleasant and painful experience. That is why, in later chapters, we have to look at the other questions, particularly those concerning the fruit of the experience. (That was Jesus' primary test – see Matthew 7:15–23). The fruits, as I have already hinted, were in all cases beautiful.

The fourth reaction: they may be true – but so what? – is perhaps the most typical.

We live, spiritually, in a strangely complacent age. All around us terrible things are happening – war, terrorism, drought, flooding and famine, HIV, global warming – the list is seemingly endless. Yet we are seldom shocked. Our postmodern age gazes at a pot-pourri of religious experiences with eyes full of gentle mockery. We do not want to be disturbed from our spiritual slumber. Like the citizens of ancient Athens, we enjoy talking about, and listening to the latest ideas (Acts 17:21). We dislike any religious pathway that seems to point to a single truth. We, too, much prefer to believe in "an unknown God".

Stories about angels, and supernatural encounters, are of passing interest (useful to enliven dinner parties, casual conversations, Christmas sermons, and evangelistic conversations) but to most people of no more significance than the sighting of a rare bird, an unusual orchid, or even the misfortunes of some well-known family.

In Scripture, and I believe in present day experience, angels come unexpectedly both to stir people into action, and to bring a much needed sense of awe and reverence into worship and daily living.

Perhaps my mind is too mathematical, but to me, if one of my postcards, flawed jewels though they be, truly testifies to an experience of the living God, then how much more does the witness of Scripture, the central diamond in the Universe, truly point us to Jesus?

If I can believe that Mark's angel truly came to him in Norwich Cathedral Close, then I can more easily believe that Mary's angel came to her in Nazareth. If our flawed jewels shine, then how infinitely brighter is the unclouded diamond of Scripture.

And Scripture points us to Jesus, risen, ascended, glorified.

I turned round to see the voice that was speaking to me. And when I turned I saw seven golden lampstands, and among the lampstands was someone "like a son of man", dressed in a robe reaching down to his feet and with a golden sash round his chest. His head and hair were white like wool, as white as snow, and his eyes were like blazing fire. His feet were like bronze glowing in a furnace, and his voice was like the sound of rushing waters. In his right hand he held seven stars, and out of his mouth came a sharp double-edged sword. His face was like the sun shining in all its brilliance. (Revelation 1:12–16)

It is to the witness of Scripture, and above all, to the teachings of Jesus, that we now turn.

Notes

(1) Frances and Kenneth McAll, *The Moon Looks Down*, Darley Anderson, 1987.

(2) Eric Liddell, the famous missionary and Olympic gold medallist, died in captivity a few years later.

(3) Dr Kenneth McAll, *Healing of the Family Tree*, SPCK, 1982 is his classic book.

(4) John Thorn, *Road to Winchester*, Weidenfield and Nicholson, 1989, Ch. 17.

(5) Mark Stibbe, *Thinking Clearly about Revival*, Monarch, 1998, p. 24. Mark is currently Vicar of the large Anglican church of St Andrew's Chorleywood. A number of others who came to faith at this time are serving God in full-time Christian work.

(6) I am often asked, and I remain puzzled, as to why it is nearly always women who seem to need this ministry. Recent ministry to an elderly Zambian woman who, at the age of 70, was set free from spirits who had troubled her since a teenage initiation ceremony, and to another African woman troubled by a powerful spirit which arrived before her birth, when her mother visited a witch doctor, confirms my thinking (supported by many African clergy) that it is usually the women who take the initiative in these dubious spiritual matters. Many African men, not unlike their English counterparts, leave the spiritual decisions to their wives. If their wives' choice is a bad one, the way is opened for trouble from evil spirits. Frequently, they seemed to take one look at the prayer team (and it didn't seem to matter whether they were English or Zambian), and then crash to the floor, sometimes wriggling like a snake, invariably screaming, and usually overtaken by terrible, and apparently uncontrollable, violence.

(7) Robert and Rosemary Gooden live at Compton House, near Sherborne, and are the founders of 'Worldwide Butterflies'. Robert is involved in conservation as far afield as Papua New Guinea.

2

Angels According to Scripture

In this chapter, we concentrate on Jesus' teaching about angels. We see that angels are a natural part of his theology. We also examine how the biblical view of angels, and their role for good and ill, unfolds in the pages of Scripture.

Angels According to Scripture

Introduction

Angels arrive unannounced on the pages of Scripture. In the first of over 300 references, Cherubim guard the way to the tree of life, after the expulsion from Eden. After such a dramatic and sombre entrance, angelic intervention comes frequently in Genesis and continues throughout Scripture, culminating in much activity in the Revelation of St John. Teaching about angels is much less frequent, with a few texts in the Psalms, some important words in the Gospels, and a few sporadic references in Paul and Peter. By contrast, the unknown writer of Hebrews displays a considerable interest in this subject. We are not told how angels are created, nor what they look like, nor much about their hierarchies (a speculative subject beloved in some modern and ancient books).[1]

Throughout the pages of Scripture, and presumably long before creation as we understand it, angels are seen as messengers of the Lord,[2] executors of God's judgment, and as worshippers in the courts of Heaven. They can protect, guide, and guard the human race. "Are not all angels ministering spirits sent to serve those who will inherit salvation?" (Hebrews 1:14) Some of their number rebelled against God (see Isaiah

14:12–15, and Ezekiel 28, also here Chapter 8), and are respon-
sible for the spiritual opposition experienced by many in their
earthly pilgrimage. They are at their most dangerous when
disguised, and appearing to do good! We will examine carefully Paul's celebrated warning, "And no wonder, for Satan
himself masquerades as an angel of light." (2 Corinthians
11:14) Paul also warns the Colossians not to get involved with
people who delight in "false humility and the worship of
angels" (Colossians 2:18). This important text warns us that
while angels are an important, and mysterious part of God's
creation, we must not *exaggerate* their significance.[3]

This warning is repeated elsewhere in Scripture. Near the
end of the Bible, John falls down to worship at the feet of the
angel who had shown him his great vision. But the angel said
to him, "Do not do it! I am a fellow-servant with you and your
brothers the prophets and of all who keep the words of this
book. Worship God." (Revelation 22:9, and see also Revelation
19:10)

Jesus mentions angels a number of times. Angels are a
natural part of his theological understanding and experience.
His teaching about them is clear, unprecedented in either the
Old Testament, or as far as we can tell, in contemporary Jewish
thinking. His parables, and his general teaching, give us some
very important insights into such diverse matters as guardian
angels, our future state, angelic emotions and limitations, and
their role in the end times.

Guardian angels

We begin by looking at the question of guardian angels, both
from the lips and life of Jesus, and throughout the rest of Scripture. We shall return to this matter, with testimonies, in Chapter
6. There are a number of biblical texts which support the belief
that people have guardian angels. In the Old Testament there
are at least four – Jacob's first blessing for his favourite son,
Joseph; Daniel's account to the Persian king of his protection

from the lions; and the famous verses of Psalm 91 quoted, or perhaps we should say misquoted, by the Devil to Jesus during the temptations in the wilderness. Psalm 34 promises protection to believers. I have often been strengthened by verse 7, particularly after any sort of deliverance ministry.

Jacob had many experiences of angels. The first was his famous dream (Genesis 28:10–19), which we shall consider below when we look at Jesus' conversation about angels with Nathaniel. Then some years later after his uncomfortable departure from his Uncle Laban (Genesis 31), he was preparing for a potentially worse encounter with his estranged brother Esau.

Scripture records that Jacob went on his way, and the angels of God met him. When Jacob saw them he said, "This is the camp of God." (Genesis 32:1–2)

Despite this angelic encounter, Jacob was extremely nervous. The next day, he made elaborate arrangements to try and pacify Esau. He also spent some time praying in a somewhat hesitant manner (see Genesis 32:9–12).

That night he had an extraordinary wrestling match with someone he wrongly assumed to be a man. After it was all over, he realised that he had actually met God. His name was changed from Jacob to Israel, and his character began to change. He was still very nervous when he met his brother Esau the next day. His guilty conscience was doubtless caused by his duplicity on earlier occasions (see Genesis Chapters 25 and 27).

Years later, on his death bed, Jacob blessed Joseph, and his two sons, with words which invoked the protection and blessing of the "Angel who has delivered me from all harm".

May the God before whom my fathers Abraham and Isaac walked, the God who has been my shepherd all my life to this day, the Angel who has delivered me from all harm – may he bless these boys. May they be called by my name and the names of my fathers Abraham and Isaac, and may they increase greatly upon the earth. (Genesis 48:15–16)

The Angel, here, is presumably the Angel of the Lord. Here, as
in other Old Testament passages, the Angel of the Lord is virtually indistinguishable from God himself. After all the experiences of his life, his many failings and restorations, and many
angelic encounters, it was quite natural for Jacob to bless his
favourite son, and grandchildren, in this way.

Daniel, also, had a number of encounters with angels. After
he had been thrown into the lions' den, the king arrived at the
first light of dawn to see what had happened. When Darius
arrived, he called to Daniel in an anguished voice,

> Daniel, servant of the living God, has your God, whom you serve
> continually, been able to rescue you from the lions?" Daniel
> answered, "O king, live for ever! My God sent his angel, and he
> shut the mouths of the lions. They have not hurt me, because I was
> found innocent in his sight. Nor have I ever done any wrong before
> you, O king. (Daniel 6:20–22).

Daniel had been protected by the Angel of the Lord. The angel
acted as a highly effective guardian throughout his ordeal.

Earlier, the Psalmist had written a great hymn of praise about
God's protection and love. He included specific words about
the work of angels:

> If you make the Most High your dwelling – even the Lord who is
> my refuge – then no harm will befall you, no disaster will come
> near your tent. For he will command his angels concerning you to
> guard you in all your ways; they will lift you up in their hands, so
> that you will not strike your foot against a stone. You will tread
> upon the lion and the cobra; you will trample the great lion and the
> serpent. (Psalm 91:9–13)[4]

The Psalmist also wrote of the protection the Angel of the Lord
brings to those who trust him.

> I will extol the Lord at all times; his praise will always be on my
> lips.

> My soul will boast in the Lord; let the afflicted hear and rejoice.
>
> Glorify the Lord with me; let us exalt his name together.
>
> I sought the Lord, and he answered me; he delivered me from all my fears.
>
> Those who look to him are radiant; their faces are never covered with shame.
>
> This poor man called, and the Lord heard him; he saved him out of all his troubles.
>
> The angel of the Lord encamps around those who fear him, and he delivers them.
>
> Taste and see that the Lord is good; blessed is the man who takes refuge in him.
>
> Fear the Lord, you his saints, for those who fear him lack nothing.
>
> The lions may grow weak and hungry, but those who seek the Lord lack no good thing.
>
> (Psalm 34:1–10)

This beautiful psalm[5] gives us confidence that when we are on the Lord's business, we will be protected. Personally, I have found this of great comfort when dealing with spiritually troubled buildings, and people. Obviously, we are not promised blanket cover – there are times when God allows his servants to suffer. But, in general, we can *expect* God's protection, as long as we seek it and remain within his will.

These four texts make a strong case for angelic protection – certainly for the servants of the living God. Later, in the New Testament, all the Apostles were rescued by an angel of the Lord (Acts 5:19). Even more significantly, the final references to Peter, in the Acts, recount his rescue by an angel. The incident is described, graphically, in Acts 12:1–17. It shows that the early church had a very strong belief in guardian angels, so strong in fact, that when the rescued Peter knocked at the door of John Mark's house, and talked to the servant girl, Rhoda, she was unable to convince the believers that it was really Peter who was at the door. Despite the fact that they had been earnestly praying for his release, they assumed that the nocturnal visitor "must be his angel" (Acts 12:15). Their curious reaction, which doesn't reflect well on the faith of the believers, strengthens the case for taking the story literally.

St Chrysostom[6] has a delightful comment on this passage. He says that the believers were allowed to make the mistake of thinking it was Peter's angel, because otherwise after his rapid exit "for another place" (Acts 12:17),[7] they would have assumed that it was indeed an angel, and not the real Peter who had visited them. Chrysostom also affirms, without any doubt, "This is the truth, that each man has an angel." There are modern parallels to this story which we shall mention in Chapter 6.

The mystery of this story, as in so many others involving angels, is not so much in Peter's miraculous escape, but in James' execution. Where was his angel? This is a serious question which we will discuss fully in Chapter 6. Meanwhile, we should note two more New Testament texts. Later in Acts, during the ferocious storm at sea, Paul is strengthened by the visit of an angel. At the height of the crisis, Paul tells the crew:

> Last night an angel of the God whose I am and whom I serve stood beside me and said, "Do not be afraid, Paul. You must stand trial before Caesar; and God has graciously given you the lives of all who sail with you." (Acts 27:23–24)

The writer of Hebrews says, "Are not all angels ministering spirits sent to serve those who will inherit salvation?" (Hebrews 1:14) which suggests that one of the *normal* functions of angels is to help believers. This text is largely ignored in today's church. It certainly teaches that angels are far more present than most of us realise. One bishop used to remark, semi-seriously, that he was delighted to see a half-empty church, it left more room for the angels. He did believe in their existence, and told me that he saw one, once, when celebrating Holy Communion.

In Jesus' life, the question of guardian angels arose both in the temptation narrative, and in the Garden of Gethsemane (see

further in Chapter 3). On one occasion, Jesus indirectly
mentioned guardian angels:

> See that you do not look down on one of these little ones. For I tell
> you that their angels in heaven always see the face of my Father in
> heaven. What do you think? If a man owns a hundred sheep, and
> one of them wanders away, will he not leave the ninety-nine on the
> hills and go and look for the one that wandered off? And if he
> finds it, I tell you the truth, he is happier about that one sheep than
> about the ninety-nine that did not wander off. In the same way,
> your Father in heaven is not willing that any of these little ones
> should be lost. (Matthew 18:10–14)

What Jesus meant by "their angels in heaven" has been much
debated (see Chapter 6 for some diverse views). All are agreed
that here, Jesus, in contrast to the similar parable in Luke 15, is
teaching that even the humblest believers have direct access to
God. Commentators are uncertain as to how literally to take the
reference to angels. Their views usually reflect their own theological presuppositions. In view of the strong teaching in the Old
Testament about angelic protection, I think that we should take
this teaching literally. Children, and the childlike in faith, have
protective angels! However, the existence of guardian angels *does
not guarantee* protection. It does imply that God cares and is
concerned for all the little ones – children, ordinary believers . . .

Earlier in his Gospel, Matthew has recorded the grim story
of the massacre of the innocents (Matthew 2:16–18). This
ghastly story, and the pages of human history, show all too
clearly that such protection is not automatic. Indeed, it cannot
be unless we have a universe in which evil is eliminated. It may
have been some comfort to the grieving mothers in Bethlehem,
prophesied by Jeremiah 31:15, if they were able to believe that
their children were now in the presence of the Lord.

Jesus faced up to the questions of both political and acciden-
tal death in his teaching about Pontius Pilate, and the Tower of
Siloam.

Now there were some present at that time who told Jesus about the Galileans whose blood Pilate had mixed with their sacrifices. Jesus answered, "Do you think that these Galileans were worse sinners than all the other Galileans because they suffered this way? I tell you, no! But unless you repent, you too will all perish. Or those eighteen who died when the tower in Siloam fell on them – do you think they were more guilty than all the others living in Jerusalem? I tell you, no! But unless you repent, you too will all perish." (Luke 13:1–5)

His message here was not about angelic protection, or the lack of it, but about the urgent need to repent. Life can be very short, and death very sudden.

At the time of Jesus' greatest crisis, at the point of his arrest, he said:

Do you think I cannot call on my Father, and he will at once put at my disposal more than twelve legions of angels? But how then would the Scriptures be fulfilled that say it must happen in this way? (Matthew 26:53–54)

Here, perhaps, lies the beginning of a solution to the mystery of angelic protection. Angels are always available, certainly for children and believers, but are not always *permitted* to intervene. Satan was permitted to cause havoc, and guardian angels were restrained, both when Herod murdered the children around Bethlehem, and when Jesus was arrested. Satan sifted the disciples, destroyed the Messiah, only to find that God's full plan of salvation had been unveiled. As we shall see below, even the angels did not understand what was happening.

Angels rejoice

However, angels can also rejoice – notably when "one sinner repents". St Luke gives us a rather different version of the parable of the lost sheep (Luke 15:3–7 see above and compare Matthew 18:10–14). He concludes with Jesus' remark that

". . . there will be more rejoicing in heaven over one sinner who repents than over ninety-nine righteous persons who do not need to repent". The text continues with another familiar parable:

> Or suppose a woman has ten silver coins and loses one. Does she not light a lamp, sweep the house and search carefully until she finds it? And when she finds it, she calls her friends and neighbours together and says, "Rejoice with me, I have found my lost coin." In the same way, I tell you *there is rejoicing in the presence of the angels of God over one sinner who repents*. (Luke 15:8–10)

This delightful parable, which expresses a woman's joy at finding part of a lost wedding gift, is like its predecessor (the lost sheep), and the one that follows (the lost son) about repentance and the subsequent celebrations in heaven. When anyone is truly saved, heaven rejoices! Jesus uses the word joy of deep spiritual experiences. Once, John the Baptist applies it to Jesus as the bridegroom (John 3: 27–30). Once Jesus is described as "full of joy" (Luke 10:21) – and that is after the successful evangelistic mission of the 72. The idea of joy amongst the angels is important. It gives us another glimpse of the wonderful variety and richness of heaven. A friend of mine lost his wife after a long and fruitful marriage. Sometime later, he had a dream based on the parable of the lost son. He saw his wife welcomed in heaven, given the new robe, the ring, the shoes, and the party. The dream showed him that his wife's homecoming, however painful to him, was a source of rejoicing in heaven.

Patricia St John[8] has a lovely story of a woman who dreamed about an angel watching five people at prayer. The first was a beautifully dressed woman kneeling in church, the second a man deep in apparently sincere prayer, the third a woman in tears, the fourth a tramp, and the fifth a small boy. Each prayer was accompanied by a bird with folded wings. The bird was there to take the prayers to heaven. The smart woman's bird was quite dead – she only went to church to observe people and to be noticed. The man's bird could never quite take his prayers to heaven, because of the bitterness in his heart. The sad woman's bird had great difficulties because she doubted God's love and care for her. The little boy's tiny bird had no difficulty in taking his brief prayers to heaven. But it was the tramp's bird, which was weak and dingy, that caused the angel to laugh for joy. The tramp hardly seemed to be speaking, but suddenly his bird rose and flew into the sunshine. "The man doesn't know how to pray at all," said the angel. "He has never prayed in his life. He doesn't know what words to use. But his heart is heavy with sin and needs. His thoughts are crying out for mercy and forgiveness. And just at this moment all the angels of God are rejoicing because another sinner has come home."

The writer of Hebrews adds to the theme of angelic joy.

> You have not come to a mountain that can be touched and that is burning with fire; to darkness, gloom and storm; to a trumpet blast or to such a voice speaking words that those who heard it begged that no further word be spoken to them, because they could not bear what was commanded: "If even an animal touches the mountain, it must be stoned." The sight was so terrifying that Moses said, "I am trembling with fear."
>
> But you have come to Mount Zion, to the heavenly Jerusalem, the city of the living God. You have come to thousands upon thousands of angels in joyful assembly, to the church of the firstborn, whose names are written in heaven. You have come to God, the judge of all men, to the spirits of righteous men made perfect, to Jesus the mediator of a new covenant, and to the sprinkled blood that speaks a better word than the blood of Abel. (Hebrews 12:18–24)

The contrast between the Holy Mountain where even Moses was filled with terror, and the Holy City where angels are found in joyful assembly is very graphic. The angels, and the redeemed, are able to joyfully worship the Lord in the beauty of holiness. There is joy in heaven, not only when one sinner repents, but also in praise and worship throughout eternity. (See also Revelation Chapters 4 and 5.)

The theme of angelic joy is important. Of course, eternity is a solemn concept, but we must believe that there will be many wonderful and joyous experiences. The image most frequently used by Jesus was that of a feast (see Matthew 25:1–13, 22:1–14, etc.).

We shall be like angels

Towards the end of Jesus' ministry, he had a significant encounter with the Sadducees – a religious group who opposed the Pharisees. In particular, they had no belief in any future life. Their question to Jesus is both absurd and hypocritical. Matthew records the incident as follows:

> That same day the Sadducees, who say there is no resurrection, came to him with a question. "Teacher," they said, "Moses told us that if a man dies without having children, his brother must marry the widow and have children for him. Now there were seven brothers among us. The first one married and died, and since he had no children, he left his wife to his brother. The same thing happened to the second and the third brother, right on down to the seventh. Finally, the woman died. Now then, at the resurrection, whose wife will she be of the seven, since all of them were married to her?"
>
> Jesus replied, "You are in error because you do not know the Scriptures, or the power of God. At the resurrection people will neither marry nor be given in marriage, they will be like angels in heaven. But about the resurrection of the dead – have you not read what God said to you, 'I am the God of Abraham, the God of Isaac, and the God of Jacob'? He is not the God of the dead, but of the living."
>
> When the crowds heard this, they were astonished at his teaching. (Matthew 22:23–33; virtually identical teaching is given in Mark 12:18ff, and Luke 20:27ff)

In the midst of dealing, very patiently, with the scepticism of the Sadducees, Jesus taught that, at the resurrection, people will be "like the angels in heaven". This teaching is reinforced by St Paul in his great chapter on the resurrection, 1 Corinthians 15, particularly in verses 42, 49 and 52. Some people are disturbed that, in Jesus' teaching, there is no place in heaven for marriage. The intimacy experienced in human marriage is replaced by the far greater intimacy of union with Christ, and the universal love and joy of Paradise. We need not infer from this teaching that we shall not be able to recognise one another, but simply that our relationship with one another will be quite different. Peter, and the others, had no difficulty in recognising the heavenly visitors, Moses and Elijah, on the Mount of Transfiguration!

The Sadducees had no belief in a future life (thus their question to Jesus was utterly cynical). By contrast, the Pharisees had a very literal belief in the bodily resurrection. Jesus challenged both parties, and left us with the vision of a very beautiful future expressed, dramatically, to the penitent thief, when he said, amidst the agony of the Cross, "I tell you the truth, today you will be with me in Paradise." (Luke 23:43)

A similar promise is given to the angel[9] of the church in Ephesus. "To him who overcomes, I will give the right to eat from the tree of life, which is in the paradise of God." (Revelation 2:7) St Paul, recounting his great ecstatic vision (2 Corinthians 12:1–6), is "caught up to paradise". Elsewhere, more soberly, he elaborates Isaiah 64:4 with a great and wonderful statement, "No eye has seen, no ear has heard, no mind has conceived what God has prepared for those who love him" (1 Corinthians 2:9–10a), adding quietly "but God has revealed it to us by his Spirit".

Jesus reinforces all this, referring to his own forthcoming death, he says, "In my Father's house are many rooms" (John 14:2). William Temple,[10] in a famous comment on this passage, says that the rooms should literally be translated as "caravan wayside resting places" which gives an impression of a spiritual journey in the life to come, not unlike Theresa of Avila's interior castle with its seven rooms.[11]

These verses ought to kill, once and for all, the foolish notion that heaven will be boring. Anyone who begins to glimpse the wonder of angels, or the beauty of Paradise, will join Paul in longing to be part of the future world. Paul has great confidence in the future life – which is a characteristic of those who have experienced such matters in this life. He writes succinctly:

"For to me, to live is Christ and to die is gain." (Philippians 1:21)

Elsewhere, he writes realistically:

"For now we see through a glass, darkly; but then face to face." (1 Corinthians 13:12, KJV)

Our experience of God in this world may be very limited, but each ray of Divine sunlight gives us great hope for all that lies ahead. Each true angelic encounter, or for that matter any other experience of God's grace, lifts our spirits and helps us to keep faith amidst the gloom of a dangerous and unhappy world.

All of this should more than satisfy. With the rock-solid evidence of Jesus' resurrection, and scriptural teaching about Paradise, angels and other powers, we can be sure that our earthly pilgrimage can have a glorious end. It is enough to know that our incorruptible spiritual bodies (1 Corinthians 15:42–50), will be like those of angels. Further speculation is both faithless and foolish. Faithless because it goes beyond what is revealed in Scripture, foolish because such knowledge is forbidden (Deuteronomy 18:9 etc.) – the unfortunate King Saul (1 Samuel 28) did not profit from his foolish visit to the witch of Endor.

Jesus and Nathanael

Jesus' fascinating conversation with Philip and Nathanael concludes with these words to Nathanael. "You believe because I told you I saw you under the fig-tree. You shall see greater things than that." He then added, "I tell you the truth, you shall see heaven open, and the *angels of God ascending and descending on the Son of Man.*" (John 1:50–51 – my italics) There is a dramatic emphasis, somewhat lost in modern translation. In the Greek, Jesus says amēn, amēn, a doublet repeated on many especially solemn moments in this Gospel.[12] Jesus had called Nathanael "a true Israelite, in whom there is nothing false" – probably making a direct contrast with the patriarch Jacob whose life and speech were full of such memorable falsehoods. Jacob, of course, had had a famous dream of angels ascending and descending a ladder (see Genesis 28:10–end). What was Jesus promising Nathanael? Certainly, that he would see marvellous things, certainly, that he would discover that, in effect, the heavens were opened, and that communications between God and man had been radically altered by the coming of Jesus. The Rabbis taught, based on the story of Jacob's ladder, that the angels first ascend the ladder, taking the prayers and petitions of believers to God, and then descend with the mercy and judgment of God. Jesus was obviously familiar with this teaching. To some extent, after the gift to individual believers of the Holy Spirit, this idea became superfluous. Paul writes, "For through him [Jesus] we both have access to the Father by one Spirit." (Ephesians 2:18) This important text on prayer expresses the same teaching, but through the agency of the Holy Spirit, rather than angels. As we shall see in the next chapter, the Holy Spirit is the *normal* means of communication from God to believers, but he does *sometimes* choose to use angels.

Did Jesus promise Nathanael a literal fulfilment of this text? In the fourth Gospel, Jesus' words, and actions, usually have both a literal and a symbolic meaning. Certainly, Nathanael witnessed the work of angels. Not only would he have heard the story of the empty tomb, and the angel rolling away the stone (Matthew 28:2); but also he was granted at least one Resurrection appearance (see John 21:1ff). He was presumably one of the Apostles who witnessed the angels at the Ascension (Acts 1:10–11), and also one of those who was released by the

Angel of the Lord (Acts 5:19). It seems likely that Nathanael
became familiar with angels by personal experience, as well as
by a general belief in them. All of which accords well with the
theology of the day.

Angels and judgment

Four of the sharpest of Jesus' parables – the Wheat and the
Tares (Matthew 13:24–30, and 36–43); the Net (Matthew 13:
47–50); the Rich Man and Lazarus (Luke 16:19–31); and the
Sheep and the Goats (Matthew 25:31–46) – give angels a
largely destructive role in the Judgment at the end of the Age.
Angels do, however, carry Lazarus to Abraham's side in
heaven. We are told little about their function, and not much
about the nature of the future life. As the theologian, Reinhold
Niebuhr[13] has wisely said, "It is unwise for Christians to claim
any knowledge of either the furniture of heaven, or the temper-
ature of hell."

The parable of the rich man (traditionally called Dives) and
Lazarus is particularly vivid. Scholars have long debated the
meaning of the parable. Did Jesus mean it to be taken literally?
Is it a powerful parable about social justice: the rich (represented by Dives and his careless brothers) will get their deserts
in the world to come? The poor (represented by Lazarus) get
justice in heaven alongside Abraham? Is this the ultimate
description of Hell – a place of torments, flames, thirst, and
with no future hope? Is the real point of the parable in the last
verse "They will not be convinced even if someone rises from
the dead"?

Virtually all the hardest teaching about the future world
comes from the mouth of Jesus. The Epistles are strangely
silent: only Hebrews (mainly Chapter 12), 2 Peter, and Jude,
together with extensive parts of Revelation have much to say
on the subject. The question of judgment is outside the scope of
this short book. One thing is certain, the parables of Jesus
ought to destroy the very foolish notion that angels are merely

comfortable spirits who can be summoned to protect, and guide, mankind.

Angelic limitations and emotions

It is quite a shock to find that many of the references to angels in the New Testament often contain warnings, and some of the references are amongst the most obscure. We have already mentioned (see above) Paul's solemn warning about not worshipping angels, and his equally clear observation that Satan can transform himself into an angel of light. The early church, particularly in the first three centuries, faced a considerable challenge from Gnosticism. The Gnostics formed many disparate groups, with two contrasting emphases. Some were extremely ascetic, attempting to subdue bodily passions by sharp discipline; others were extremely amoral, teaching that as the body was unimportant almost any behaviour was acceptable. Their foundation was a common belief in "inner light", and secret mysteries mediated in some cases by Jesus to the Apostles, and in others by the direct revelation of *angels*.[14] Both the warnings from Paul mentioned above, probably indicate that some aspects of early Gnostic teaching affected the New Testament church, particularly in Colossae.

Two of Paul's most famous texts mention angels. The great chapter on love begins, "If I speak in the tongues of men and of angels, but have not love, I am only a resounding gong or a clanging cymbal" (1 Corinthians 13:1), which is scarcely complimentary to angels. It is possible that "tongues of angels" was a colloquial expression for glossolalia in the troubled Corinthian church, in which case Paul's comment is more understandable. Even more dramatically, the great passage at the end of Romans 8 (see verses 31–39), which is rightly often read at funerals, ends with a great crescendo

> For I am convinced that neither death nor life, neither angels nor demons, neither the present nor the future, nor any powers, neither

height nor depth, nor anything else in all creation, will be able to
separate us from the love of God that is in Christ Jesus our Lord.
(Romans 8:38–39)

But what did Paul mean? How can angels *separate* us from the
love of God? The contrasts in the text (death and life, angels
and demons, present and future) make it virtually certain that
Paul is not referring to evil angels.

Paul may just be using hyperbole, to emphasise that neither,
good nor evil, can ultimately separate the believer from God's
love. Alternatively, he may have in mind the Colossian problem
(see again Colossians 2:18) where over-enthusiastic believers
seem to have put visions, and supernatural experiences, above
obedience to Christ and his teaching. Such visions may start by
being God-given, but human pride easily opens the gateway to
deception. Mark Stibbe's warning testimony from Finland (see
Chapter 9, p 226) is a modern example of this problem.

There are a few other obscure texts which we should
mention. Jude v. 6 and 2 Peter 2:4 refer to fallen angels – possibly based on some obscure interaction between men and angels
recorded in the early verses of Genesis 6. 1 Corinthians 11:10
tells women that they must cover their hair when prophesying
"for this reason, and because of the angels". Paul's main arguments concern the strict social customs of the time. Commentators are divided as to whether uncovered hair provides
temptation for fallen angels (as perhaps in Genesis 6), or
offends the dignity of worshipping angels. Uncovered hair,
particularly in Corinth, robbed Middle Eastern women of
dignity (as it still does today), exposed them to unwonted
contact, and possibly to the accusation of being prostitutes.

With some relief, we now turn to a much clearer, and very
important text in 1 Peter.

Angelic longing

Peter writes "Concerning this salvation, the prophets, who

spoke of the grace that was to come to you, searched intently and with the greatest care, trying to find out the time and circumstances to which the Spirit of Christ in them was pointing when he predicted the sufferings of Christ and the glories that would follow. It was revealed to them that they were not serving themselves but you, when they spoke of the things that have now been told you by those who have preached the gospel to you by the Holy Spirit sent from heaven. *Even angels long to look into these things."* (1 Peter 1:10–12 – my italics).

This arresting statement is taken up by Charles Wesley in his great hymn "And can it be that I should gain an interest in the Saviour's blood?" Verse 2 reads:

> 'Tis mystery all! The Immortal dies
> who can explain His strange design?
> In vain the first-born seraph tries
> to sound the depth of love divine. .
> 'Tis mystery all let earth adore,
> let angel minds enquire no more.

Angels long to look, angel minds enquire! What St Peter means, and what Charles Wesley's great hymn illustrates, is that angels have great limitations. Angels did not understand how the great Old Testament prophecies were to be fulfilled; angels did not know what God's plan of salvation was, and consequently angels gazed and wondered at the mystery of Jesus' sufferings and death.

Angels long to look! Like the disciples at the empty tomb on the first Easter Day, they appear to be bending down to look and to wonder. They have a great and overwhelming interest in the mystery of the salvation of mankind. The message of the Gospel is that salvation is a deep mystery – hidden from both men and angels – see, for instance, Romans 16:25, 1 Corinthians 2:7–8, and Ephesians 3:2–6.

Another hymn writer puts it poetically:

> Crown him the Lord of love,
> Behold his hands and side,
> Those wounds yet visible above
> In beauty glorified.
> No angel in the sky
> Can fully bear the sight,
> But downward bends his burning eye
> At mysteries so bright.[15]

This is so important for our understanding of angels and their role in God's universe. If angels, as it were, strained over the walls of the celestial city to marvel at the mystery of the Cross and of our salvation; this is deeply moving. It is a truly marvellous matter that angels, the faithful messengers of God, did not fully understand the depths of God's love for faltering mankind, until they witnessed the glory and the suffering of his Son. They also appear as silent observers of the sufferings of the Apostles. Paul writes:

> For it seems to me that God has put us apostles on display at the end of the procession, like men condemned to die in the arena. We have been made a spectacle to the whole universe, to angels as well as to men. (1 Corinthians 4:9)

This verse proved of great comfort to one suffering member of the hidden Chinese church. (See Chapter 4, p 103ff.)

We shall judge angels

An even more remarkable text which suggests considerable limitations in angelic understanding and power is found in the midst of a broadside from Paul to the Corinthian church about the impropriety of Christians going to law against other Christians (see 1 Corinthians 6:1–6).

Jesus had promised the disciples a powerful role in the final judgment. "I tell you the truth, at the renewal of all things, when the Son of Man sits on his glorious throne, you who have followed me will also sit on twelve thrones, judging the twelve tribes of Israel" (Matthew 19:28), which contrasts somewhat with the role of the angels in the parable of the sheep and the goats (Matthew 25:31–46).

Here Paul takes the matter further (1 Corinthians 6:3). He probably has in mind a great passage from Daniel 7:9–27 where the part that the saints will play is described in vv 26–27.

But the court will sit, and his power will be taken away and completely destroyed for ever. Then the sovereignty, power and greatness of the kingdoms under the whole heaven will be handed over to the saints, the people of the Most High. His kingdom will be an everlasting kingdom, and all rulers will worship and obey him.

David Prior writes:[16]

The sheer grandeur of this perspective on the consummation of the kingdom of God, and the part to be played in it by "saints" like these Corinthian bickerers, must have made Paul wince whenever he thought about the scene in Corinth: like Daniel, he might have declared, 'Here is the end of the matter.' How, in the name of the Most High God, could these folk at Corinth sink that low? *Do you not know that the saints will judge the world?* It all becomes farcical, if not blasphemous, to go to *court* about *trivial cases.*

Paul is still not finished. So far are the Christians at Corinth from forgetting their destiny in the kingdom of God that they have not registered that even angels are to be in the dock. Where does that leave squabbling about "everyday affairs"? Angels have a difficult role to play at the best of times. They give the best of their energies to the worship of heaven and the service of the saints. *But they have immense difficulties understanding the glories of salvation. Indeed, Peter imagines them peering down from heaven trying to penetrate the mysteries of what it means to be redeemed.* But, by and large, "the manifold wisdom of God", seen in the "unsearchable riches of Christ", is beyond the ken of "the principalities and powers". It is the task of the redeemed people of God, including the church of Corinth, to communicate this divine wisdom to these angelic beings.

As Paul has already explained, this wisdom is in "Jesus Christ and him crucified", and there are fallen angels who cannot stomach the fact. It was their pride that had them originally cast out of the kingdom of God, and they still await divine judgment for that rebellion. "Corinthian Christians, do you not know that we are to judge those angels? How could you have forgotten such basic Christian teaching and plummeted to the depths of sitting in judgment on one another?"

Angels and the Second Coming

Jesus made it crystal clear that angels will be involved at the Parousia – the Second Coming. However, unlike many foolish "prophets" over the last 2000 years, they *know not* 'that day or hour' (Mark 13:32). This is important as a number of spurious angel stories purport to give details of an imminent return of Jesus (see p 208f).

All of us would be wise to follow the saintly Bishop Ken,[17] who in his hymn "Awake my soul and with the sun" wisely writes "live this day as if thy last". That is the only safe way to prepare for the Second Coming (or for death, which is far more likely!).

When the great day comes, Jesus will be accompanied by his angels. He will reward "each person according to what he has done". (Matthew 16:27). Those who have acknowledged Jesus before men, he will acknowledge before the angels of God (see Luke 12:8, also Luke 9:26, and Mark 8:38). Angels are an essential part of God's creation. Their role, which at the moment is largely invisible, will become gloriously apparent at the end of time.

Conclusions

Jesus taught about angels; they were part of his world, part of his spiritual experience, part of his *natural thinking*. However, the Holy Spirit (see Luke 11:13; and John Chapters 14–16), rather than a guardian angel, was his *principal* gift to believers.

He didn't teach his followers either actively to seek angels, nor to rely on their protection. Angels, according to Jesus, and the wider witness of Scripture, are a wonderful part of God's creation. They will have a major role to play in the end times. The Revelation of St John, of course, has much to say on these matters. The presence of angels cannot be ignored; nor, for us in our present state, should it be exaggerated.

We shall now consider how Jesus, and to an apparently greater extent, the New Testament church, experienced the presence and protection of angels.

Notes

(1) See, for instance, *Encyclopaedia of Angels,* Rosemary Guiley, Facts on File, 1996. The section under the heading about the early Greek writings of 'Pseudo Dionysius' contain a good summary of much speculative thought.

(2) First, for example, in the Abraham cycle of stories in Genesis.

(3) See, for instance, the brief discussion of Gnosticism later in this chapter (p 49).

(4) This text is, characteristically, misused by Satan in the Temptation narrative (Luke 4:9–13).

(5) The hymn 'Through all the changing scenes of life' is a metrical psalm based on these verses. See also my *Healing & Deliverance*, Monarch, 1999, p. 64f. for further comments on this important text.

(6) From a sermon of Chrysostom (347–407) on this passage.

(7) "Another place" has been much debated. It could mean Rome. The arguments are complex. See John Wenham,

Redating Matthew, Mark, Luke and John – a Fresh Assault on the Synoptic Problem, Hodder and Stoughton, 1991.

(8) Patricia St John, *Would You Believe It?* Pickering & Inglis, 1983, p. 91.

(9) The meaning of the "angel" in the texts about the seven churches in Revelation, Chapters 2 and 3 is uncertain. It is difficult to believe that the author means that there is an actual angel presiding over a particular church. If that were the case, St John is highly critical of the angel's work, which is unlikely. The angel here is probably symbolic, the message is clearly to the members of the churches.

(10) William Temple, *Readings in St John's Gospel*, Macmillan, 1959, p. 226.

(11) Theresa of Avila (1515–1582) *The Interior Castle* is a classic book about prayer and the spiritual life, written in the 16th century. Theresa's journey, of course, is in *this* life, but she has a deep mystical sense of what lies ahead.

(12) See John 3:3, for instance.

(13) Quoted by Dr Alison Morgan, *What Happens When We Die?*, Kingsway, 1995, p. 235.

(14) The *Encyclopaedia of Angels*, *op. cit.* pp. 71–74 has one of its largest, and largely uncritical, articles on the Gnostic view of angels. It is clear that many New Age ideas about angels are based on Gnostic teaching, one of whose most notable proponents was said to be Simon Magus (see Acts 8 and the *Encyclopaedia*, p. 72).

(15) "Crown Him with many crowns" M. Bridges, verse 3.

(16) David Prior, "The Message of 1 Corinthians", *The Bible Speaks Today*, IVP, 1988, p. 109f.

(17) Thomas Ken (1637–1711) hymn writer, saintly Bishop of Bath and Wells.

3

Angels Mainly According to Luke

In this chapter, we examine the role of angels mainly in the Gospels, and in the Acts of the Apostles. We note Luke's particular interest in our subject, and consider why angelic appearances seem to be more frequent in the life of the early church than in the life of Jesus.

Angels Mainly According to Luke

The case for angels needs making in today's sceptical society. If it can be made, by extension the case for the Virgin Birth and the Incarnation become stronger. Luke was well placed to make this case. Writing about the Day of Pentecost, he records the amazed onlookers as saying "We hear them declaring the wonders of God in our own tongues!" (Acts 2:11). Some years later, as Paul's travelling companion, he would personally witness some of these wonders.

Luke joins Paul's second missionary journey just after Paul has received a vision "of a man of Macedonia standing and begging him, 'Come over to Macedonia and help us'" (Acts 16:9). In the next verse, the narrative changes from "they" to "we". The author of Acts has joined the expedition!

In Philippi, where Luke apparently stayed until rejoining Paul (compare Acts 16:40 and Acts 20:6), many miracles occurred. The conversion of the wealthy Lydia, the deliverance of the slave girl, and the remarkable events in the gaol, combined to make a strong church.

Later, Luke witnessed more miracles – notably the raising of Eutychus. He was not the last person to fall asleep during a long sermon (see Acts 20:7ff), but the consequence was unusually dramatic. Later, Luke described Paul's voyage to Rome in extraordinary detail. He seems to be making the point that even the elements combined to make it almost impossible for Paul to travel to Rome. At the height of the storm, an angel (see Acts 27:23–24 and p 81 below), strengthened Paul. Then, on the little island of Malta, more miracles occurred. A viper fastened itself on Paul's hand, but the apostle was unharmed. As a result, Paul's reputation is enhanced. This, in turn, led to the healing of the father of the chief official of the island, and then of all the other sick people (see Acts 28:1–10).

Is it surprising that Luke shows a particular interest in prayer, the work of the Holy Spirit, and angelic encounters?

Angels appear in the prologue (the events surrounding John the Baptist's birth), the Incarnation (as messengers to both Mary and Joseph), the Nativity (both as a celestial choir, and also to warn the Holy Family of impending danger). In Jesus' lifetime, such was his relationship with his Father, their presence was very rare. Apart from his teaching about them, they appeared in the wilderness, the Garden of Gethsemane, and in great glory at the time of the Resurrection.

Christmas angels

Luke's Gospel, after a careful preamble (see Luke 1:1–4 and compare with Acts 1:1), opens with the events surrounding the birth of John the Baptist. The cycle of angelic stories concerning the birth of John the Baptist has great similarities with events recorded in the Old Testament.[1]

"The angel of the Lord" (a typical figure of speech[2]) appears to Zechariah (Luke 1:8ff) to promise him that his wife will, unexpectedly, bear a son who will be "great in the sight of the Lord", and amazingly, "filled with the Holy Spirit even from birth". Zechariah, not unreasonably, and in somewhat similar fashion to Sarah (Genesis 18:12) and Abraham (Genesis 17:17), was more than a little dubious. The angel then reveals himself by name as Gabriel, and punishes Zechariah with nine months of silence for his lack of faith.

The pregnancy and birth are successfully accomplished. Mercifully, Elizabeth (Luke 1:60) and Zechariah (Luke 1:63) both know that the baby is to be called John; and amidst much rejoicing, Zechariah's tongue is loosed.

In Luke, the angelic appearances continue with the events surrounding the Incarnation and Nativity of our Lord. By contrast, Matthew mentions just three times that "an angel of the Lord" appeared unto Joseph – always in a dream; while Mark and John begin their Gospels with a theological proclamation of faith (see Mark 1:1 and John 1:1–14).

This cycle of angelic appearances is very well known, so well known that the stories can easily lose their wonder and breed unhealthy scepticism. A few restless angels, bored shepherds, distracted wise men, a grumpy innkeeper, produced by tired teachers for an end of term carol service don't usually encourage feelings of awe and reverence. Parents, often complaining that their child should have played Mary, are usually more concerned with photographs than theology.

Of course, there are glorious exceptions. Some children have an amazing intuition and sense of the supernatural (see Ch. 6, p 153ff). Many teachers, and Sunday School helpers, against all the odds, produce something sparkling and original each year. But because of this prevailing scepticism, the case for angels (and by extension for the Incarnation and the Virgin Birth) needs to be made. A few relevant stories of modern encounters with angels can help restore faith in this the greatest of all angelic encounters.

According to Luke there are just two angelic encounters in the actual Nativity story. First, the Angel Gabriel (see Daniel 8:16, 9:21 and earlier Luke 1:19) appears to Mary. This earth-changing event is described in just a few words by St Luke.

In the sixth month, God sent the angel Gabriel to Nazareth, a town in Galilee, to a virgin pledged to be married to a man named Joseph, a descendant of David. The virgin's name was Mary. The angel went to her and said, "Greetings, you who are highly favoured! The Lord is with you."

Mary was greatly troubled at his words and wondered what kind of greeting this might be. But the angel said to her, "Do not be afraid, Mary, you have found favour with God. You will be with child and give birth to a son, and you are to give him the name Jesus. He will be great and will be called the Son of the Most High. The Lord God will give him the throne of his father David, and he will reign over the house of Jacob for ever; his kingdom will never end."

"How will this be," Mary asked the angel, "since I am a virgin?"

The angel answered, "The Holy Spirit will come upon you, and the power of the Most High will overshadow you. So the holy one to be born will be called the Son of God. Even Elizabeth your relative is going to have a child in her old age, and she who was said to be barren is in her sixth month. For nothing is impossible with God."

"I am the Lord's servant," Mary answered. "May it be to me as you have said." Then the angel left her. (Luke 1:26–38)

Mary, like others when meeting angels, is perplexed and uncertain. Her question "How will this be, since I am a virgin?" is deemed by Gabriel a reasonable question. Unlike Zechariah (Luke 1:18ff), Mary is given a straight answer with no hint of a rebuke.

Meanwhile, Joseph is considerably troubled. Pre-nuptial pregnancy was not good news – particularly when he knew that he couldn't be the father! Joseph was granted a dream, sufficiently detailed to set his righteous mind at rest. In this particular dream, an angel of the Lord appeared to him[3] (Matthew 1:20ff).

The next angelic appearance was to the shepherds. First an angel of the Lord appears to them, and then a great choir of angels gave them, and us, a beautiful hymn, "Glory to God in the highest and peace to his people on earth", used to this day by the mainstream churches every Sunday in their Communion services. The shepherds were very much on the fringe of Jewish society, and the angelic appearance to this group should

remind us that angels don't necessarily appear to religious
people. They appear at God's bidding, to do His work and to
proclaim His glory. (See Luke 2:8–20.)

No wonder that Mary "treasured up all these things and
pondered them in her heart". Angelic experiences, and testimonies, will strengthen a believer's faith, especially if they
confirm what has already become known in other ways.

The other angelic experiences were again granted to Joseph
in dreams (Matthew 2:13ff). In each case they concerned guidance, first for protection from Herod, and secondly as a sign
that it was time to return home to Nazareth. God sometimes
speaks to people in dreams, both in Scripture, and in ordinary
experience.

Mary and Joseph already had experience of angels, but after
the traumas of the journey to Bethlehem, the birth in the stable,
and the hostility of Herod, this must have been important
confirmation to them of God's favour and protection.

Angels in Jesus' ministry

By contrast, St Mark's Gospel begins in the wilderness. The
wilderness had been a place of fear and failure for the Jewish
people. They had wandered there for 40 years during the
Exodus and, despite many miracles, a whole generation had
turned its back upon God. Then out of the same wilderness, the
strange wild prophet John the Baptist emerges, prophesies the
coming of the Messiah, baptises adult Jews (something quite
unheard of), and baptises Jesus. Jesus commended by the Voice
of the Father, and empowered by the Spirit, is driven into the
wilderness, tempted and tested by Satan, and attended by wild
beasts and angels.

Satan uses Scripture to test Jesus, including a well-known
proof text about angelic protection (Psalm 91:11–12).

Then the devil took him to the holy city and had him stand on the
highest point of the temple. "If you are the Son of God," he said,

"throw yourself down. For it is written, 'He will command his angels concerning you, and they will lift you up in their hands, so that you will not strike your foot against a stone.'" Jesus answered him, "It is also written: 'Do not put the Lord your God to the test.'" (Matthew 4:5–7)

Jesus knew well that angels *could* protect him (see earlier on Matthew 26:53, Chapter 2 p 41), but that guardian angels could not be expected to in *inappropriate* circumstances. Guardian angels are not available on demand, and their protection cannot be assumed even by the Son of God. Satan delights to make people misuse spiritual power.[4] Mark concludes his brief, but dramatic account, with the words, "He was with the wild animals, and angels attended him." (Mark 1:13) The closest parallel to this description, in the Old Testament, is found in 1 Kings 19:5–7 where an angel supplies Elijah, in the wilderness, with food and strength. In Elijah's case, the angelic intervention was after a great spiritual triumph, all too quickly followed by terror and depression. His ministry was almost over. By contrast, Jesus not only triumphed over Satan, but his faithful obedience marked the beginning of his public ministry – a ministry, according to Mark, of constant conflict with the demonic forces, and constantly sustained by his relationship with God the Father.

Angels, and wild animals, (especially snakes) often appeared in the wilderness. The angel of the Lord had appeared to Moses in the burning bush (Exodus 3:2). After this great beginning, the journey into the wilderness, which began so well, became a time of grumbling, idolatry, rebellion, and sexual disaster. The architect of this last failure was none other than the prophet Balaam (see Revelation 2:14 and Numbers 31:16 etc.). Balaam, deep into occult practices (Numbers 24:1), is hired to prophesy against the advancing Israelites. Seduced by money, he sets out, only to be blocked by his recalcitrant donkey. The donkey is considerably more spiritually alert than his master (a not uncommon phenomenon in haunted houses where animals are often more sensitive to the presence of evil than their human owners). The donkey is aware of the angel long before Balaam! Balaam then infuriates his host Balak by prophesying success for Israel. Like Caiaphas (John 11:49–50), he even includes a Messianic prophecy, "A star will come out of Jacob; a sceptre will rise out of Israel" (Numbers 24:17). Unfortunately, he doesn't learn from his angelic encounter, and despite having prophesied success for Israel, he encourages the Midianite women to seduce Israel. This tawdry story should warn us that angelic experiences do not necessarily convert people.

There are no further direct appearances of angels in the Gospel narratives until the Garden of Gethsemane, and the first Easter day. This should not surprise us, since Jesus' relationship with God was so close ("I and the Father are one." John 10:30). The point is often made that the cluster of angelic announcements at the beginning and end of the Gospels underlines the particular work of God in redemption and through revelation. In Scripture, angelic encounters are *never* asked for. Angels appear aiding believers in distress, and announcing God's plans to his servants. There is however one oblique reference to angels connected with Jesus' healing presence:

A tradition of angelic intervention

Some time later, Jesus went up to Jerusalem for a feast of the Jews. Now there is in Jerusalem near the Sheep Gate a pool, which in Aramaic is called Bethesda and which is surrounded by five covered colonnades. Here a great number of disabled people used to lie – the blind, the lame, the paralysed and they waited for the moving of the waters. From time to time an angel of the Lord would come down and stir up the waters. The first one into the pool after each such disturbance would be cured of whatever disease he had. One who was there had been an invalid for thirty-eight years. When Jesus saw him lying there and learned that he had been in this condition for a long time, he asked him, "Do you want to get well?"

"Sir," the invalid replied, "I have no-one to help me into the pool when the water is stirred. While I am trying to get in, someone else goes down ahead of me." Then Jesus said to him, "Get up! Pick up your mat and walk." At once the man was cured, he picked up his mat and walked. (John 5:1–9)

Leon Morris in his massive commentary[5] states that verses 3b and 4 "and they waited for the moving of the waters. From time to time an angel of the Lord would come down and stir up the waters. The first one into the pool after such disturbance would be cured of whatever disease he had . . ." are omitted from nearly all important ancient manuscripts and that they were inserted to give a clearer explanation of local expectations.

Clearly Jesus knew about the tradition – not least from the man's pathetic statement about never being first into the waters when they are stirred. The healing at the pool is important theologically for a number of reasons. Jesus asks the man a very pertinent question "Do you want to get well?" For some reason, he alone is chosen to be healed. There is no clear reason for this. Jesus often dealt with individuals, many of whom like this man seemed particularly unworthy recipients of his grace. In evangelism, healing, and in the matter of guardian angels, discussed in the previous chapter, we cannot avoid the obvious evidence of God's sovereignty and choices. At the conclusion, Jesus gives him a stern warning, "See, you are well again. Stop sinning or something worse may happen to you." This is reminiscent of the statement in Luke 11:26 about seven worse spirits returning after an exorcism.

There is a distinct impression that the man who had been ill for 38 years was neither very hopeful of healing (which is quite understandable), nor even particularly desirous of healing – after all, it was simpler, and easier, to remain a beggar. There is also a strong hint that although he was physically healed, he was not spiritually whole. By contrast, see the story of the healing of the woman with the issue of blood. She, too, had been ill for a long time, but Jesus specifically declared her to be whole (see Mark 5:25ff). At the very end of this story (John 5:15) the

man went away and told the Jews that it was Jesus who made
him well. The result was that Jesus was now locked into a
deadly conflict with the Jewish leaders in Jerusalem. The man,
who had been healed in a far more remarkable way than if he
had entered "the troubled waters", slips away into obscurity.
But, like Balaam, it is doubtful if the supernatural encounter
had affected his spiritual state.

Supernatural encounters whether with angels, or Jesus
himself, are no guarantee of experiencing new birth. Jesus went
further than this, warning in the Sermon on the Mount, that even
performing signs in his name is no guarantee of divine acceptance (Matthew 7:15–23; see also Acts 19:13–14, Acts 8:13ff).

The idea of an angel stirring up the waters is interesting.
Throughout the centuries many springs have been associated
with healing, and there is some evidence of their efficacy. Jesus
makes no effort to correct the local superstition, and we should
assume that he accepted this particular tradition of angelic
involvement. If he had regarded it as a false superstition, he
would have condemned it as strongly as he condemned the
false traditions of the Pharisees (see Mark 7:9ff, for instance).

The Transfiguration

The Transfiguration (Luke 9:28–36, Mark 9:2–13, and
Matthew 17:1–13) is not about angels. But remembering Jesus'
teaching to the Sadducees that believers will become like
angels (see above, pp 44ff), we can treat the presence of Moses
and Elijah as similar to an angelic appearance. The Transfiguration is a turning point in the Gospel narratives. It created a
great impression on Peter (see 2 Peter 1:17), and the dazzling
white clothing is similar in description to that of the angels in
the resurrection stories. Before the great encounter on the
mountain, Jesus had spent most of his time teaching and healing in Galilee; afterwards he sets his face to Jerusalem. Characteristically, Luke records that it began while Jesus was praying.
(Luke 9:28–29).

It is probable that the amazing vision, granted to Jesus' three closest disciples, took place on Mount Hermon. It was over 3000 metres high, and close to Caesarea Philippi, where Peter had recently acknowledged Jesus as "the Christ, the Son of the living God" (Matthew 16:16). Jesus had gone there to pray, he must spend time with God to make sure that he was right, and that the path to Jerusalem, and the cross, was really the way of victory. The Transfiguration provided that assurance, not only for Jesus, but also for Peter, James and John. As at his baptism, his role as son and servant is reinforced by a voice from heaven. Moses and Elijah appear, talking with Jesus, on the mountain. They were recognised as the supreme representatives of the Law and the Prophets of Israel. In this vision, they spoke to Jesus. In Scripture, both are connected with the end of time. Both had left this life in a strange way. The grave of Moses was never found (Deuteronomy 34:5–6); and the Epistle to Jude has a curious verse (v. 9), based on Jewish Apocryphal writings, about a dispute between the Archangel Michael and the Devil over his body. Elijah ascended into heaven (2 Kings 2:11). The expectation was that in the last days a prophet like Moses would arise (Deuteronomy 18:15) and that a prophet similar to Elijah would return (Malachi 4:5).[6]

The presence of God was made clear by the dazzling white clothing, the cloud, and the voice from heaven. Moses and Elijah disappear, and the awestruck disciples are left in the presence of God and his Son. It is hardly surprising that the disciples are overcome, and it is very moving that "Jesus came and touched them" (Matthew 17:7).

The theology of the Transfiguration is one of glory inexorably linked with suffering. Jesus made this clear to the three on the way down from the mountain. Sadly this great story is sometimes misused by spiritualists, and by those who believe in reincarnation. These two beliefs, in different ways bypass the Cross, and distort the biblical record. The next angelic encounter is at an even more decisive juncture.

The garden of Gethsemane

> Jesus went out as usual to the Mount of Olives, and his disciples
> followed him. On reaching the place, he said to them, "Pray that
> you will not fall into temptation." He withdrew, about a stone's
> throw beyond them, knelt down and prayed, "Father, if you are
> willing, take this cup from me, yet not my will, but yours be done."
> An angel from heaven appeared to him and strengthened him. And
> being in anguish, he prayed more earnestly, and his sweat was like
> drops of blood falling to the ground. When he rose from prayer
> and went back to the disciples, he found them asleep, exhausted
> from sorrow. "Why are you sleeping?" he asked them, "Get up and
> pray so that you will not fall into temptation." (Luke 22:39–46)

This was the decisive moment in Jesus' earthly life. Up until
now, Jesus strides through the pages of Scripture, the complete
master in all circumstances. He appears, and disappears, at
will. He silences both earthly opponents and demonic ones, he
heals the sick, raises the dead, has authority over nature, and
teaches so sublimely, that even today non-Christians will often
admire and want to follow his teaching.[7]

A little while earlier, Jesus had walked through Jerusalem
freely for the last time. Accompanied by his disciples, they had
left the light of the upper room, and walked out into the darkness of the narrow streets of the Holy City. They had passed the
Temple, its golden vine glinting in the light of the full Passover
moon. Quickly, they had descended the steep path (which can
still be walked today), crossed the little brook called Kidron,
and climbed up a steep slope. At the top of the ridge, there was
a choice. Jesus could have turned right, and walked back to his
friends in Bethany, and then returned north to Galilee, or he
could have turned left into the Garden called Gethsemane, well
known to him and to Judas Iscariot.

There, Jesus faced the greatest spiritual crisis of his life. He
left his disciples nearby. He then spent an hour in intense
prayer, while his disciples spent the time falling in and out of

sleep. This contrast is much beloved of the great renaissance painters. We know from John that earlier he prayed for the unity of the church, for his disciples, and for all future believers (see John 17). We know from Matthew, Mark, and Luke, that he prayed with incredible intensity to his Father. He even asked for a lightening of his spiritual load, praying: "Father, if you are willing, take this cup from me; yet not my will, but yours be done." (Luke 22:42)

We cannot begin to grasp the intensity of this sacred time of prayer. Our feeble struggles, our little uncertainties, fade into complete insignificance when compared with this foaming spiritual cup (see Mark 10:38 where James and John totally fail to understand the significance of Jesus' solemn words). What we should never underestimate is the strength of this temptation and testing. All that was needed for Jesus to escape was a late-night stroll away from the Garden along the ridge to the north of Jerusalem. The encounter with the Devil in the wilderness was as nothing compared with this. In the wilderness, Jesus had been ministered to by angels; here, in the gathering gloom, "an angel from heaven appeared to him and strengthened him." (Luke 22:43)[8]

In the wilderness, Jesus had faced three temptations – to misuse his power for his own physical needs, to misuse his power and rely on Divine protection to perform a miraculous sign, and to receive earthly power by bowing down to the "Prince of this World".

In the Garden, we might consider that Jesus faced three even more deadly temptations – to use his power to walk away from trouble (as he had rightly done in Nazareth – see Luke 4:30), to call on a legion of angels and rely on Divine protection, or to do, perhaps, what Judas longed for, and to receive earthly power by acknowledging the Prince of Darkness, and leading a rebellion against the Romans.

The solitary angel, in contrast with the ministering angels in the wilderness,[9] came to *strengthen him*. The effect was to *intensify* the spiritual struggle, as Luke makes clear. We are not told what, if any, message the angel brought.

Could it be that the angelic presence was the answer to Jesus' final prayer, "Yet not my will, but yours be done"? Could it be that the angel, silently, or with a spoken word, conveyed the Father's final answer? The shadow of the Cross, prophesied to Mary by Simeon, prophesied by Jesus to the twelve, was now to become a terrible reality. The cup of God's wrath (Isaiah 51:17, 22) poured out against the sin of the world, now had to be drunk to the full. Was that the message that the angel brought, and which brought forth such holy agony in the quiet moonlit garden?

The angel's presence heightens the already unbearable tension. One writer[10] describes the scene as follows:

At this critical moment angelic strength supplemented Jesus' human resources. We get some indication of the intensity of his feeling when we read of sweat like great drops of blood falling down upon the ground. The word "agony" is found only here in the New Testament. Why was Jesus in such perturbation as He faced death? Others, including many who owe their inspiration to the Master, have faced death quite calmly. It cannot be death as such that caused this tremendous depth of feeling. Rather it was the kind of death that Jesus would die, that death in which He was forsaken by God (Mark 15:34), in which God made Him to be sin for us (2 Corinthians 5:21).

The presence of the angel underlines the intensity of the spiritual battle. Jesus who has often prayed through the night (Luke 6:12, for instance), prays and waits.[11] While the Son of God strives, the disciples sleep, and when the crisis comes, they melt into the darkness, unable to help. The whole outcome of the world's salvation rested on Jesus waiting, and then drinking the cup to the full. It is wonderfully mysterious that the Father gave the Son the sign of a *solitary* angel.

And then the crowd came. Jesus, still fully the master of circumstances, declared prophetically "I am He" (John 18:6). At this moment, he disclosed his Divinity, probably using the exact Aramaic expression that God had used to Moses when he revealed his name amidst the burning bush (Exodus 3:14). At this, the soldiers fell back stunned; the disciples led by the impetuous Peter engaged in a futile fight. Jesus, now completely passive, allowed the soldiers, and their officers to do their worst. His final words to his disciples included, "Put your sword back in its place, for all who draw the sword will die by the sword. Do you think I cannot call on my Father, and he will at once put at my disposal more than twelve legions of angels?" (Matthew 26:52–53)

Legions of angels could have been summoned; but that would have been to dance to the Devil's tune more certainly than if he'd jumped from the pinnacle of the Temple. Once again, Jesus had to reject the idea of calling upon divine protection.

The disciples all fled, including the mysterious young man (presumed to be John Mark, in whose mother's house the early church met, Acts 12:12) who fled away naked. (Mark 14:51–52) Jesus was left alone to face the worst that the world and the Devil could offer. A long dark night was to follow, then a day of twisted cruelty accompanied by supernatural darkness. No angels, mostly unfaithful friends, jeering crowds, and brutal soldiers. This was the cup that the sons of Zebedee had imagined that they could drink (Matthew 20:22). This is the cup that all of us, tempted by quick fixes and cheap grace, want to avoid. This is the cup that broke the power of the legions from Hell, and opened the way of victory. Paul puts it very clearly:

When you were dead in your sins and in the uncircumcision of your sinful nature, God made you alive with Christ.. He forgave us all our sins, having cancelled the written code, with its regulations, that was against us and that stood opposed to us; he took it away, nailing it to the cross. And having disarmed the powers and authorities, he made a public spectacle of them, triumphing over them by the cross. (Colossians 2:13–15)

That triumphal procession took place on the third day, and this time there were angels present!

Angels at the tomb

Each of the four Gospels tells us of angelic experiences around the tomb. Critics and cynics have had a field-day dissecting the differences and apparent discrepancies in the four accounts. "A young man dressed in a white robe" (Mark 16:5); "An angel of the Lord" (Matthew 28:2); "Two men in clothes that gleamed like lightning" (Luke 24:4); "Two angels in white, seated where Jesus' body had been" (John 20:12) – four slightly different pictures of what the women saw who came to the tomb "very early in the morning".

This is hardly surprising. Whenever men and women encounter supernatural beings, there is a measure of confusion. A careful reading of Genesis 18, leaves us wondering exactly how many people were present. Angels often do look like human beings. Only subsequently, often after a mysterious disappearance, do people realise the full significance of what has happened. The discrepancies in the accounts of the first Easter Day render the narrative more, not less, authentic.

The four Gospels, as one, bear witness to an empty tomb, a risen Christ, and an awestruck, transformed group of followers. Holy fear and joyful surprise are present in all their hearts. The best texts of Mark's Gospel end with the words (referring to the women who had come to the tomb) "they were afraid" (Mark 16:8).

Mark's words mean that the women were filled with awe. Many times in his Gospel, people were filled with this holy fear. Notably at the first recorded exorcism (Mark 1:27); after the healing of the paralytic man (Mark 2:12); when he stilled the storm (Mark 4:41); when Jairus' daughter was raised (Mark 5:42); when he walked on the water (Mark 6:51); after the healing of a man who was deaf and mute (Mark 7:37); during the Transfiguration (Mark 9:6); after his hard teaching to the rich young ruler (Mark 10:24); after the cleansing of the Temple (Mark 11:18).

It is entirely fitting that Mark's account of the Resurrection should end with the faithful women, trembling and bewildered, overcome by amazement and wonder.

Matthew records that the women "hurried away from the tomb, afraid yet filled with joy" (Matthew 28:8). Luke says "In their fright the women bowed down with their faces to the ground" (Luke 24:5). John records Mary Magdalene racing away from the tomb, displaying what appears to be a mixture of fear and wonder "They have taken the Lord out of the tomb, and we don't know where they have put him!" (John 20:2)

The accounts tell us how the great stone was moved by an angel, and the devastating effect of his appearance on the guards (Matthew 28:2–4). Matthew includes the interesting sentence that the guards, strangely reminiscent of Sennacherib's army (see the next chapter) "became like dead men"! Mark and Luke intend their men, described as dressed in white to be understood as angels. One fine commentator puts it as follows:[12]

The feature which shows that the evangelist means an angel is the factor of revelation (Mark 16:6–7). God often uses visible means to reveal himself, and the angel fits into this pattern. As frequently in the Old Testament and the Jewish literature from the later period, the angel appears as the divine messenger. This conclusion is supported by the detail of the white garment. In the colour symbolism of the New Testament white is primarily the heavenly colour and is mentioned almost exclusively in eschatological or apocalyptic contexts. In this instance the white clothes are not properly a description, but an indication of the dazzling nature of their glory (for instance as in the Transfiguration account in Mark 9:3. See also Revelation 6:11; 7:9,13). The presence of the angel underscores the character of the Resurrection of Jesus and anticipates the Parousia when the Son of Man will come in the glory of the Father "with the holy angels" (Mark 8:38; see also Mark 13:26).

The angels in their brilliant white clothes remind us of the glory of the Transfiguration. Their presence at the empty tomb almost concludes their work in Jesus' earthly ministry.

The overwhelming evidence of history is that "Jesus is risen!" (Mark 16:6). This is not the place for a detailed discussion of the evidence; but just for a moment consider the state of the disciples on the Saturday evening. Sheltering behind locked doors for fear of the Jews, they had no friends in Jerusalem except a few women, and a few closet disciples like Joseph of Arimathea and Nicodemus. Could such a group, with their improbable story about a crucified carpenter who was the Messiah, have "turned the world upside down" (Acts 17:6 KJV) unless the Resurrection story was true? How was James, the brother of the Lord, an early Christian martyr, changed from an embarrassed sceptic to a devout follower – unless Paul's simple words written circa AD55 "Then he appeared to James" (1 Corinthians 15:7) are true? If the Resurrection story is true, then it is hardly surprising that the event was accompanied by angels, even if their number is uncertain.

Angels in Acts

Luke concludes his account of Jesus' earthly ministry with a brief account of the Ascension (Luke 24:50–53). After a few preliminaries, he begins his next volume with a more detailed account of the same event. He concludes this event with a very restrained account of the first angelic visitation to the disciples.

After he said this, he was taken up before their very eyes, and a cloud hid him from their sight. They were looking intently up into the sky as he was going, when suddenly two men dressed in white stood beside them. "Men of Galilee," they said, "why do you stand here looking into the sky? This same Jesus, who has been taken from you into heaven, will come back in the same way you have seen him go into heaven." (Acts 1:9–11)

For the angelic hosts the period of inquiry was over; now they understood fully the purposes of God, and his strangely wonderful dealings with disobedient mankind. No wonder the writer of Hebrews could say:

> What is man that you are mindful of him, the son of man that you care for him? You made him a little lower than the angels; you crowned him with glory and honour and put everything under his feet. (Hebrews 2:6–8; Psalm 8:4–6).

We have already referred to a number of angelic appearances in the Acts of the Apostles (see Ch. 2, p 38f). This occurred naturally as we thought about guardian angels. However, the whole book is full of revelations, visions, and supernatural encounters.[13] We shall now look at the martyrdom of Stephen (Acts 6 and 7), the ministry of Philip (Acts 8), the conversion of Cornelius (Acts 10 and 11), and the death of Herod (Acts 12:23). Finally, we shall again touch on Paul's experiences, as we try to sort out the apparent confusion between the work of the Holy Spirit and the work of angels.

The death of Stephen

Stephen was accused of "blasphemy against Moses and against God" (Acts 6:11). When facing the Sanhedrin, his opponents saw "that his face was like the face of an angel" (Acts 6:15).

One commentator[14] writes that this was "not the mild, gentle look that is often seen in paintings of angels; not the fierce look of an avenging angel, but a look that told of inspiration within, clear eyes burning with the inner light. We can hardly doubt that it was Saul (Acts 7:58) who remembered that look, a look which burnt into his soul until he too was turned to accept Jesus as his master and learnt in his own life to experience the presence of the Holy Spirit."

Stephen's speech, which infuriated his hearers, has several surprising references to angels. The first (Acts 7:30) refers to the well-known incident of the angel of the Lord appearing to Moses at the burning bush. The second states that an *angel* spoke to Moses on Mount Sinai (Acts 7:38), and the third says that the Law was put into effect through angels (Acts 7:53).

Both Paul (Galatians 3:19) and the writer of Hebrews (Hebrews 2:2), follow Stephen in asserting that angels mediated the Law. Angels are not mentioned in Exodus 20 (the giving of the Ten Commandments), nor in Moses' report in Deuteronomy 5. But Moses' first speech (Deuteronomy 33:1ff – my italics) begins

> The Lord came from Sinai and dawned over them from Seir; he shone forth from Mount Paran. He came *with* myriads of holy ones . . .

There is much debate as to whether the text should read "with myriads of holy ones", or "from myriads of holy ones".[15] Such distinctions reflect the cautious reverence of the biblical writers. Frequently, the appearances of God, himself, were described in angelic terms. A good example occurs in Judges 13, where Manoah (see v. 22) believes that he has seen God, whilst elsewhere the writer refers to "the Angel of the Lord".

For our purposes, Stephen's demeanour, his face shining like an angel, his vision of the exalted Jesus (Acts 7:56), and his willingness to forgive his murderers (Acts 7:60) are far more important than rabbinical arguments about who gave the Law to the rebellious people of Israel.

Stephen's death was the first example of Christian martyrdom.[16] His death bore extraordinary fruit. The angels did not rescue him, but the Holy Spirit was moving nearby.

> And Saul was there, giving approval to his death. On that day a great persecution broke out against the church at Jerusalem, and all except the apostles were scattered throughout Judea and Samaria. Godly men buried Stephen and mourned deeply for him. But Saul began to destroy the church. Going from house to house, he

dragged off men and women and put them in prison. Those who had been scattered preached the word wherever they went. (Acts 8:1–4)

Saul's reaction is fascinating. Was this the action of a fanatical man who had been thoroughly disturbed by the sight of a martyr with the face of an angel?

One side effect of Saul's campaign was to drive the church out from Jerusalem, and so begin to fulfil the command of Acts 1:8. The most effective worker was Philip. After a fruitful, and controversial ministry in Samaria, Philip encountered an angel.

Philip and the Ethiopian

Now an angel of the Lord said to Philip, "Go south to the road – the desert road – that goes down from Jerusalem to Gaza." So he started out, and on his way he met an Ethiopian eunuch, an important official in charge of all the treasury of Candace, queen of the Ethiopians. This man had gone to Jerusalem to worship, and on his way home was sitting in his chariot reading the book of Isaiah the prophet. The Spirit told Philip, "Go to that chariot and stay near it." (Acts 8:26–29)

It is interesting to see the difference between the role of the angel of the Lord (v. 26) and the Holy Spirit (v. 29). Luke is careful to make this distinction. Philip is given an *external* angel to get him out of Samaria and on to the desert road, but it is the Spirit, presumably working *internally* within Philip's soul, who points out the scripture-reading eunuch in his fine chariot. Clearly the Holy Spirit is working at "both ends of the line", and the eunuch is deeply receptive to Philip and his message.

The story ends in a measure of textual confusion. "When they came up out of the water, the Spirit of the Lord suddenly took Philip away" (Acts 8:39). The very early Western text[17] reads, "The Spirit of the Lord fell upon the eunuch and the angel of the Lord snatched Philip away." This reading rounds the story off better, and preserves the clear distinction between the angel and the Holy Spirit found at the beginning of the story.

The conversion of the first Gentile

The conversion of Cornelius is another of the great turning points in Acts, and once again an angel plays a significant part.

> At Caesarea there was a man named Cornelius, a centurion in what was known as the Italian Regiment. He and all his family were devout and God-fearing; he gave generously to those in need and prayed to God regularly. One day at about three in the afternoon he had a vision. He distinctly saw an angel of God who came to him and said, "Cornelius!" Cornelius stared at him in fear. "What is it, Lord?" he asked. The angel answered, "Your prayers and gifts to the poor have come up as a memorial offering before God. Now send men to Joppa to bring back a man named Simon who is called Peter. He is staying with Simon the tanner, whose house is by the sea." When the angel who spoke to him had gone, Cornelius called two of his servants and a devout soldier who was one of his attendants. He told them everything that had happened and sent them to Joppa. (Acts 10:1–8)

Once again, the Holy Spirit is working at "both ends of the line". Peter, who needs far more persuading, has a curious vision (Acts 10:9–16) which makes no sense until the Holy Spirit tells him that, "Three men are looking for you"! The first result of this dramatic encounter was that Peter invited his Gentile visitors to stay, the second was the clear conversion of a Gentile household. It is impossible to overemphasise what a barrier, both social and spiritual, had to be overcome; comparable perhaps, in modern times, to the problem of apartheid in South Africa (see Ch.4, p 102f).

There is a clear distinction between Cornelius' vision of an angel, and the Holy Spirit's work with Peter. At the end of the story, the Holy Spirit takes over (Acts 10:44–48), intervening even before Peter has finished preaching!

Acts soon reaches another climax. Saul of Tarsus has been converted (Acts 9), the Gentile church is growing (Acts 11:19–30), and Herod arrests Peter and James (Acts 12:1–3). This unpleasant incident is fully in keeping with the family record. Earlier members of the dynasty had slaughtered the innocents (Matthew 2:16–18), and executed John the Baptist (Matthew 14:1–12). Herod then suffered a dramatic death!

> Then Herod went from Judea to Caesarea and stayed there a while. He had been quarrelling with the people of Tyre and Sidon; they now joined together and sought an audience with him. Having secured the support of Blastus, a trusted personal servant of the king, they asked for peace, because they depended on the king's country for their food supply. On the appointed day Herod, wearing his royal robes, sat on his throne and delivered a public address to the people. They shouted, "This is the voice of a god, not of a man."
>
> Immediately, because Herod did not give praise to God, an angel of the Lord struck him down, and he was eaten by worms and died. (Acts 12:19b–23)

Luke laconically continues, "But the word of God continued to increase and spread." Herod was not the last tyrant to discover that persecution doesn't eliminate the church. Interestingly, the Jewish historian Josephus, writing circa AD90, also says in effect that "God's judgment fell upon Herod because he glorified himself instead of God."[18]

The differing work of the Spirit and the angels

Finally, we return to some of Paul's experiences.

> Paul and his companions travelled throughout the region of Phrygia and Galatia, having been kept by the Holy Spirit from preaching the word in the province of Asia. When they came to the

border of Mysia, they tried to enter Bithynia, but the Spirit of Jesus would not allow them to. So they passed by Mysia and went down to Troas. During the night Paul had a vision of a man of Macedonia standing and begging him, "Come over to Macedonia and help us." After Paul had seen the vision, we got ready at once to leave for Macedonia, concluding that God had called us to preach the gospel to them. (Acts 16:6–10)

The guidance received by Paul and his companions can seem confusing. The Holy Spirit (v. 6) keeps them out of the province of Asia, the Spirit of Jesus (v. 7) prevents them from entering Bithynia, and the visionary man of Macedonia (v. 9) summons them to Philippi!

Again, we should assume that Luke has made a careful distinction between different types of guidance. One understanding of the differences would run as follows:

The Holy Spirit spoke prophetically, through one of the party, and said "Don't go to the province of Asia." The risen Christ appeared in a dream to Paul, or, more likely, one of the others, and said, "Bithynia is not my chosen place at this time." Then Paul had his celebrated vision of the man of Macedonia who summoned them across the Aegean Sea to Philippi.

All this would have been of particular interest to Luke. It is here that the narrative changes from "they" to "we". Luke was present in Troas, and remained in Philippi after Paul and the others were escorted out (see Acts 16:38–39).

This interpretation fits well with Paul's own testimony. He is quite clear that his conversion experience (Acts 9:1ff; Acts 22:4ff; Acts 26:9ff; 1 Corinthians 15:8; 1 Corinthians 9:1; Galatians 1:16 etc.) was the equivalent of the resurrection appearances granted to the twelve and their closest companions (Acts 1:22). In the introduction, I mentioned that Paul had at least five other remarkable experiences of guidance. We have just discussed "the man of Macedonia"; referring to Corinth (Acts 18:9–10) Luke writes "One night the Lord spoke to Paul in a vision: 'Do not be afraid; keep on speaking, do not be silent. For I am with you, and no-one is going to attack and harm you, because I have many people in this city.' " In Jerusalem, (Acts 23:11), the Lord again comes to Paul in a vision saying "Take courage! As you have testified about me in Jerusalem, so you must also testify in Rome." In even more dangerous circumstances, after days without food, Paul, a non-sailor, exercises apostolic leadership in a seafaring situation.

> After the men had been gone a long time without food, Paul stood up before them and said, "Men, you should have taken my advice not to sail from Crete; then you would have spared yourselves this damage and loss. But now I urge you to keep up your courage, because not one of you will be lost; only the ship will be destroyed. Last night an angel of the God whose I am and whom I serve stood beside me and said, 'Do not be afraid, Paul, you must stand trial before Caesar; and God has graciously given you the lives of all who sail with you.' So keep up your courage, men, for I have faith in God that it will happen just as he told me. Nevertheless, we must run aground on some island." (Acts 27:21–26)

The angel protected, or prophesied the protection of, the men; but the ship was lost. I have noted this sort of outcome in three other places. (See p 27, p 109 & p 145.)

Luke has recorded five visionary experiences in Paul's life – on the road to Damascus, in Troas (leading him to Philippi), in Corinth, in Jerusalem, and on board ship. He is well able to distinguish between the different types of experience.

In the midst of all this, Paul experienced the wonderful reve-lation, which he shares, cautiously, with the Corinthian church. He received many such revelations (see 2 Corinthians 12:1 and 7), and he was not permitted to share them in *detail*.

> I must go on boasting. Although there is nothing to be gained, I will go on to visions and revelations from the Lord. I know a man in Christ who fourteen years ago was caught up to the third heaven. Whether it was in the body or out of the body I do not

know – God knows. And I know that this man – whether in the
body or apart from the body I do not know, but God knows – was
caught up to paradise. He heard inexpressible things, things that
man is not permitted to tell. I will boast about a man like that, but I
will not boast about myself, except about my weaknesses. Even if I
should choose to boast, I would not be a fool, because I would be
speaking the truth. But I refrain, so no-one will think more of me
than is warranted by what I do or say.

To keep me from becoming conceited because of these surpass-
ingly great revelations, there was given me a thorn in my flesh, a
messenger of Satan, to torment me. Three times I pleaded with the
Lord to take it away from me. But he said to me, "My grace is
sufficient for you, for my power is made perfect in weakness."
Therefore I will boast all the more gladly about my weaknesses, so
that Christ's power may rest on me. That is why, for Christ's sake,
I delight in weaknesses, in insults, in hardships, in persecutions, in
difficulties. For when I am weak, then I am strong. (2 Corinthians
12:1–10)

As a consequence of these revelations, Paul was troubled by the
much debated "thorn in my flesh". Whatever it was, and no one
can be certain, the effect was to make Paul even more dependent than ever on God's grace.

This glorious text should give us great confidence in the reality of Paradise, great caution in what and how we share revelations, and the grim realisation that angelic visions do not make
for an easy spiritual life.

"If you think you are standing firm, be careful that you don't
fall." (1 Corinthians 10:12)

Angels in the Gospels and Acts

In conclusion, we should ponder the relative frequency of
angelic experiences in the Acts and the Gospels. In Acts, the
Holy Spirit is ever present, but it seems that at key times, God
granted the infant church special visions and visitations.

By contrast, in the Gospels, angels seldom appear to Jesus.

Three times he heard the voice of God,[19] only twice, in the wilderness and in the garden, was he visited by angels. Consistently, he *knew* by the internal witness of the Spirit, what God would have him do and say (Mark 1:38; Mark 3:13; Luke 4:21ff, Luke 10:22; John 1:51, John 7:38 etc.).

Jesus Christ was, and is, God's Revelation, of Himself, to the world. He did not *need angels*; whereas angels were, and are, an essential part of God's continuing revelation to mankind. A revelation which is disclosed by the written word of Scripture, declared by faithful preaching; and often accompanied, as in Acts, by signs and wonders.

Mary, Joseph, the women at the empty tomb, the disciples on the day of the Ascension, Peter, Philip, Cornelius, Saul of Tarsus (Paul), were all granted angelic guidance and help at crisis points in their earthly pilgrimage.

So it has been throughout history. Angels come and go; their occasional interventions *always unsought*, yet always greatly welcomed. It is to this evidence that we now turn.

Notes

(1) See, for instance, the birth of Samson. (Judges 13.)

(2) See Genesis 16:7, and many other texts. (See also below.)

(3) The New Testament writers are careful to distinguish between angels who appear in dreams and visions, and those who are actually present. It may seem a fine distinction, but it is one that we should maintain.

(4) A point well made by Susan Howatch in her novels *Glittering Images* and *Glamorous Powers*, HarperCollins, 1987, 1988.

(5) Leon Morris, *The Gospel According to John*, Eerdmans, 1971, p. 302.

(6) Michael Green, *Matthew for Today*, Hodder & Stoughton, 1988. p. 163ff gives a wonderful commentary on this great event.

(7) Roy Hattersley, a distinguished Minister in the Labour

Government of the 1970s, makes this point in his recent biography of John Wesley. On Radio 4, Sunday 6th October 2002, he said that as an atheist, he admired Jesus' teaching, and wished that more people believed and went to church.

(8) This text, not found in many of the best manuscripts, should be retained. It is far more likely that later scribes would have deleted it, because it seemed to show too much of the human Jesus, than that some pious writer would have inserted it. The account in Mark is graphic enough, even without the presence of an angel. See also long discussion in C. P. Evans, *Saint Luke*, SCM, 1990, p. 811, and Leon Morris, *Luke*, Tyndale Commentaries, 1974, p. 311. Both are uncertain whether the text is original. The story is almost certainly part of the original Passion tradition, and, on balance, Morris concludes, is probably part of Luke's original Gospel.

(9) See Matthew 4:11 and Mark 1:13. Luke, curiously, does not mention the angels in the wilderness.

(10) Leon Morris, *Luke*, Tyndale, 1974, p. 312.

(11) W. H. Vanstone, *The Stature of Waiting*, Darton, Longman & Todd, 1992, has a brilliant discussion of this whole incident.

(12) William Lane, *The Gospel of Mark*, Marshall, Morgan & Scott, 1974, p. 587.

(13) Jack Deere, *Surprised by the Voice of God*, Kingsway, 1996, p. 53 makes the point that every chapter in Acts, except Chapter 17, gives an example, or a reference to, supernatural revelatory communication from God to his servants.

(14) F. F. Bruce, *The Book of the Acts*, Marshall, Morgan & Scott, 1954, p. 136, quoting L. E. Browne.

(15) The New Testament writers usually use the Greek version of the Old Testament called the Septuagint. The NIV translation of Deuteronomy 33:2 follows the Septuagint in making the crucial change that He (God) came with (rather

than from) myriads of holy ones. Jewish contemporary commentaries support this understanding. See F. F. Bruce, *op. cit.*, p. 163, note 84.

(16) It is clear that throughout history, God has permitted the martyrdom of many of his saints, and that their blood is often efficacious. See p 168ff for an account of the martyrdom of Polycarp in the second century which had a profound effect on the sub-apostolic church.

(17) See Bruce, *op. cit.*, p. 185, notes 40 and 41.

(18) See John Stott, *The Message of Acts*, IVP, 1990, p. 213.

(19) See Luke 3:22, Luke 9:35, John 12:28 (where some of the crowd mistake the voice of God for that of an angel).

4

Of Mice and Angels

In this chapter, we look at the role of angels in battles, and political conflicts, in both Scripture and history. We consider the intellectual difficulties of such experiences, especially in the many cases where God apparently does not choose to intervene.

Of Mice and Angels

The claim that God sometimes intervenes, through his angels, in human conflicts seems, to many, more appropriate to the myths of ancient Greece and Rome, than to the history of the Christian era.

However, the evidence of scripture, ancient and *modern* history is sufficiently powerful to make a strong case. The Old Testament is unequivocal; the New Testament (especially Revelation) sees a battle mainly in the heavenly realms; early Christian history tells of the surprising conversion of Constantine – widely attributed to a sign that he saw in the sky before a crucial battle; modern history produces persistent stories of angelic encounters attributed to a wide range of people – George Washington in the midst of the American War of Independence, British soldiers in the First World War, widely attested stories from recent war zones, and potential war zones in Rhodesia, Vietnam, and South Africa.

We will let the events speak for themselves, and then attempt the far harder task of analysing how to respond to them theologically. We begin with one of the most decisive elements in Old Testament history.

In 701 BC, the Jewish nation faced one of its greatest crises. The Assyrians, the ethnic cleansers of their time, had already captured Samaria, deported the leaders of the Northern Kingdom, and were repopulating the region in such a way as to ensure future tension between the Jews and the Samaritans, up to and beyond Jesus' lifetime. Now, in the person of Sennacherib's arrogant field commander (see Isaiah 36–37; and the parallel accounts in 2 Kings 18, and 2 Chronicles 32), the Jews were threatened with total annihilation. If the Assyrians had triumphed, it is very difficult to see how the Jewish faith, let alone the Jewish nation, could have survived. Lord Byron described what follows in his epic poem:

> The Assyrian came down like the wolf on the fold,
> And his cohorts were gleaming in purple and gold;
> And the sheen of their spears was like stars on the sea,
> When the blue wave rolls nightly on deep Galilee.
> Like the leaves of the forest when Summer is green,
> That host with their banners at sunset were seen:
> Like the leaves of the forest when Autumn hath blown,
> That host on the morrow lay wither'd and strown.
> For the Angel of Death spread his wings on the blast,
> And breathed in the face of the foe as he pass'd;
> And the eyes of the sleepers wax'd deadly and chill,
> And their hearts but once heaved, and forever grew still!
> And there lay the steed with his nostril all wide,
> But through it there roll'd not the breath of his pride;
> And the foam of his gasping lay white on the turf,
> And cold as the spray of the rock beating surf.
> And there lay the rider distorted and pale
> With the dew on his brow, and the rust on his mail;
> And the tents were all silent, the banners alone,
> The lances unlifted, the trumpet unblown.
> The widows of Asshur are loud in their wail,
> And the idols are broke in the temple of Baal;
> And the might of the Gentile, unsmote by the sword,
> Hath melted like snow in the glance of the Lord![1]

Herodotus,[2] the Greek historian, recording a similar defeat, tells how the king of Egypt, deserted by his military leaders, entered his sanctuary and appealed with weeping to his god. The god appeared and cheered him, and an army of tradespeople was raised to fight Sennacherib in Pelusium. That night a multitude of field mice ate up the quivers, bow strings and shield-straps of the Assyrians. As they fled, the next day, many of them were killed.

In the ancient world, the mouse is a symbol of sudden destruction, and even of plague. Consequently, some theologians have assumed that the Assyrian army was destroyed by some contagious disease. What is certain is that Sennacherib hastened home and was eventually assassinated. The power of Assyria was reduced, Jerusalem survived another hundred years, until the Babylonians under Nebuchadnezzar, deported them to a more merciful form of captivity in 597 BC.

As we study these accounts, and various explanations, we have three choices – a rational destruction by plague, a curious natural disaster inflicted by mice, or a remarkable deliverance by the Angel. While we dwell on what may be unpalatable choices, we should remember that the greatest Jewish Festival, Passover, commemorates an earlier Divine deliverance of the Jewish people (see Exodus 12:29ff).

If we are to take the inspiration of Scripture (2 Timothy 3:16ff) seriously, then we have little choice. We must accept the triple witness of the Old Testament accounts, and realise, once and for all, that angels have a destructive, as well as a comfortable, role. William of Occam (1285–1347),[3] the influential medieval philosopher, taught that when dealing with these sorts of situations, the simplest situation should be accepted. If we accept the idea that God, sometimes via his angels, does intervene then the other two explanations become obsolete. The idea of mice gnawing all the Assyrian bow strings is completely absurd; and plague, although likely in some of the swamp areas between Egypt and Israel, should be ruled out from the biblical accounts which speak so clearly of an *instant* change in the situation.

A similar, but less destructive, intervention had occurred

earlier (see 2 Kings 6:8ff). The king of Aram, infuriated by Elisha's supernatural knowledge of his plans, sends an army to capture him. Early one morning, Elisha's servant discovered that the city where they were living was now surrounded by a large army. In a panic, he alerted his master. The prophet had a simple reply: "Don't be afraid. Those who are with us are more than those who are with them."

Elisha then prayed for his servants eyes to be opened, and then the servant was able to see "the hills full of horses and chariots of fire". The end was unusually peaceful, the men of Aram were temporarily blinded, led into the city of Samaria, given food, and sent home with their vision restored. As we shall see there are modern parallels to this story.

The conversion of Constantine

In 321, Constantine who, on the death of his father, had been declared Emperor in York in 305, still didn't control Rome. His rival, Maxentius, had superior forces, and the security of Rome. Constantine, with a complete lack of prudence, marched through Italy to do battle.

He had begun his reign, like his father, as a worshipper of "the Unconquered Sun". There were strong Christian influences around him. His mother, Helena, was a notable Christian, and his half-sister was called Anastasia (the Greek word for Resurrection).

In 311, according to a conversation that Constantine had with the church historian Eusebius, he saw a cross across the midday sun inscribed with the words, "By this sign conquer". He immediately won an important victory against the Franks at Rouen.

The campaign in 312 was marked by another vision for Constantine, and crass stupidity by Maxentius. Constantine had a dream telling him to put the Chi-Rho[4] ($\mathcal{X}$) monogram on the shields of his soldiers; Maxentius, with superior numbers of men, left the safety of Rome, and foolishly chose to line up his soldiers with their backs to the River Tiber. Constantine's army prevailed, and he became a strong supporter of the Christian cause. The course of Christian history was changed (not necessarily for the better, some would argue). Once Christianity became the state religion of the Roman Empire, "conversion" was often brought about by force in contrast to the response to the signs and wonders of the first three centuries.

The Christians believed that the one God, whom they worshipped, had given Constantine a sign, and a remarkable victory. One modern historian remarks:[5]

> The problem of presentation is a very old one. Consider Constantine's conversion and (or by?) the fiery vision in the sky. Whether the appearance of the cross of light was only a subjective experience, or whether it was objective reality the historian cannot decide.

A battle won by faith and not by force

Bede[6] records a victory won by the Britons, without bloodshed, under the leadership of a saintly bishop called Germanus in 429. The account bears a striking similarity to that of Jehoshaphat's victory recounted in 2 Chronicles 20.

Bede records how the Britons, who felt inferior to the Saxons and the Picts, called on Bishop Germanus, who had a powerful reputation for being involved with miracles of healing, to help them. They prepared for battle by a serious keeping of Lent, and the baptism of much of the army.

After the feast of Easter, Germanus took command, and organised an ambush. The enemy, confident of an easy victory, advanced towards the place where they expected to attack and overwhelm the main British force. As they passed the place of the ambush, the Bishop shouted, "Alleluiah" three times. The whole army joined in, and the enemy panicked as the surrounding hills echoed with the sound. The enemy fled, throwing their weapons away, and many tried unsuccessfully to cross a river.

On this occasion, a victory was won by faith and not by force!

Bede also records a victory of King Oswald,[7] a godly man who knelt before a wooden cross, and prayed for victory. In later years, many miracles of healing, and release from demonic possession, were associated with the spot where the king had prayed. Oswald, rather like King Josiah (see 2 Kings 23), was later killed in another fierce battle in 642. Before we get too exercised by accounts of miracles at the site of the battle, and at the site of the graves of holy people, we would do well to remember a similar account in the pages of Scripture:

> Elisha died and was buried. Now Moabite raiders used to enter the country every spring. Once while some Israelites were burying a man, suddenly they saw a band of raiders; so they threw the man's body into Elisha's tomb. When the body touched Elisha's bones, the man came to life and stood up on his feet. (2 Kings 13:20–21)

Bede was a careful historian and wrote, "As the laws of history demand, I have laboured honestly to transmit what I could learn from common report for the instruction of posterity."[8] It is, of course, impossible to know how accurate Bede's sources were, and difficult to know how much he wrote with theological lessons in mind. Nevertheless, his "history" seems less surprising where we read similar accounts from much more recent times.

We now jump forwards many centuries. Holland in the 17th century was one of the most devout Protestant countries. In 1672, she faced a formidable coalition of the armies of France, England, Münster and Cologne. Having survived earlier terrible attacks from Spain, she now seemed doomed to defeat.[9]

On Easter Eve, 14th April, a believing widow called Grietje Klass went to bed. I have summarised an account written down in 1704, and now translated into English.

> Grietje went to bed much afraid. At half-past-nine, a great light filled her bedroom. She saw an angel (which she described in great

detail) wearing a white gown, who was very tall, and stood about ten feet from her bed. She heard him speak (although whether it was an external voice or an internal one she wasn't sure). "Thus shall God preserve Holland." The angel stayed some time, perhaps half-an-hour. Then the angel spoke again, "The angel of the Lord encamps around those who fear him, and he delivers them." She recognised the words as coming from Psalm 34. Grietje was very afraid, but gained peace when she shared the vision with many other people. Many people heard her account, and the description of the angel, long before Holland was unexpectedly, and unaccountably, delivered from her enemies.

An angel in America

Another well-known story about angels in wartime concerns George Washington.[10] In the winter of 1777, after a series of military defeats, George Washington, the American leader in the War of Independence fought against England, was in despair. This account of what happened is abridged from an account given by one of his staff officers, Anthony Sherman. Sherman, a youth of 18 at the time, told the story many years later at an Independence Day parade in 1858. He was then 99 years old!

One day – I remember it well – when the bitterly cold wind was whistling through the leafless trees, and the sun shone brightly in a cloudless sky, he stayed in his room on his own all afternoon. When he came outside I noticed that his face was paler than usual, his soul seemed to be full of something of extraordinary importance. Dusk was falling when he sent a servant to the rooms of the officer of the guard with a request to come to him. When he arrived we talked for about half an hour and then Washington said to us: "I do not know whether it is because of my anxiety, or something else, but this afternoon, as I was sitting at my table writing an urgent report there was something in the room that disturbed me. I looked up and saw an extremely beautiful woman standing opposite me. Because I had given strict orders that I was not to be disturbed I was so surprised that it was a while before I could utter a word to ask her why she was there. I repeated my question a second, third and even fourth time, but my mysterious guest gave no answer, except to slightly raise her eyes. At the same time a strange feeling made it impossible for me to do anything. Once again I tried to speak to her but I had lost my tongue, even my mind was paralyzed. A new influence mysterious, powerful, irresistible, took possession of me. The only thing I could do was to stare at my unknown visitor steadily, without moving.

"Gradually it seemed as though the atmosphere was filled with strange vibrations and became luminous. Everything around me seemed to become more ethereal and the mysterious visitor herself became more airy and yet more distinct to my eyes than before. I began to feel like someone who is dying, or rather I had sensations which I sometimes imagine are like those which accompany death. I did not think, I was only conscious of staring fixedly and mindlessly at my guest. Then I heard a voice say: 'Son of the Republic, look and learn!' "

There followed three detailed visions, each of which, was proceeded by the solemn words "Son of the Republic, look and learn!" The first concerned the War of Independence. The second, clearly, concerns the Civil War (1861–1865). Sherman's account of it given just before the Civil War started was as follows:

I turned my gaze to America and saw villages and towns and cities appearing one by one until they were scattered over the entire country from the Atlantic Ocean to the Pacific Ocean. Then the dark, shadowy angel turned his face to the south and I saw an ominous ghost approaching our country from Africa. He glided slowly and heavily over every town and city and then the inhabitants prepared for battle against each other. As I looked I saw a shining angel bearing a crown of light with the word "Union". He carried the American flag which he placed between the people of the divided nation and said: "Remember that you are brothers." Immediately the inhabitants threw down their arms and made friends, united under the national banner.

The third vision, consisted of a colossal, and unexpected attack, on the land of America. Eventually, it concluded with the words:

> The dark cloud rolled back together with the armies which it had brought with it, leaving the inhabitants of the land victorious. Again I saw how villages, towns and cities arose where they had formerly been, while the shining angel planted the banner he had brought with him among them and called out in a loud voice: "As long as the stars continue to exist and the dew falls on earth from heaven, the Republic will go on." He took the crown from his head with the word "Union" flashing on it and placed it on the banner, while the people knelt down and said, "Amen."
>
> Straight away the scene started to blur and dissolve and finally I saw only the swirling mist rising up as I had seen in the beginning. When this also disappeared I once again gazed upon the mysterious visitor who said in the same voice I had heard at first: "Son of the Republic, what you have seen is explained as follows: The Republic will suffer three great disasters. The most terrible is the second of these and when it is past the whole of the world together will not be able to triumph over it. Let every child of the Republic learn to live for his God, his country and the Union." With these words he vanished and I stood up from my chair and felt that I had seen a vision which showed me the birth, the progress and the destiny of the United States.

The first part of the vision encouraged George Washington, a deeply prayerful man, at the darkest time in the great struggle against England; the second was about the ghastly Civil War, which was mainly fought over the question of the abolition of slavery. The ghost from Africa presumably refers to the Negro slave trade, which caused so much suffering, and so tarnished the Christian cause in America. The third is hard to interpret. America is so strong, that an invasion seems all but impossible – unless of course the vision presaged the events on and beyond September 11, 2001. There are, not surprisingly, an extraordinary number of stories surrounding that tragic day (see p 107).

Angels in the First World War

The First World War was perhaps the most bloodthirsty, and unnecessary, event in the history of the human race. The terrible experiences in the trenches, and the ultimate humiliation of Germany in the Treaty of Versailles, had other devastating consequences.

Theologians, and ordinary people, lost faith in the God of Scripture. This precipitated a decline in Western Christendom, which continues unabated even today. The people of Germany welcomed Adolf Hitler to restore their fortunes. But amidst the carnage of the war, there were many stories of angels.

From the British side, there are an incredible number of accounts of angels[11] being seen amidst the horrors of the First World War. Of course, any such accounts raise huge questions. But the evidence is well documented (see also p 156). One of the most striking, and least well known, occurred very near the end of the war. In the Spring of 1918, the Germans tried to end the war with a massive assault. They broke through, and the Allied troops were retreating in disarray. The Household Brigade Magazine describes what happened as follows:[12]

At the focal point of the enemy's advance, at Bethune, the Germans concentrated on a slight rise beyond the town, yet the ground there was absolutely bare and none of the men were there; nevertheless enemy machine guns and shells raked it from end to end with lead. As suddenly as it had started the enemy's fire ceased, and in the complete silence there rose a lark's thrilling song of thankfulness. The dense line of German troops, which had started to move forward to their victory in mass formation, halted dead. As the British watched they saw it break! The Germans threw down everything they had and fled in frantic panic!

A senior German officer gave the following extraordinary account of the events:

The order had been given to advance in mass formation, and our troops were marching behind us singing their way to victory, when Fritz, my lieutenant here, said, "Herr Kapitan, just look at that open ground behind Bethune. There is a brigade of cavalry coming up through the smoke drifing across it! They must be mad, these Englishmen, to advance against such a force as ours in the open! I suppose they must be cavalry of one of their Colonial Forces, for look! They're all in white uniforms and are mounted on white horses!"

"Strange," I said, "I've never heard of English having any white cavalry whether Colonial or not. Anyway, they've all been fighting on foot for several years past, and in khaki, not white. "Well, they're plain enough," he replied. "But look! Our guns have got them in their range now, they'll be blown to pieces in no time."

We actually saw the shells bursting among the horses and their riders which still came forward at a quiet walk, in parade-ground formation, each man and horse in his exact place. Shortly afterwards our machine guns opened a heavy fire, *raking the advancing cavalry with a hail of lead*; but they still came, and not a single man or horse fell. Steadily they advanced, clear in the shining sunlight, and a few paces in front of them rode their leader, a fine figure of a man, whose hair, like spun gold, shone in an aura around his head. By his side was a great sword, but his hands lay quietly holding the reins, as his huge white charger bore him proudly forward. In spite of heavy shelling and concentrated machine-gun fire, the white cavalry advanced remorselessly as fate, like the incoming tide on a sandy beach. Then a great fear fell over me. I turned to flee; yes, I, an officer of the Prussian Guard, fled panic stricken, and around me were hundreds of terrified men, whimpering like children, throwing away their weapons and accoutrements in order not to have their movements impeded . . . all running. Their one desire was to get away from that advancing white cavalry, but above all from their awe-inspiring leader whose hair shone like a golden aureole. That is all I have to tell you. We are beaten. The German army is broken. There may be fighting, but we have lost the war; we are beaten by the white cavalry . . . I cannot understand . . . I cannot understand.

During the days that followed, many German prisoners were examined and their account tallied in substance with the one given here.

From the British side, the whole event seemed inexplicable. *They didn't see any white cavalry*, with or without riders. But they did see, and hear, the Germans start firing at a completely empty area of open ground, then a sudden panic amidst the well-drilled, disciplined Germans, followed by the complete cessation of a shattering bombardment.

Elisha's servant (2 Kings 6:8) could have enlightened both sides!

The Second World War

There are a number of other stories of small nations being protected by angels at times of great difficulty. Certainly in Finland, in 1939, against all the odds, the Finnish army repulsed the might of the invading Soviet Union. There are a number of persistent stories about angels assisting in the battle. Dr Moolenburgh[13] also tells a story of a German invasion into neutral Switzerland, being stopped supernaturally in May 1940.

While there are many fewer documented stories from the Second World War, there is also a deep sense that Britain's survival in 1940 was due to prevailing prayer, and some unusual events.

The shattering defeat of the British Expeditionary Force ought to have been followed by its capture and annihilation on the beaches of Dunkerque. For some reason, Hitler failed to give the order to attack, and an extraordinary combination of calm weather and cool heads enabled thousands of small boats to rescue the stranded army. Your writer's father was amongst those rescued.

The Battle of Britain, fought in the air in August and September in 1940, was similarly a victory against all the odds. Strange stories were told of supernatural intervention.[14] According to Billy Graham, Air Chief Marshall Lord Dowding, who was in charge of the operation, believed the victory was miraculous, and that angels had sometimes been directly involved.

Without that victory, England would certainly have been invaded, and in all probability would have had to negotiate a humiliating peace.

Angels in recent history

Corrie Ten Boom,[15] herself a miraculous survivor of a German concentration camp, who was certainly familiar with the work of angels, tells of an event during a rebellion in the Congo. A group of rebels advanced on a school where two hundred children of missionaries lived. She writes, "They had planned to kill both children and teachers. In the school, they knew the danger, and therefore went to prayer. Their only protection was a fence and a couple of soldiers; while the enemy, who came closer and closer, numbered several hundreds. When the rebels were close by, suddenly something happened. They turned and ran away! The same thing happened on each of the next two days. One of the rebels was wounded, and he was brought into the missionary hospital. When the doctor was dressing his wounds, he asked the soldier, 'Why did you not break into the school as you had planned?' The soldier replied, 'We couldn't do it; we saw hundreds of soldiers in white uniforms, and we became scared.' Of course, in Africa soldiers do not wear white uniforms." Corrie concluded, very reasonably, "They must have been angels. What a wonderful thing that the Lord can open the eyes of the enemy so that they see angels!"

My friend John Knight[16] tells of two similar incidents which occurred in the late 1970s when he was working as a priest in Zimbabwe (Rhodesia, as it was then).

Military intelligence had learnt that the largest ever guerilla force to enter Zimbabwe was about to cross into the country in our area – a densely forested and mountainous area. Many small "details" or "sticks" of men were out searching for signs of this group. A young Christian we knew, and his friend, formed a two-man stick, with radio, and were searching through their allotted section. They came over a hill and were well down the slope before realising that the thick undergrowth of the valley floor was "crawling" with men. They had unexpectedly walked into the hide-out of nearly a thousand guerillas who had with them a small mountain of war material.

At the same moment, they too were spotted, and a battle royal ensued. Our two young friends could only do one thing – dive into a small contour on the hillside, and start returning the fire. They started praying. Their radio was not picking up any friends. In moments, the three or four magazines they each had for their weapons were expended. They knew that only God could help them now. All of a sudden, they realised that all the shooting had stopped. Looking carefully out of their meagre hiding place, they were scarcely able to believe what met their eyes. The large group was moving swiftly back towards the border, leaving much of the heaviest material behind. In subsequent follow-up operations, one man was caught and interrogated. Amongst other things, they asked why the group had run off down the valley. The guerilla explained that when they saw the whole hillside "alive" with soldiers in white uniforms, they knew that they were heavily outnumbered, and so made a run for it!

On another occasion when these "soldiers in white" appeared, they brought protection to an elderly couple living in a lonely homestead. Feeling a little more nervous this particular evening, the couple knelt down to pray as usual before going to bed, and asked that God's angels would protect them from danger. In the early hours of the following morning a guerilla band attacked a neighbouring homestead a couple of miles away, and met with more than they bargained for. It was occupied by security force personnel! In the battle that followed, the security forces took, as a prisoner, one of the men they wounded. In the interrogation that followed, the guerilla explained that they had decided to attack the neighbouring farmstead, but when they got there, they found it surrounded and heavily guarded by soldiers in white, so they abandoned their first plan and moved against the homestead that – unbeknown to them – was actually guarded by the security forces!

Angels in Vietnam[17]

Another story from the 1960s comes from Vietnam:

> An evangelist, a Vietnamese called Saul, had led five villages to
> faith. They had already had one miraculous escape when he led
> them by boat away from certain death at the hands of the Vietcong.
> They then founded a new village, near the base of an American
> garrison. Very soon, the Vietcong discovered their presence, and
> they were surrounded by heavily armed guerillas. The Americans
> were unable to defend them. The villagers conducted a vigil of
> prayer which lasted three days and three nights. Unexpectedly, the
> Vietcong retreated – quite suddenly.
>
> A while later, a Vietcong soldier was wounded. He ended up in
> an American hospital, where the story of the village, which had
> such a surprising liberation, was well known. The doctor treating
> the wounded soldier, gained his confidence and asked him,
>
> "Why didn't you attack the village, it was not armed?"
>
> The soldier replied, "We couldn't do anything, while large
> groups of soldiers in white uniforms were regularly patrolling the
> village."
>
> No soldiers wore white uniforms during the Vietnam War.

Angels in South Africa and China

In the final decades of the 20th century, the church faced huge
pressure in many parts of the world. In South Africa, the
churches played a very important part in the dismantling of
apartheid. In China, the underground house church movement
made remarkable progress. Some of this is described in two
remarkable books by Michael Cassidy and Brother Yun.[18]

Cassidy tells the story of a South African colonel deep in
prayer on 23rd March 1994, just a few weeks before the South
African elections, which were to bring Nelson Mandela to
power. The situation was very tense, many were praying, many
despairing.

Colonel Johan Botha, a Christian, who after witnessing the

appalling riots in Soweto in June 1976, had turned to God with even deeper intercession, was praying (unusually for him) in English.

He said, "God, what is it that you want for us, and what do you want for South Africa?" Immediately, he saw an angel, bathed in a brilliant indescribable light. The angel instructed him the need for chains of prayer services, and stressed that he had fourteen days. Fourteen days later was 6th April, Founders' Day in South Africa. Johan took his story to President de Clerk, who encouraged him. His testimony gave great impetus to a Day of National Prayer which even the newspapers regarded as a crucial factor in the peaceful outcome of the elections.

Such days of prayer have restarted in South Africa, and their influence is spreading to other African states.

The Heavenly Man

In England, all of us were aware of the struggles against apartheid in South Africa. We could rejoice at stories of reconciliation and hope, and at miraculous visitations like the one to Colonel Botha. Occasionally, we heard rumours of what God was doing in China. The reality far exceeded what most of us could have expected. One of the most remarkable leaders of the underground church was Brother Yun, who was given the nickname "the Heavenly Man". Twice Yun escaped from prison in a way reminiscent of Peter in Acts 12. The first occasion was in 1983. The house church, especially around Henan was growing. The leaders had a fantastic dedication to the Lord, often expressed in fasting and prayer. At one prayer meeting, Yun experienced spiritual warfare at first hand.

Before we left for Shaanxi that evening we asked God to prepare the hearts of the people to receive his Word. While praying, I suddenly saw a terrible vision that shook my soul. The others told me I startled them when I shouted out, "Hallelujah!

Jesus' blood has overcome you!"

Everybody stopped praying and asked me what the matter was.
With sweat on my brow I told them, "I saw a terrible evil vision. A
black, heinous creature came after me. It had a horrible twisted
face. It pressed me down on the ground and sat on my stomach so I
couldn't get up. With one of its hands it grabbed my throat and
started choking me. With its other hand it grabbed some steel
pliers and tried to shut my mouth with them. I could hardly
breathe. Then I saw a great strong angel fly toward me. With all
my strength I poked my fingers into the eyes of the evil creature. It
fell to the ground, and I was carried away to safety by the angel. I
shouted, 'Hallelujah! Jesus' blood has overcome you!' "

Soon afterwards, Yun was arrested. He was dragged through
the streets, paraded bloody and bruised, through a town in a
way that reminded him of the experience of the Apostles (see 1
Corinthians 4:9). Back in prison, he felt that God was calling
him to act as though he was mad – just like David in the court
of Acish, King of Gath (see 1 Samuel 21:10–15).

Many spectators had crowded outside the prison window and
looked in. One officer went to another room and made a telephone
call to Henan, to try and find out who I was from the authorities
there. The other interrogators went with him to hear what was said.
They left me alone in the room and shut the door. I was still tightly
bound by rope, so they saw no chance I could escape. The onlookers also gave their attention to the telephone call, and crowded
outside the window of that room to listen.

At that moment, with everyone's eyes off me, the Holy Spirit
spoke to my heart, "The God of Peter is your God." I remembered
how angels had opened the prison gates for Peter to escape. *"Are
not all angels ministering spirits sent to serve those who will
inherit salvation?"* (Hebrews 1:14)

The rope that bound my arms behind my back suddenly snapped
by itself! I didn't tear the ropes off, but kept them loosely in place. I
decided to try to escape, and if caught I would claim I was trying to
go to the toilet. With my arms still positioned behind my back, I used
my mouth to turn the door handle and I walked out of the room!

At that moment God gave me faith and courage. I reminded myself that the blood of Jesus Christ protected me. I walked through the middle of the onlookers in the courtyard. Nobody stopped me or said anything to me! It was as though God had blinded their eyes and they didn't recognise who I was.

I walked through the courtyard to the toilet block in the northern part of the compound, about 30 feet away from the interrogation room. As quickly as I could, I pulled off the rope from around my body. My hands, arms and shoulders were still numb from being bound by rope for so long.

Because the front gates had been locked, the only way out of the compound was over an eight-foot high cement wall. The wall had sharp glass embedded in the top. I stood there for a moment, stared at the wall and prayed, asking the Lord to heal my hands and body.

I decided to try to leap over the wall. I saw no other choice. I was trapped and at any moment the officers would come and grab me. What happened next is not possible from a human perspective, yet God is my witness that what I am about to tell you is the truth.

First I pulled myself up onto the wall as high as I could manage. I looked over the top and saw that on the other side was a ten feet wide, open septic tank. As I hung grimly onto the side of the wall, all of a sudden, I felt as if somebody hoisted me up and threw me over! I jumped so far that I even cleared the septic tank! A Scripture came to mind, *"With your help I can advance against a troop; with my God I can scale a wall."* (2 Samuel 22:30)

The God of Peter wonderfully helped me leap over the wall and escape! I believe the same angel I had seen in my vision helped to lift me up.

Yun completed his escape, and continued to minister to the hidden house churches of his district, and further afield. He had many extraordinary adventures, arrests, imprisonments, and suffered terrible torture. His testimony reads very like Paul's in 2 Corinthians 11:16ff. His final imprisonment in China was in Zhengzhou maximum security prison in Henan. As usual, he was tortured, and on this occasion, he had to be carried around the prison by friends, as his legs had been broken. He felt very discouraged, and constantly cried out to the Lord. On 4th May,

1997, God intervened dramatically. First, he was given a severe warning and a great promise of freedom from Jeremiah 15:19–21. Then he had a powerful vision, even though he was wide awake. He saw his wife, just released from prison, binding his wounds and preparing medicine. In the vision, she said to him, "Why don't you open the iron door?" Before he could reply, she walked out of the room, and the vision ended. He heard the Lord say, "This is the hour of your salvation." A fellow believer, Xu, who had carried him around the prison twice said, "Yun, you must escape." It was completely impossible. Apart from his broken legs, his escape involved passing through three normally locked doors, walking across a large courtyard, and out through the main gate, onto a busy street. But after so many different signs, he knew that he had to attempt the impossible.

He describes in great detail what happened. He was able to pass through the first gate because a prisoner came in the opposite direction, and the guard was distracted by a phone call. The second and third gates, unaccountably, were open and he walked past guards who seemed totally unaware of his presence.

He walked across the courtyard (not realising until later that his broken legs had been healed), and the main gate was open! A taxi drew up outside, and he was able to direct the driver to the house of some believers. The believers, unlike those praying for Peter's release, were expecting him, as was his wife. The authorities failed to find him; they were hindered by a huge rainstorm just as they discovered his escape! Eventually he escaped from China with a false passport, including a photograph to which he bore no resemblance.

Although there were no discernible angels in his second escape, the way he walked past the security guards and the open gates, is very similar to Acts 12:10.

September 11, 2001

The destruction of the World Trade Center in New York by suicide bombers gave the American people, and their friends in the Western world, their biggest shock for many years. The events unleashed a whole series of responses, the outcome of which is completely unpredictable. People could ask: where were the guardian angels? We know that many people were killed, though many fewer than through the eruption of the volcano near Goma in Congo a few months later. We know that many professing Christians were among the victims. We know that a number of Christians had warnings that something was about to happen. One relief worker had dreams of a huge disaster, and a sense that he would be called to work in Afghanistan, something that seemed highly unlikely before September 11. When I was in Nairobi in December 2001, I was told that a Kenyan had telephoned his mother on 10 September to say that he was now willing to go anywhere that the Lord called him – the next day he was among the victims. That last phone call gave great comfort to his family.

On September 11, Sujo John[19] reached work at 7.30 a.m. His new place of work was in an office on the 81st floor of the World Trade Center's north tower. At 8.04, he sent a friend an e-mail saying "I have a call of God on my life", adding that he needed to do more than merely attend church each Sunday. At 8.45 a.m. one of the hi-jacked planes hit the north tower, one wing sliced through his floor killing several of his colleagues. He joined the flight down the stairs, passing the brave firemen running up. On the 53rd floor, he tried, unsuccessfully, to telephone his wife. She was pregnant with their first child, and was coming into work at the south tower. At 9.03 the second plane hit the south tower, almost exactly where she worked. Sujo reached the base of the tower, and was just about to exit through a revolving door, when the whole building collapsed. He was trapped with about fifteen other terrified people. As the building collapsed, he shouted to them, inspired by his deep-

ened commitment to Christ, "We're going to die. Do you know
the Lord? Call upon the Lord and you will be saved!" People
started crying out "Jesus, Jesus". He was trapped for about 20
minutes; he expected to be killed at any moment. The others
didn't survive, but Sujo said, "I felt the peace of God as never
before, because I knew they were in a better place. He was
trapped under about three feet of dust and debris, and could
hardly breathe, but amidst the dense smoke and fumes, he spotted the torchlight of a man in a FBI jacket who was prone, but
still alive. They both thought they were going to die. Together,
they started to pray, and as they did so, they spotted through the
gloom, the flashing red light of an ambulance. When, somehow, they reached the ambulance, they found that half of it had
been crushed. Sujo believed that God had placed that flashing
light to show them a way out. He left the disaster without a
scratch, convinced that his wife and unborn child would have
been killed in the other half of the disaster. In fact, his wife had
arrived for work just after the second tower was hit, and found
her way to work barred. If she had arrived a few minutes
earlier, she would almost certainly have been killed.

Sujo has learnt from his experience, and is now preaching to
thousands, helping a grieving nation turn back to their God for
salvation, comfort and guidance. As I write this, my mind goes
back to the King's Cross tube disaster nearly 20 years earlier. A
young man called Lionel, a Christian in a very strongly Christian family, was killed there. I used to know him well; he was a
member of a youth group that I had run in a previous church.
There will always be these paradoxes. Later, we will look at an
even more difficult question – where were the angels in
Auschwitz?

An angel in Pakistan?

One of the many consequences of the attack on September 11,
coupled with the American-led military response in
Afghanistan (and Iraq), has been an enormous increase in

OF MICE AND ANGELS

tension between Christians and Muslims. In England, many
Muslims have felt unwelcome and some have suffered physical
attack; in Pakistan there have been several examples of murder-
ous attacks on Christian churches and schools. In July 2002,
the Christian school at Murree,[20] which mainly teaches the children of missionaries, was attacked by terrorists. The attack was
carefully premeditated and ingenious. The fastest way to
remove missionaries from the country would have been to kill
their children. The attack went wrong. Despite the tragic death
of six Pakistanis (some Christian, some Muslim) there seems to
have been a remarkable amount of protection. If the terrorists
had come ten minutes earlier, they would have found the
whole school out playing during their break. As it was, they
were back in their classes. Though the attackers had grenades,
they did not use them. When they tried to enter the classrooms,
they failed (for no adequate reason – one door was locked and
they failed to open it, but didn't notice a nearby door that was
open). When they had shot the guards and run through the
property, and had everything at their mercy, they inexplicably
ran away. One parent was shot in the hand, but was then
directed to safety by two large men in an unknown uniform
who seem to have been angels – no soldiers of that description
have been traced, and the uniform that the parent described
is unknown in Pakistan. Apparently, the terrorists were
trapped crossing a river. Pursued by local soldiers, and opposed
by villagers on the opposite bank, they apparently blew
themselves up.

This incident raises, even more sharply, a familiar question
(see p 27 and p 145). Why, if God intervened directly to protect
the children, were six people, all doing their duty, killed? Why
is angelic intervention sometimes partial?

How does God intervene?

What are we to make of all this? Can we really believe that
God intervenes in such ways? Logically, I believe, we must.

Some will want to believe that God is the completely detached
God of the Deists (the universal watchmaker who set the
universe going, and then sat back to see what would happen).
But if we believe in the Incarnation, then we are committed to a
belief in a God who is deeply involved in the everyday life of
the world. We need not be surprised by the activities of angels,
rather more by our inability to see them. In the first chapter,
rational people testified to personal encounters, which were
highly significant for them. In this chapter, we have written
about people, some in leadership, some in private life, who
have testified to encounters with far greater consequences. We
cannot really accept one and reject the other. We can only see
the tiniest fraction of the whole. Many physicists, as their
knowledge increases, become aware of the increasingly large
number of things that they don't know. In a similar way, as
we discover a little more about the largely unseen spiritual
world, we should be increasingly aware of our own *lack* of
knowledge. We would do well to humble ourselves in the face
of a Creator, who deigns, occasionally, to let a few of his
people, and sometimes even their opponents, see a glimpse of
heavenly things.

The Bible teaches us that there are myriads of angels, unseen
and all around us. Jesus (Matthew 26:53) could have called up
more than twelve legions of angels. On the opposite side, those
of us who have the privilege of praying within buildings for
them to be cleansed from evil powers know that prayer in the
name of Jesus cleanses places from evil powers. We don't see
them leave (occasionally people feel them go); but the results
are clear. If this is true, then how much more certain we can be
that "the angel of the Lord encamps around those who fear
him, and he delivers them" (Psalm 34:7). Angels may seldom
be seen, either in battle, or in great political events, but that
doesn't mean that they are not present.

Very tentatively, I would offer two lines of thought. The first
is that God's purposes are often best served by the patient
sufferings of his people. Paul makes this point when discussing

his much debated thorn which is set in the midst of writing about his great revelation of Paradise (2 Corinthians 12:1–10). Peter makes the same point and tells his readers to "rejoice that you participate in the sufferings of Christ" (see 1 Peter 4:12–19) when writing to the beleaguered Christians in Rome. He also has a strong theology of the Devil.

> Be self-controlled and alert. Your enemy the devil prowls around like a roaring lion looking for someone to devour. Resist him, standing firm in the faith, because you know that your brothers throughout the world are undergoing the same kind of sufferings.
>
> And the God of all grace, who called you to his eternal glory in Christ, after you have suffered a little while, will himself restore you and make you strong, firm and steadfast. (1 Peter 5:8–10)

Soon after writing these words, Peter, who had had several miraculous escapes, would suffer a terrible death with many of his fellow believers in Rome.[21]

Oscar Cullmann[22] offers a second line of thought. He writes:

> The devil is bound to a line, which can be lengthened even to the point where, for a while, Satan can make himself independent and has to be fought against by God. Going slightly beyond the Revelation of St John, this means that the whole fearful character is to be attributed to the evil, which temporarily looses itself from these bonds. If this event is taking place in accordance with the divine plan, then God himself limited his omnipotence for this interim period, without giving it up in the long term.

Cullmann, and others like him, are affirming the biblical teaching[23] that there are strong spiritual powers, with territorial authority, whose control depends on the spiritual state of different regions and countries. This accords well with modern experience where believers have met overwhelming spiritual opposition in places untouched by the Gospel, and clearly under the control of occult forces.

Here, perhaps, lies an answer to the dark question "Where were the angels in Auschwitz?"

We do know of miraculous interventions in the Second World War, even in concentration camps;[24] but we also know that the events in Auschwitz, and elsewhere, have cast a dark shadow on Western civilization. They have left a shadow of collective guilt, which seems to affect our political thinking and theological judgment, 60 years later.

If we accept Cullmann's thesis, then Auschwitz becomes the deadliest illustration of Satan's unrestrained freedom and malice – malice primarily directed against the "Chosen People", against Christian leaders and, of course, against the Son of God.

This in no way excuses the Nazi leaders, nor other tyrants and their henchmen. The Nazi leaders with their hatred of the Chosen People, their disdain for Christianity – typified by the very choice of the swastika as their emblem – and their propensity for occult practices, fulfilled the condition of Cullmann's thesis. Sadly, they were neither the first, nor the last, rulers to act in this way.

Scripture teaches that God's freedom to intervene is greatly increased by the prayers of believers. Hezekiah's prayer (Isaiah 37:14–20) before the destruction of the Assyrian army; and the believers' prevailing prayer for the release of Peter (Acts 12:5, 12) are obvious biblical examples of surprising outcomes in desperate circumstances.

Conversely, when people open themselves up to the ways of Satan, there is a sharp increase in evil, and *apparent* lessening of God's presence. There are many examples of this in the Old Testament, also in the power struggles in the Acts of the Apostles.[25]

Cullmann[26] draws his book to a conclusion with these powerful thoughts:

We have seen that it is God's will that we should always pray. But that means that the situation is as it was in such terrible events as we experienced say, in the time of Hitler, when we noted the temporary victory of evil and the temporary absence of God, and had to have courage to pray. What we know of Dietrich Bonhoeffer's prayers in the last moments before his execution may serve as an example here.

Even then we have to pray. For here prayer has a quite special effect, which transcends all the functions that we have illuminated so far. I have said that, as creatures of the God who is love, we must unite with his loving will in prayer through our praying. But we go almost beyond the bounds of human possibility as we enter into the action in his battle against evil. Given the provisos enjoined by God's sovereignty, we may venture to say that through our prayers we become God's helpers in the battle against evil in the world. All individual and collective prayers for peace belong here.

Oscar Cullmann lived through the war in Nazi Germany. Writing in 1944, in his book *Christ and My Time*, he coined a much used analogy. After D-Day the decisive battle of the war had been fought, but victory (for the opponents of his country) had not yet come.[27] A strong case can be made for saying that England's survival was miraculous (see above), but the victory involved much suffering, and much bloodshed on all sides. The angels, largely unseen, were involved – just as certainly as in the First World War, where there is so much anecdotal evidence. There are many biblical passages which teach us about the largely unseen spiritual battle. In the New Testament, we could turn to any of the following: Ephesians 6:10–20, Romans 8:31–39; Colossians 2:9–15; Luke 10:18–20; Mark 13 (especially v. 22 and v. 27). In the Old Testament a passage from the Book of Daniel is best explained by assuming that it records an unseen spiritual battle.

On the twenty-fourth day of the first month, as I was standing on the bank of the great river, the Tigris, I looked up and there before me was a man dressed in linen, with a belt of the finest gold round his waist. His body was like chrysolite, his face like lightning, his

eyes like flaming torches, his arms and legs like the gleam of
burnished bronze, and his voice like the sound of a multitude.

I, Daniel, was the only one who saw the vision; the men with me
did not see it, but such terror overwhelmed them that they fled and
hid themselves. So I was left alone, gazing at this great vision; I
had no strength left, my face turned deathly pale and I was help-
less. Then I heard him speaking, and as I listened to him, I fell into
a deep sleep, my face to the ground.

A hand touched me and set me trembling on my hands and
knees. He said, "Daniel, you who are highly esteemed, consider
carefully the words I am about to speak to you, and stand up, for I
have now been sent to you." And when he said this to me, I stood
up trembling.

Then he continued, "Do not be afraid, Daniel. Since the first day
that you set your mind to gain understanding and to humble yourself before your God, your words were heard, and I have come in
response to them. But the prince of the Persian kingdom resisted
me twenty-one days. Then Michael, one of the princes, came to
help me, because I was detained there with the King of Persia."
(Daniel 10:4–13)

It is particularly interesting to note that Daniel's companions
did not see the angel, but sensed the supernatural presence and
were terrified. The angel then explained that his ability to help
was delayed until he was assisted by the Archangel Michael.

God, who made the absolute decision to create us, has also
taken the decision to limit his power. The only alternative is a
completely pre-planned clockwork universe. Creation, as every
parent knows, involves risks and heartache, as well as love, joy,
and fulfilment. In our fallen world, we shall inevitably experience a mixture of darkness and light. Jesus was no stranger to
this – referring to Satan as "the prince of this world" (John
14:30 etc.). In the Acts of the Apostles, Paul had many major
spiritual battles. In Cyprus (Acts 13:4–12) with Elymas a
sorcerer, and false prophet; in Philippi (Acts 16:16–40) with
the slave girl who could predict the future; and in Ephesus
(Acts 19) with many obvious practitioners of sorcery, and who

were full of evil spirits. In each place, the outcome was *not entirely favourable*. After the events in Cyprus, the young John Mark went home to Jerusalem, precipitating a huge row between Paul and Barnabas. In both Philippi and Ephesus, Paul had to make a somewhat undignified departure, leaving the local Christians to pick up the pieces and establish the church.

Similarly, although for six people and their families, the incident in Pakistan had a tragic outcome, we may still believe that there was a remarkable measure of Divine protection in the school in Pakistan. In the First World War, many soldiers saw the "Angel of Mons"; some survived, many died.

The Revelation of St John (Chapter 12:7–9) describes the terrible opening battle in the heavenly realms. If that was, or is, the state in heaven, we need hardly be surprised that the evidence of angelic intervention in earthly battles is sporadic, and the outcome sometimes seemingly incomplete. We see at best through a glass darkly, and are often totally unaware of the angelic protection around us. We would be foolish to deny the presence and involvement of angels at a national level, but any attempts at a systematic theology of such encounters will certainly end in grief.

Notes

(1) Lord Byron (1788–1824) was not renowned for either his faith or his lifestyle. These elegant verses are probably deriding what he would have regarded as one of the most unbelievable episodes in Scripture.

(2) Herodotus *Annals* ii:14.

(3) William of Occam (1285–1347) celebrated for his metaphorical razor, a philosophical view which eliminated all possibilities which were not absolutely essential. For a fuller description see Alister McGrath, *Christian Theology*, Blackwell, 1994, pp. 45–6 and p. 258ff.

(4) Chi-Rho, the first two letters of the word "Christ", in Greek, was a popular Christian sign. Significantly, a few

years later, in 315, Constantine issued coinage using this sign.

(5) Ramsay MacMullen, *Christianising the Roman Empire AD100–400*, Yale University Press, 1984, p. 24.

(6) See Bede, *Ecclesiastical History of the English People* translated by Leo Sherley-Price, Penguin, 1955, p. 62. Bede (673–735) was a monk, a biblical scholar, and "Father of English History".

(7) Bede *op. cit.* p. 142.

(8) Bede *op. cit.* p. 27.

(9) Dr H. C. Moolenburgh, *Meetings with Angels*, C. W. Daniel, 1992, p. 136.

(10) Moolenburgh (*op. cit.* p. 138f.) He makes the point that the American magazine *Destiny* regularly republishes this significant story. I have abridged his account.

(11) The Angels of Mons are discussed in detail in many books. See, for instance, Rosemary Guiley, *Encyclopaedia of Angels*, Facts on File, 1996. See further in Ch.6, p. 156.

(12) Dr Victor Pearce, *Miracles and Angels*, Eagle, 1999, p. 131ff. Based on an original document from the Household Brigade Magazine.

(13) Moolenburgh *op. cit.* pp. 147–8.

(14) Billy Graham, *Angels, God's Secret Agents*, Hodder & Stoughton, 1995, p. 123.

(15) Corrie Ten Boom, *Marching Orders for the End Battle*, Fort Washington, 1960, p. 89f.

(16) John Knight, *Rain in a Dry Land*, Hodder & Stoughton, 1987 p. 134ff.

(17) Moolenburgh *op. cit.* p. 188, quoting from Een Niew Geluid, 1968. There is a similar story in Law, *The Truth about Angels*, Charisma House, p. 44. The two accounts are probably of the same incident reported slightly differently.

(18) Michael Cassidy, *A Witness for Ever*, Hodder & Stoughton, 1995, p. 160, and Brother Yun, *The Heavenly Man*, Monarch, 2002, from Chapters 6 & 22.

(19) This account is based on Martin Fletcher's report in *The Times*, Saturday 24th November 2001.

(20) I am indebted to Michael and Rosemary Green for this account. They visited Pakistan shortly after this incident to attend their son's ordination by the Bishop of Lahore. Their grandchildren were amongst those who escaped from the tragedy at the school.

It is important to note that moderate followers of Islam *helped to protect* the children, and to corner the terrorists. In many parts of the world religious extremists, whether Hindu, Sikh, Muslim, Jewish, and Christian, use the banner of their religion to promote evil acts. Such conduct is always based on a narrow interpretation of their holy texts, and fuelled by perceived injustice to their fellow religionists. One of many obvious examples would be the sufferings of the Muslims, and the Christian minority, in the Palestinian refugee camps. Political and practical injustice in Palestine, coupled with a particular understanding of the Koran, is the seedbed for recruitment to the cause of the Islamic freedom fighters. Mix that with the dangerous teaching that death in a religious cause earns a place in Paradise, and a lethal spiritual cocktail has been concocted.

(21) The death of the leading Apostles caused considerable problems for the early church. 1 Clement, written in AD96, says that "sinful jealousy" caused both their deaths (see Section 5 of his letter). There is strong archeological evidence to support Peter's martyrdom in Rome. See especially John Walsh, *The Bones of St Peter*, Victor Gollancz, 1983, and Dr Guaducci, *St Pierre Retrouvé*, Editions St Paul, 1974 trans. from Italian original published by Arnoldo Mondadavi, Editore-Milano. This is important evidence corroborating the spread of the Gospel to Rome in the mid-1st Century.

(22) Oscar Cullmann, *Prayer in the New Testament*, SCM, 1995 p. 141.

(23) Peter Wagner, *Territorial Spirits*, Sovereign World, 1991,

has a much fuller discussion of this important subject.

(24) Corrie Ten Boom's account of Ravensbrück in *The Hiding Place* is an example of God's prevailing presence in a concentration camp.

Moolenburgh, *op. cit.* gives many examples of angelic protection of individuals, both in occupied Holland, and in Germany towards the end of the war.

(25) See, for instance, 2 Chronicles 33:1–9, Acts 19, etc.

(26) Cullmann *op. cit.* p. 141f.

(27) Cullmann *op. cit.* p. 47.

5

Angels and Conversion

In this chapter, we look at the part played by angels, and visions, in some people's conversions. We also note examples of God's protection of his servants, especially when involved in evangelism.

Angels and Conversion

We have already seen (Chapter 3) the part played by angels and visions in the conversion of the Ethiopian eunuch, Saul of Tarsus, Cornelius, and in the evangelism of Philippi. Throughout history, a small, but significant number of conversions have taken place because of the direct intervention of angels, or because of visions. All true conversions are miracles of grace. God challenges people in a variety of ways. We are concerned, here, with the evidence that *sometimes* conversions take place in ways that seem unusual.

We begin with an experience of Monica.

Monica's vision

Monica was born in North Africa in the fourth century. She was patient, and gentle. She had to put up with a violent husband, and a cantankerous mother-in-law. Her witness led to the conversion of both of them. Her prime concern, however, was her wayward and brilliant son. He was living a dissolute life, and his career was going nowhere. When praying, she had a vision. She dreamt that she was standing on a measuring stick (which symbolises the rule of faith). She was full of anguish. A youth appeared, and enquired what was wrong. Monica explained about her son, Augustine. Then she saw her son standing with her on the same stick. She heard a voice saying that where she was, her son would be. She understood this to mean that, in time, he would share her faith.

Monica persisted in believing, while her son grew more and more successful, and apparently further away from the Kingdom of God.

Nine long years later, Augustine had his dramatic and well-known conversion. He was to become the greatest theologian of his age. Soon afterwards, he sat with his mother as she was dying. They both experienced a great sense of the Divine presence.

But despite this, and his mother's earlier vision, Augustine was very cautious about such experiences. Writing about his conversion, he says:

> Whom could I find to reconcile me to thee? Should I have approached the angels? What kind of prayer? What kind of rites? Many who were striving to return to thee and were not able of themselves, have I am told, tried this and have fallen into a longing for curious visions and deserved to be deceived.
>
> Being exalted, they sought thee in their pride of learning, and they thrust themselves forward rather than beating their breasts. And so by a likeness of heart, they drew to themselves the princes of the air, their conspirators and companions in pride, by whom they were deceived by the power of magic. Thus they sought a mediator by whom they might be cleansed, but there was none. For the mediator they sought was the devil, disguising himself as an angel of light. And he allured their proud flesh the more because he had no fleshly body.[1]

Despite this cautious approach to the supernatural, Augustine wrote much about the afterlife. Later, in (see p 170ff), we shall look at one of his lesser known works, where he shares his thoughts and a strange vision of Paradise that one of his baptismal candidates had experienced.

For many years, Augustine wrote and taught that the age of

miracles was past. Then, near the end of his life, he started to
notice the miracles, mainly of healing, that were taking place in
his home city. He recorded some of them in great detail. When
Augustine was dying, a man came to see him to ask the Saint to
pray for his healing. Augustine wanted to decline saying that
he, personally, had no healing gift. The man told him that he
had received a *vision*, and that in it he had been told to seek out
Augustine to receive prayer for his healing. Hearing that,
Augustine agreed to pray for him. The man was completely
healed, and Augustine died soon afterwards.

The conversion of King Edwin

The conversion of King Edwin (585–633), later King of
Northumberland, is described in great detail by Bede.[2] Edwin
had been exiled by his predecessor, and had taken refuge with
Redwald, King of the East Angles. A friend warned Edwin that
Redwald had been bribed to murder him. Despite this warning,
Edwin refused to flee, and sat alone outside King Redwald's
palace.

In the middle of the night, he saw a man approaching whose
unexpected arrival caused him great alarm. The stranger told
Edwin that he knew about all his troubles and asked him three
questions. First, he asked what reward Edwin would give to
someone who could persuade his host, Redwald, not to harm
him. Secondly, how would he react if as a result of this protection, Edwin became the greatest known king amongst the
English nation? Thirdly, if this prophecy proves to be true,
would Edwin follow the guidance that he would then be given?
Edwin promised due rewards, and that he would follow the
guidance of anyone who could protect him and raise him to the
throne. The unknown man then laid his right hand on Edwin's
head, saying:

"When you receive this sign, remember this occasion and
our conversation, and do not delay the fulfilment of your
promise." Then, the man vanished, and Edwin realised that it

was not a man but a spirit (presumably an angel) who had appeared to him.

Soon afterwards, Edwin's original friend returned, told him that all was now well. Redwald supported Edwin in battle, and he was quickly established as the rightful King of Northumbria. For a long time afterwards, despite being married to a believer, Edwin dithered about accepting the Christian faith. He was inspired by the preaching of Paulinus, later Archbishop of York. But still he hesitated, until one day Paulinus visited him.

Paulinus came up to him, laid his right hand upon his head, and enquired whether he remembered this sign. The King trembled and would have fallen at his feet. Paulinus raised him up, and in a friendly voice reminded him of the third promise that he had made many years earlier. Paulinus told him to accept the faith, and receive not only earthly blessings but a future place in heaven.

Soon afterwards, the King and his leaders were baptised. His high priest, Caifi, destroyed his own pagan altars, and Edwin reigned well until he was killed in battle in 633.

The conversion of Sundar Singh

At the beginning of the 20th century, Sundar Singh, the fifteen-year-old son of a wealthy Sikh landowner, was desperate. His mother had just died, and his own spiritual quest, which had included education at a good school run by missionaries and searching the holy writings of the Sikhs, the Hindus, and the Muslims, had led him nowhere. He prayed to God to reveal Himself to him. He had decided that if there was no answer, he would commit suicide by throwing himself in front of an express train, which would pass his home at 5 a.m. He woke at 3 a.m, took his early-morning bath, which Sikhs and Hindus always have before worship, and returned to pray. He expected one of the gods to speak to him. What happened changed his life. He could see a cloud of light breaking through the darkness. As the light got brighter, he saw the radiant figure of

Jesus, whose followers he had hated at school. He heard a
voice saying, "Why do you persecute me? I died on the cross
for you and the whole world." The cloud disappeared and he
went to wake his father to tell him what had happened. His
family was furious, eventually sending him out of the family
home with poisoned food. Sundar became a most respected
Christian evangelist, he travelled the world, had the joy of
seeing his father converted, and had a number of experiences,
during his evangelistic ministry, of angels.[3] This story illustrates the ways in which God can call and protect his servants.
We cannot presume on this, and Sundar, himself, disappeared
when crossing the mountains on his way to another evangelistic
mission in Tibet.

The angel and the Eskimo leader

About the same time, something remarkable was happening in
North-East Canada, on the edge of Baffin Island where the seer
of the local Eskimos, a man called Angutirjuaq, had heard
about a God, whom he knew as Jesusi. After a great dream of
light and darkness, he started a spiritual search to see if Jesusi
was the way to the truth. He followed a tribal custom and went
to search for seal meat, on a dark moonless night. He decided
that if he found a seal, made a kill and could share it with his
followers, then he would follow the new way. Very quickly,
despite the lack of moonlight, he found a hole where seals
come up to breathe. In the bitter cold of the Arctic night, he
managed to fall asleep. When he awoke, he was astonished,
because the ice-hole was lit up. He could even see a seal in the
hole. Far more remarkably, he was aware of three bright figures
in the sky. He harpooned the seal, made his way back to his
camp, and told his followers of his decision to follow Jesusi.
Years later, Canon John Turner arrived as a missionary.
Angutirjuaq's grandson was one of the first to respond to
clearer teaching about the way of Jesus. But then things started
to go badly wrong. As so often happens, contact with the

missionaries was followed by greater contact with Canadian traders, and that opened up the way to liquor. The Eskimo communities became renowned for drunkenness, violence and sex. By the early 1990s, the suicide rate, particularly amongst the teenagers, was rising dramatically. The few remaining Christians turned to prayer. Some of the effects of a dramatic ongoing revival can be seen on the Transformations II Video.[4] Apart from huge social changes, for the better, in schools, community, environment, and churches, there were some supernatural signs – particularly an inexplicable deep sound heard, and caught on tape, at one of their revival meetings. This strange phenomenon occurred as Looee Arreak, one of the youth leaders, started to pray for some of the young people. There was already a deep sense of repentance, and a desire to be cleansed based on the Beatitude "Blessed are the pure in heart for they will see God" (Matthew 5:8). The supernatural sound, like the sound of many voices, started softly, and then built up to a crescendo, causing everything and everyone to shake. The pastor thought that something had gone wrong with their sound switchboard. He turned it off completely and the sound continued, it was nothing to do with the human recording system. Amazingly, the tape recorder still recorded the sound – something completely impossible to explain. There was, and is, a tremendous sense of awe and wonder. In many neighbouring communities, it was also obvious that God was bringing transformation. The angels who visited the old seer, Angutirjuaq, about a hundred years ago, seem to be guarding the community, and encouraging their people's new found faith.

Celestial light in Scotland

The revival in the Outer Hebrides began in 1949, as the Holy Spirit stirred up a few people to new heights of prayer. Two old sisters, Peggy and Christine Smith, had a particular burden for their island. They believed the promise written in Isaiah 44:3

"For I will pour water on the thirsty land, and streams on the dry ground; I will pour out my Spirit on your offspring, and my blessing on your descendants." They often prayed far into the night, while seven church leaders in the parish of Barabhas met in a barn, and for many months prayed long and hard. Then it became obvious that all around people were praying. Lights could be seen in many buildings, far into the night. People started to sense God's power, there was a mighty wind, a sense of God's glory, and a supernatural light above many of the houses. The only proper response seemed to be that of the Psalmist, "Be still, and know that I am God" (Psalm 46:10). One early morning, several hundred people, from a small and scattered community, were drawn to meet for prayer outside the community police station at 4 a.m.! People were lying on the main road, crying out to God. It was as if the community was only concerned with the things of Eternity. Many people were converted, and all who were involved had their faith, and expectation, deepened.

Angels in Dartmoor

It would be hard to find a greater contrast to either Angutirjuaq or Sundar than Fred Lemon. I heard Fred give his testimony in Oxford Town Hall. It was at a healing meeting led by my old friend Fred Smith. Fred Smith[5] was no stranger to miracles – even that night a man walked in yellow with cancer, walked out looking very well, and when I contacted him some months later said that he had been completely healed; but it was Fred Lemon who had the strangest story. It ran something like this:

> In my younger days, I was a serious criminal. One day, with some others, I robbed a jewelry shop in London. Unfortunately, there was some violence; we left the jeweller almost dead. Soon after-wards, we were arrested and brought to trial. The jeweller's life hung in the balance, so did mine. If he had died, according to the law at the time, we would have certainly been hung. Fortunately,

he recovered, I was given a long stretch, and ended up in Dart-moor. It was a gloomy terrible place, and I made little attempt to socialise or to get educated. I was one of the most hopeless cases, among a group of desperate lost people. Then on 10th August 1950, I awoke to find three men standing in front of me in my cell. It was in the middle of the night, but the dark gloomy cell was flooded with light. The angel on the right, said "Fred this is Jesus," pointing to the figure in the middle. I was aware of the presence of Jesus. He started to tell me all about my past life. Strangely, I didn't feel afraid. He told me how he had died to pay the penalty for my sins, and through his resurrection that he had overcome the power of death. Significantly, at the end of a wonderful speech, he said, "If you want to become a Christian, you must drive the hatred from your heart." I knew that he was speaking the truth. I was well aware that I had an extreme hatred, especially towards some of the prison warders, and that I had even contemplated attempting to murder some of them. I had been listening with my head in my hands, but with this last sentence I looked up, the three men still looking at me were fading through the wall. There was a distinct click, and I was alone. I knew that Jesus and two of his angels had chosen to visit me. I wasn't afraid. In fact, immediately, I lay down and fell into a deep and peaceful sleep.

Fred went on to tell how his life had been instantly transformed by God's grace. It hadn't been easy, in many ways people found the new Fred more difficult to understand than the old one. Years later, after his release, Fred Lemon wrote a book,[6] and liked nothing better than to travel around giving his testimony to God's grace, and telling of the unexpected visitors in his prison cell.

Angel choirs in hospital

On 10th March 2002, I was preaching in Holy Trinity Leicester. It was my first Sunday on the staff of this large church. The Vicar invited people to come forward for prayer. Rosemary Carr, who was visiting one of her family, came up. A few days later, she wrote to me with this story:

> I was in hospital for an operation in September 1995 and the
> following occurred in the early hours of the Sunday I was there.
> There were just three of us in the ward over the weekend – an
> elderly lady dying of cancer next to me, and one other, also post
> operative, opposite us. The poor lady next to me was continually
> crying out in pain and fear, so I went to her and offered to pray
> with her for restful sleep, which she gladly accepted. As I strug-
> gled back to bed, I was assailed by nasty gargoyle-like faces, and
> knew it to be the enemy's retaliation. I cried out to Jesus to send
> his angelic protection.
>
> Almost immediately I heard distant music, which I assumed was
> a radio, but as it came nearer and louder, I realised it was an
> angelic choir – such high and beautiful notes in strangely familiar
> music – and soon, through the central aisle of the ward came a
> procession of angels, so tall and ethereally glorious, playing old-
> fashioned instruments like the lutes, etc. one sees on Christmas
> cards. I don't know how long this went on, but I was transfixed
> with wonder and praise.
>
> And then I was aware of Jesus amongst them. (I did not see his
> face, but his presence was tangible in the spirit sense.) He had not
> come for my dying neighbour as I thought, but went across to the
> other patient. She was a hospital sister from the A and E Ward.
> Two of her three teenage children were special needs children. I
> saw in the Spirit her family all around her bed, and Jesus came and
> embraced them each, one by one, and then collectively as a family.
> Then He went, and the beautiful music and accompanying angels
> also went. I had been a spectator in a very moving scene.
>
> I wrote to the elderly lady when she left for the hospice, and I
> believe my letter was a comfort to her husband when she died.
>
> It was some time before I could tell the other patient what I had
> seen Jesus do for her and her family. I invited her to Women
> Aglow at Christmas 1995, and shared the special blessing I felt she
> had received. She said "So long as none of my children was left
> out." And, of course, no one is excluded by Jesus. Now she is a
> member of our church and of my home group, and going from
> strength to strength.
>
> God is good!

This story is particularly interesting, featuring both the presence of the spiritual opposition, and a choir of angels. The testimony of my correspondent obviously brought spiritual blessing to the dying old lady, and appears to have helped the hospital sister become a Christian.

An angelic vision before a renewal

My friend Roger Simpson, now Vicar of St Michael-le-Belfry in York, sent me this story concerning an earlier part of his ministry:

I went to St Paul's and St George's in 1989. It was a large episcopal church at the far end of Queen Street, right in the centre of Edinburgh. The church had fallen on hard times and had a congregation of between 20 and 30. Another church called St Thomas' had invited me to plant a church into the city centre and they gave us 50–60 of their people. After we had been there about a month or two, and the congregation had already begun to grow rapidly, I had one of those encounters that you never forget. I had just baptised Duncan Campbell's[7] great-grandson at one of the morning services, and as I was standing on the door, an elderly lady said to me, "I need to speak to you." I went to visit her the next day. She lived in a very posh flat in Herriot Row, and she told me the most amazing story. She had come back from India with her husband after the war, and they had gone to live in the family home on the Isle of Skye. While there, her husband had died, and the episcopal priest who visited them on the island was from St Paul's and St George's. As a result, she moved to Edinburgh, joined the church, and over the next fifteen years she saw the congregation get smaller and smaller. The priest was very discouraged, and during one Evensong (she told me that there were about nine people in the congregation), in the middle of the prayers, she looked up in this huge church, and she saw many, many angels hovering over the church. There was tremendous brightness and glory, and then "in the Spirit", she saw hundreds of people crowding to get into the church. Then the vision passed. She stayed in that church for another ten years, and eventually the congregation had to move

into the little chapel underneath the nave. She thought she was
going mad, but she carried on praying. After the vicar left, she then
went away to the Isle of Skye. She came back a year and a half
later, and stood on the pavement, with all the students who were
queuing to get into the church! She wept and wept. Her vision was
fulfilled, and the church grew over the next seven years to 800
people.

The miracle of conversion

Every conversion, each rebirth of a dead church, each revival,
whether or not it is accompanied by supernatural signs, is a
miracle. Jesus made that clear when at the end of his perplex-
ing conversation with Nicodemus, he said "The wind blows
wherever it pleases. You hear its sound, but you cannot tell
where it comes from or where it is going. So it is with everyone
born of the Spirit." (John 3:8)

The Apostles understood this when they prayed for boldness,
signs and wonders. Their prayers were answered by a supernatural shaking of the building (see Acts 4:23–31).

Recently I listened to Michael Cassidy preaching in Bath.
After all the miracles in South Africa surrounding the dismantling of apartheid,[8] he was somewhat pessimistic of the current
state of affairs. Miracles, visions, and signs, have to be
sustained by hard work, and a continued openness to God's
more normal means of grace. He did however strike an optimistic note, with an account of a visit to a predominately
Muslim country, where the Christians were engaging in fervent
prayer. There had been some remarkable conversions – mainly
of Muslims who had dreams and visions of the Risen Christ.

Soon after writing these words, a missionary visiting our
church told me this story:

A devoted Indonesian Muslim on his third pilgrimage to Mecca
was travelling with a party of others in a coach. As they drove
along from Mecca to Medina he started talking to the coach driver.
When the driver discovered that the Indonesian was on his third

pilgrimage, he remarked that this must have cost him a great deal of money. On being assured that it was indeed very expensive to come on the pilgrimage, the driver went on to ask why the Indonesian didn't give his money to the poor instead, as the Christians do!

The Indonesian was so surprised that he didn't know what to say. Later that day he told others about this strange conversation. When they heard it, they became very angry because they were sure that the driver must have been a Christian, and a Christian was not allowed to be among them, for otherwise their pilgrimage could lose its value! However, when the driver was called to reassure them that he was a Muslim, the Indonesian was even more confused, as the coach driver – whom all the other passengers recognised – was not the man he had been talking to that day in the coach.

The Indonesian returned home still in a state of confusion over the incident. Some time later, he was visiting the home of a Christian friend and saw a picture on the wall, which he recognised as that of the "coach driver". When he asked who this man was, he was told that the picture was of Jesus. As a result of this experience, the man, and about 50 of his relatives and friends, came to faith in Christ.

For obvious reasons, I have given no identification of the source or the people involved. Christians are facing terrible persecution in parts of Indonesia. There is a great spiritual battle taking place there. Intense prayer is being accompanied by remarkable signs (see also p 159ff), and persecutions. Our visitor told us of young Christians refusing to deny Jesus and dying for their faith, of churches being destroyed, and yet of much growth in holiness and evangelism.

It would be helpful to know if Sundar Singh's conversion was preceded by intense prayer – perhaps by his former schoolteachers. It would be helpful to know if the missionaries who had somehow got a message to Angutirjuaq were also engaged in deep prayer for his people. It would be good to suppose that the chaplains, and other Christians among the Dartmoor staff, were busy interceding for Fred Lemon. Were the local Chris-

tians praying for the Indonesian on his pilgrimage? The truth is
that we do not know. What we do know, from Christian history
past and present, is that where there is intense prayer, there is
much more evidence of God moving powerfully and unexpectedly in individuals and communities.

There are many known examples of faithful people praying,
and seeing remarkable transformations taking place. Rather
fewer, perhaps, have been accompanied by such powerful
visions.

We now turn to the matter of the protection of evangelists.
Countless stories are told of this nature, but the one that I have
chosen is unusual. The situation was not life-threatening, but
very awkward, and the people involved were crossing out of
danger into an apparently Christian country – but one that can
be strangely hostile to evangelism.

God protects evangelists

An example of God's protection comes from Albania. In the
1950s, Albania was declared to be world's first official atheistic
state. The Christians were villified, and persecuted. Outside,
some intercessors felt called to prayer. A few intrepid tourists[9]
carried Bibles into this dangerous country, and tried to make
contact with Christians. Then communism collapsed, and the
country began to open up. About the same time, in 1990, a
Somerset businessman, Ian Loring, was facing a personal
crisis. An unpleasant business career had come to a dramatic
end, and he had been fired. At the age of 27, he was unem-
ployed, and not particularly employable. In a Bristol shopping
centre, he saw and heard a typical open-air gospel presentation.
He was singularly unmoved, impressed neither by the clever
reverse lettering used by the evangelist Korki Davey, nor by the
testimony of a converted Irishman "from the mire to the choir".
About two months later, reflecting on an increasingly uncertain
future, and relaxing in the bath, he was startled to hear a quiet
authoritative voice: "Do not store up for yourself treasure on

earth where moth and rust destroy. But store up for yourself treasure in heaven. For where your treasure is, there will your heart be also. No one can serve two masters. Either he will hate the one and love the other, or he will be devoted to the one, and despise the other. You cannot serve both God and Money." (See Matthew 6:19–25.)

Ian knew that, for whatever reason, God had chosen to speak to him. In early 1991, after some training in evangelism, he found himself travelling towards Albania. The group's first attempts at evangelism took place in a railway siding in Northern Greece, where they found, and fed, a group of hungry Albanian refugees. They gave the group some copies of Luke's Gospel. The next night they returned with more food; but the refugees had been fed in quite a different way. Their leader said, in Albanian, "Last night, I read your book to the men. I told them that it was important for them to listen. In the morning when I awoke, they were looking at me. No one was saying anything! Their faces were different. I said to them 'You all saw him too, didn't you?'" He continued, "Last night, he stood there by the fire. His clothes were white and clean. He said to us 'You are my sheep, and I am your shepherd. Come to me', and he held out his hands."

This was an extraordinary encouragement to Ian and his team. Often the work was hard, and very dangerous, occasionally there were other conversions through the direct intervention of God. On one occasion, he needed a different sort of help. Crossing from Albania into Northern Greece could be hazardous, as the Greeks weren't too keen either on Protestant evangelists, or their evangelical literature.

Caralee and I felt deeply in need of a rest in Thessaloniki. I had been leading a huge number of Bible studies, and the constant stream of visitors from the growing church fellowship to our room in Little Paris, sometimes from 8 a.m. through to 11 p.m., was draining. So was the feeling of living in a fishbowl, being constantly watched by others: along with Mike Brown, we were the only foreigners living in the market town for the region's 250,000 people. Sometimes, when we reached Greece, we would sleep for 24 hours at a stretch to recover.

On this day, when we reached the Greek side of the border, we discovered their customs officers were on strike. I asked a policeman if it was still okay to pass through, and he told me it was fine by him. However, as Caralee began to drive past the customs point, a man in a light grey uniform jumped up on to the footplate, yanked open my door and dragged me down on to the road. As my side hit the ground, he was going berserk, shouting, punching me in the stomach and kicking me in the back and kidneys. I was completely stunned by the assault. Other customs officers were gathering around, and I could hear Caralee screaming at them.

When the beating had finished, my sides were raw and I felt sick and in shock. We were made to park up our vehicle and led away towards a police Land Rover. We had driven through the customs officers' picket line, and the man, a stocky colonel with a high forehead, was shouting that he was going to have us arrested.

"You have tried to enter our country with violence," he raged, scarlet-faced. I couldn't believe the accusation. We were driven away from the border point with the colonel and a police officer sitting stiffly in the front. I looked at Caralee: she had tears in her eyes. Two of my ribs were too sensitive to touch, and I didn't know what was going to happen to us. The officer was offering no explanations, and the colonel kept repeating his charge.

After a short drive the car drew into the Greek town of Kastoria and pulled up outside the courthouse. The colonel marched us roughly inside the building. We sat there waiting for an unbearably long time in a plain room with a single wooden bench. I felt deeply upset and afraid: we were in a foreign country, unable to speak the language and facing a trumped-up charge. Caralee's hand felt warm as I held it, and we prayed together furiously.

The colonel entered shortly and presented us with a document and a black Biro. "Sign this . . . here," he shouted gruffly. It was written in Greek, which neither of us could read, but I assumed it was some admission of our offence. Another policeman was attempting to translate but saying little more than, "Sign here please."

As I pushed the document away, my hand was shaking. "Look," I said angrily, "we'd like to speak to a lawyer."

"You haven't got a lawyer," the colonel snapped sarcastically. "You're in Greece now. You'll sign it, or else you'll be forgotten about!" It was an ominous statement.

At that very moment, a tall, olive-skinned man in a blue pin-striped suit entered the room. Under his arm he held a buffed brief-case and an Oxford legal dictionary. "I'll be your lawyer," he announced in an upper-class English accent.

No one said a word: everyone was equally stunned. The man spoke quickly in Greek, and the colonel and the officer left the room. He sat down next to Caralee without introducing himself. "Tell me what has happened," he said, and I explained the events of the last couple of hours with a huge sense of relief.

"Wait here," he replied, "I shan't be long."

Half an hour later we entered the courtroom with the man now representing us. "Sit here with me," he said, "You will be all right. Just say that you are sorry when I tell you."

There were three judges presiding over the session that day in Kastoria courthouse: two men, and a woman sitting in the middle, all of them dressed in black and red legal robes. The policeman spoke first, then the customs colonel, and then our lawyer. The colonel spoke again with a red face, raising his voice angrily. Our lawyer spoke once more, and then the room went silent. Neither Caralee nor I could understand a word of what was being said.

As I waited, I felt tense and cold. I shuffled uncomfortably in the chair and cast my eyes around the room. Directly behind the woman judge was a large Orthodox painting of the resurrected Christ with his arms outstretched towards us. Across the courtroom roof, the painting fanned out to depict a grey-bearded God the Father looking down from a patch of blue sky between the clouds. I studied the painting for a long minute. A strong sensation came over me that in this room Jesus was going to be both our judge and our advocate, and my spirits began to lift.

The woman judge stood up and slammed her hammer down on the bench. She turned towards us and announced: "You are without blame, and free to go. I'm sorry." The sense of relief and vindication was phenomenal. She then turned to the colonel and began to berate him at length. He seemed to shrink a little before her and turned even redder in the face.

Outside the courtroom, we shook our lawyer's hand firmly. "Could we have your card? We still don't know your name," I enquired. "What do we owe you?"

"Oh, it's all right," the man replied, already stepping away. "You would have done the same for me." Then he was gone through the front door of the courthouse.

I looked at Caralee and she at me. It was a little strange. The police officer escorted us back to the car, and the colonel sat without speaking in the front. As we drove towards the border, he reached back and offered his hand. I shook it, lightly at first, but then with firmness as he looked at me with his pride now diminished.

The whole incident left a deep impression on us. It seemed to underline in our hearts God's amazing care, even if we strayed over the edge – in this instance through a picket line. And as for our free lawyer who had so quickly disappeared, who was he? An angel with an Oxford legal dictionary?

The next time we arrived at the border, the colonel greeted me like an old friend, hugging me warmly and offering me a glass of ouzo. It was as if, like children, we'd had a fight and made up and now he respected me. Whenever I needed help getting people or goods through the border from then on, it was the colonel's pleasure to make the process smooth.[10]

It seems to me, that it is far more likely that Ian's lawyer was an angel than an actual English-speaking lawyer who turned up at the right time, with the necessary diplomatic skills to rescue two very frightened evangelists in a remote part of Greece.

This story fits the category of angels who appear as human beings. Only afterwards do the recipients of their help realise the true nature of their helpers.

This story, while not strictly about conversions, illustrates the presence of angels, and other supernatural powers, when serious evangelism is undertaken, particularly in hostile situations. While we can never presume on such protection, it is apparent that God intervenes directly far more often than most easy-going, rationalistic, Western Christians expect! As we have seen, the early church faced this situation – not least after the execution of James, and the arrest of Peter.

Notes

(1) Augustine Confessions Book Ten, chapter XLII. For his conversion see Book Eight. Augustine on miracles, see *City of God*, Books 8–10. Translated by H. Bettenson, Penguin, 1984; quoted by me in *Thinking Clearly about Healing and Deliverance*, Monarch, 1999, pp. 169ff.

(2) Bede, *A History of the English Church and People*, translated by Leo Sherley-Price, Penguin, 1955, p.120ff.

(3) See any standard life of Sundar Singh. I am grateful for the summary of his life in David Shrisunder's "Encounters with Angels" 1995, obtainable from the author by e-mail at Shrisunder@abbeypress.net.

(4) Transformations Videos are produced by the Sentinel Group, and distributed by Gateway Christian Media Ltd PO 11905, London NW10 4ZQ. Both the revival amongst the Eskimos and the revival in the Hebrides appear in great detail.

(5) See Fred Smith, *God's Gift of Healing*, New Wine Press, 1986.

(6) Fred Lemon, *Breakout*, Lakeland, 1977.

(7) Duncan Campbell was the evangelist who, humanly, was used as the evangelist in 1949 in the Outer Hebrides (see p. 125f). For other stories about revival, prayer and visions, see Mark Stibbe, *Thinking Clearly about Revival*, Monarch, 1998.

(8) See, amongst others of his writings: Michael Cassidy, *A Witness for Ever*, Hodder & Stoughton, 1995.

(9) Beverly Barton (Eadon, as she then was) used to amaze my congregation in Shepton Mallet with her intrepid witness in Albania in the 1980s.

(10) Muthena Alkazraji, *Christ and the Kalashnikov*, p. 60ff, Marshall Pickering, 2001. Used by permission of Zondervan Inc. Many other stories of protection of evangelists can be found in Christian literature, often in situations of considerable danger.

6

Angels Intervene

In this chapter, we consider the theological arguments
about guardian angels. We give some more examples of
angelic help and protection. We try to test these experiences
against the gold standard of Scripture, and we look briefly
at some testimonies, which give a glimpse of angels at
worship.

Angels Intervene

Angels intervene in many different ways and in a variety of situations. Popular understanding focuses on the role of guardian angels. In this chapter, we concentrate mainly on this aspect of angelic dealings with our world. This seems to be only a small fraction of the work of angels which appears to be mainly concentrated in the courts of heaven.

Guardian angels

We have looked briefly in Chapter 2 at Jesus' teaching about guardian angels. The Bible clearly teaches that angels are around us, often protect us, but doesn't go as far as saying that each human being has a guardian angel, who is on constant sentry duty. Michael Green[1] has a very helpful comment on the crux passage in Matthew 18:10–14. He points out the similarities, and the differences, between the parable of the lost sheep as told in Luke 15, and here in Matthew. The Lucan passage is evangelistic – three wonderful parables about the Father's heart for seeking the lost; and the joy in heaven, in the presence of the angels when one sinner repents. By contrast, in Matthew, Jesus is teaching about relationships in the kingdom. In this great chapter, Jesus teaches about the need for humility

(vv 1–4); how to welcome people (vv 5–6); wholeheartedness
(vv 7–9); pastoral care (vv 10–14); openness (vv 15–20);
forgiveness (vv 21–22); freedom from resentment (vv 23–35).
It is within this context, that we can understand Jesus' teaching
about angels. Green continues:

> He is speaking to his disciples, those who were later to become
> leaders in the community. He has been telling them not to put
> stumbling blocks in the way of the apparently unimportant, and to
> be utterly ruthless with sinful tendencies in themselves. And now
> he encourages them to care for the lonely, the lost and the sick, the
> discouraged. They are sheep without a shepherd, and God cares
> enormously for each one. That is symbolised by the fact that "in
> heaven the angels always behold the face of my Father who is in
> heaven".
>
> This would have immediately rung a bell with his Jewish listen-
> ers, for there was a highly developed angelology among the Jews
> of that day. Nations have their angels (Daniel 10:13ff). Churches
> have their angels (Revelation 2: 1ff). Individuals have their angels
> (here). The rabbis believed that even the flowers had angels to
> represent them before God! It is a delightful way of expressing the
> unceasing love and care of the Creator for his creatures, and there
> is a strong note of accessibility as well. The "face" of the Eastern
> ruler was hard to approach. He was a busy and important person.
> But the angels always behold his "face". They have unrestricted
> access to his presence. God cares very much for the little members,
> the stray sheep of his flock. Do the leaders care? That is the thrust
> of this passage.

Jesus is making a very similar point in John 1:51 (see Chapter
2, p 46f) where he teaches that the windows of heaven are
open, and angels descend and ascend on the Son of Man.

Historical viewpoints

Not surprisingly, the church has come up with many different
interpretations of this passage. Here is one summary of the
early church's views:

The Church Fathers agreed about the existence of personal, or guardian angels. For example, St Basil the Great, citing Matthew 18:10–11, said that "each one of the faithful has an Angel who directs his life". St John Chrysostom concurred. They disagreed, however, over whether pagans and the unbaptized were entitled to guardian angels, and also where exactly a guardian angel assumed his duties with regard to a human's life. Origen, commenting on Matthew, believed that only the faithful receive guardian angels, and at one time even opined that adults in general do not have them because Jesus referred only to children. Saints Basil and Cyril of Alexandria likewise believed that only the faithful qualified. St Jerome made no distinction between souls of the righteous and souls of sinners, but agreed with St Basil that mortal sin would put guardian angels "into flight". St Ambrose said that God sometimes withdraws a guardian angel in order to give someone the "opportunity" to struggle alone, and thus gain more glory. St Thomas Aquinas qualified that view by stating that he did not believe a guardian angel would completely abandon a person, but might leave temporarily. Some Church Fathers believed that the guardian angel was installed at baptism, while others, such as Aquinas, Jerome, and St Anselm, believed that the angel appears at birth.[2]

After the Reformation, Protestant teachers were somewhat more cautious. Martin Luther wrote that "an angel is a spiritual creature created by God without a body for the service of Christendom and the church".[3] This definition contains the main thrust of angelic ministry as experienced by men and women (but ignores their work and worship in the courts of heaven).

Calvin, in one place takes much the same line:[4]

Scripture strongly insists upon teaching us what could most effectively make for our consolation and the strengthening of our faith: namely, that angels are dispensers and administrators of God's beneficence toward us. For this reason, Scripture recalls that they keep vigil for our safety, take upon themselves our defence, direct our ways, and take care that some harm may not befall us.

and elsewhere gives a very cautious exposition of Matthew 18:10:[5]

> Christ hints that there are certain angels to whom their safety (the children) has been committed . . . from this I do not know whether one ought to infer that each individual has the protection of his own angel. We ought to hold as a fact that the care of each one of us is not the task of one angel only, but all, with one consent watch over our salvation. If the fact that all the heavenly host are keeping watch for his safety will not satisfy a man, I do not see what benefit he could derive from knowing that one angel has been given to him as his especial guardian. Indeed, those who confine to one angel the care that God takes of each one of us are doing a great injustice, both to themselves and to all the members of the church, as if it were an idle promise that we should fight more valiantly with these hosts supporting and protecting us round about!

Calvin is, perhaps, being too logical. Obviously, we are called to take the struggle against "the spiritual forces of evil in the heavenly realms" (Ephesians 6:12) very seriously. Accepting the simple teaching of Scripture of the existence of guardian angels reinforces the reality of the spiritual battle; it does not remove our responsibility to pray, to seek protection, and to stand firm.

Calvin, and other Protestant writers such as Karl Barth, are highly dismissive of speculative theologies which try to sort hierarchies of angels.[6] Calvin also warns[7] against the "superstition which frequently creeps in, to the effect that angels are ministers and dispensers of all good things to us. . . . And that what belongs to God and Christ alone is transferred to them". We shall see the importance of this warning when we look at New Age teaching about "Spirit Guides" in Chapter 9. While not denying that many people have experienced help from angels, particularly in events of surprising protection, we must not fall into the trap of assuming their protection and/or guidance. We have seen, in Chapter 3, how Luke carefully distinguishes between the work of the Holy Spirit, and the particular

work of angels. Calvin's warning is important. Scripture
teaches that believers have the *constant* presence of the Holy
Spirit (Ephesians 3:16, etc.), that the Holy Spirit *sometimes*
guides by external means (Acts 13:2, etc.), and that *occasionally* angels are released from heaven for particular tasks (Acts
8:26, etc.). We now turn to a few examples of protection, and
other experiences, which support the view that there is much
unseen by us which works to help us.

The tractor at Lee Abbey

Ray and Pam Fardon, who once helped me with a Parish
Mission, told me a wonderful story of protection, and escape
from disaster. In the late 1960s, they were leading a youth
camp at Lee Abbey, near Lynton, in North Devon. Pam was
enjoying the beauty of the coastline, when suddenly her
thoughts were disturbed by the loud noise of an engine. She
looked up and saw a tractor, out of control, careering wildly
down a steep field. The driver managed to steer it through a
gate, but it was gaining speed all the time as it raced through a
second field. By now, many of the guests at the house on the
top of the hill, and many in the youth camp, were watching
with horror. They started to pray for the tractor driver who was
trying desperately to bring his machine under control. The tractor was racing towards a car park crowded with holidaymakers,
eating their picnics. Pam remembers praying, "Lord, please
change its direction." Moments later, it veered aside, missed the
car park, and somersaulted over the cliff.

Ray took a few men with him and raced down the cliff pathway, instructing everyone else to pray. Quickly, Ray found the
tractor upside down on a car parked by a chalet on the beach,
far below the original scene. The owner, a widowed mother of a
large family, had just left the car and wandered back to the
chalet, wondering why she had got out of the car. Her car was
completely crushed, but no one was hurt. Ray, and his friends,
searched for the tractor driver, but there was no sign of anyone.

A little while later, the original tractor driver, who had got out of the tractor leaving the engine running while he opened a gate, appeared on the scene. Pam and Ray and others were certain they had seen someone driving the tractor, and steering so that it avoided the car park. Pam, at the time, described a man in brown, leaning right over the steering wheel with his hands almost crossed over. Ray, Pam, and others who witnessed the scene, are quite convinced that they saw an angel driving the tractor. Like many similar other stories, it is simpler to believe that the second driver was an angel. The alternative is that a number of people all suffered hallucinations; and that, by chance, the tractor swerved to avoid ploughing into the car park.

My editor asks, pertinently, why didn't the angel stop the engine or put the brake on? I have already addressed this issue (see pp. 27, 81), and would add that angels seem concerned with *saving life* and not property. If the angel had stopped the tractor there would have been no story! If the Ethiopian eunuch had directed his chariot to Samaria, he would naturally have met Philip; again there would have been no story. God seems to allow these incidents to give us glimpses of his sovereign power.

Lee Abbey is a great place of prayer, a place where others have seen angels and heard them singing. Its founder, Jack Winslow,[8] wrote a book which includes many stories of miraculous protection, and several about angels. Many stories about angels are stories of protection, usually from extreme danger from people hostile to the Christian Gospel.

Protection for a missionary

Revd John Paton[9] was an intrepid missionary to the New Hebrides. He suffered much persecution and hardship, but eventually saw a lot of fruit for his labours. On one occasion, in the 1860s, hostile natives surrounded his headquarters. John, and his intrepid wife, prayed all night for protection, they were

alone and defenceless – only God could help them. When
daylight came, they were amazed, and relieved, to see the
attackers leave. Years later, the tribe's chief became a Christian.
Mr Paton asked him why he and his followers hadn't burnt the
house down. The chief explained that he had seen many
hundreds of men, in shining garments, standing with drawn
swords, circling the mission station. They were far too afraid to
attack. Only then did John Paton realise that God had sent his
angels to protect him and his wife.

Angels drive away a gang

When speaking recently at Lee Abbey, I was very pleased to
meet a couple who worship at St Boniface's, a church on a
housing estate near the edge of Birmingham. For years the
Quinton Estate had been very run down, church attendances (as
in most comparable situations) were very low. In 1985, Revd
Wallace Brown had arrived there as vicar. What happened in
the next fourteen years, and which continues today,[10] is a
wonderful story of courage, prayer, risk-taking, and evangelism, which should inspire every struggling church who thinks
that their "patch" is particularly difficult. For the purposes of
this book, it is their troubles with the Quinton Mob which are
relevant. The Quinton Mob were a particularly unpleasant
group of teenagers, who had nothing better to do than to sit
around the walls of the church causing mayhem.

Calling the police was useless, the gang would just melt
away, and return a few hours later. One evening, Wallace
counted about 35 of them, mostly older teenagers, swigging
beer, making a row, and generally making access to the church
and the rectory profoundly unpleasant.

Mary, Wallace's wife, was in complete despair. She prayed
deep into the night, literally spreadeagled over her lounge floor.
God led her to the book of Nehemiah. The message, which was
clear to Mary, and far from clear to Wallace, was that the walls
of St Boniface's had to be reclaimed. It was a spiritual battle,

which could only be won through prayer, and practical measures. Nehemiah posted a guard day and night to warn off Sanballat and his friends, while the walls of Jerusalem were rebuilt. Let them tell the rest of the story in their own words:

The following morning I lay in a hot bath thinking over my hurtful ridicule and discovered I was inwardly impressed by Mary's ideas. Nehemiah had come to a broken-down city. Vandals were threatening to overrun the walls and take the city. God's work was in danger of being wiped out even before it started. There were definitely parallels.

I went downstairs for breakfast, "Go on then – what does the Lord say about our situation through Nehemiah?" I asked self-consciously.

Mary accepted my unspoken apology and said, "Let's wait on God and see." She recorded the answer in her diary: "We asked God how we could put guards on our walls. He gave us the understanding to place guardian angels there. We were to do this each day. And to continue to pray, just like Nehemiah."

The very next day, Mary and I went out and prayed "on location". Feeling slightly foolish, I asked God to place guardian angels all round the walls, to make them safe, and to bring godliness to our lawns and boundaries. It felt good.

The effect was immediate and astonishing. Within a few days the gang started to break up. From the 35 swearing, screaming youths of the previous week, the number dropped to about ten and then by the following week to a mere two or three. Mary and I continued to go out and pray day by day: "Lord, keep your guardian angels round these walls, please."

And so he did. The relief was absolute. After year upon year of human failure, the terrible "siege" of church and vicarage was broken by the supernatural holy presence of God's angels. People started to come in unhindered. My family unexpectedly tasted freedom, and it was wonderful. Mary was able to walk out of the house, and I could relax. What was more, the Quinton Mob did not move to pastures new – they totally broke up! Those years of belligerent menace simply ended with one stroke of God's mighty hand.

In this case, nobody *saw* the angels; but few could doubt their presence. Occam's razor (see pp. 90, 115) again leads us to conclude that angelic intervention, in response to desperate prayer, is by far the most likely explanation.

Angels as unexpected helpers

One of the things that has most surprised me in preparing to write this book, is when you start asking about angels, how many people have themselves had experiences which seem to have involved angels.

Don Latham (see p. 27) told me how, some years ago, he was just leaving the M32 in Bristol to drive up the M4 to catch a plane at Heathrow Airport. He had allowed a reasonable amount of time, but just as he was changing motorways his smart, well-serviced car stuttered to a halt. He got out and opened the bonnet. Nothing was obviously wrong and he started to pray. He was about to travel overseas on a major speaking trip, and the inconvenience to many other people if he missed the plane would have been considerable. Almost immediately someone appeared and asked if he could help. For a short time the unknown helper fiddled around under the bonnet. He then turned to Don and told him that the car would get him to the airport, but that he'd better get it seen to as soon as he returned. On his return, Don took the car straight to his normal garage. When they had looked at it, they expressed some amazement that he'd been able to drive it anywhere.

There are many similar stories in the literature about angels; one of the most dramatic inspired the book *Where Angels Walk*.[11] The author's son, Tim, was trapped on Christmas Eve 1983, in sub-zero temperatures on a lonely highway on the coldest night in American Mid-West records. Tim, and a friend, had been driving home to see their family in Chicago. Unfortunately, the car had crawled to a frozen halt. To leave the car was to invite certain death on such a night, to wait and hope for rescue wasn't a much brighter option. They prayed, and drifted off, as if into a dream, in the cold. They were woken, not by the lights of an oncoming vehicle, but by a knock on the window and an offer of help. Their rescuer, who said nothing else, was driving a tow truck. He towed them back to where, earlier in the evening they had dropped off a friend, and where if they'd had any sense they would have asked to stay the night. When they arrived, Tim raced into his friend's house to ask to borrow money to pay for the tow. His friend commented, "I don't see any tow truck out there." Not only was there no sign of a truck, but there was only one set of tyre marks in the snow – and they belonged to Tim's car!

My former colleague, Liz[12] describes an incident of protection in Nairobi.

I arrived, with a friend who works for Tearfund, at Nairobi train station. We arrived in the middle of the night, and decided to wait until dawn to walk into the city. We began walking along a long straight road towards the place where we were staying. It was very early in the morning, and no one was around. After we had travelled about a quarter of a mile, a well-dressed Kenyan man came up and said, very politely, "May I interrupt you? I heard some men talking at the station. They said that they were going to mug you. They are waiting, just ahead, in the scrubland on the left. I suggest you wait here, at the bus stop, and a bus will come."

We were somewhat shocked, but followed his advice. We were then surprised by his sudden disappearance. The road was long and straight, and we should have been able to see him. A few minutes later a *mutatu* (Kenyan bus) arrived, and it was going to our destination. As it drove past the scrubland, we saw several men hiding behind some trees, just as our mysterious stranger had warned us. We both felt that the only explanation was that we had been warned, and protected, by an angel.

Unexpected helpers in Northern Nigeria

Baroness Cox[13] was preaching at Christchurch Clifton on the evening of Remembrance Sunday in November 2002. In the

midst of a powerful and moving sermon about the courage,
faith, and graciousness of the persecuted church in Southern
Sudan, Northern Nigeria, Indonesia, and in Nagorno Karabakh
(part of the ancient Christian Kingdom of Armenia) she
included the following story:

She was travelling from Kaduna, in Northern Nigeria, to
Abuja, to catch a plane home. The flight was important, not
only were their tickets non-refundable, but also she was due to
speak in an important debate on Africa in the House of Lords
the very next day. As often when travelling in Africa, there was
little time to spare. About a hundred miles from the airport, in
the midst of typical African bush, they met another vehicle
which flashed its lights at them. They ground to a halt, and the
other car swept on its journey. They got out, wondering what
was wrong. The ominous sight of oil gushing out from the rear
wheel greeted them. None of them had mechanical skills, and
they held a quick prayer meeting on the now deserted road. Out
of the bush, two strong, and competent, young men appeared.
Within two minutes, they had opened the back, extracted some
tools, and taken the wheel off – no mean feat! But the trav-
ellers' joy was short lived. As the wheel was being removed,
bearings hurtled out in all directions. Another brief prayer
meeting was held. Suddenly, a young boy aged about twelve,
appeared. He was carrying a black plastic bag, containing a
supply of new wheel bearings, all designed to fit a Honda vehicle! The wheel, and its bearings, was restored, and they were
instructed to test drive the car. It immediately became apparent
that another wheel needed the same treatment. Help came as
before, and they were able to continue their journey after a
delay of a mere 20 minutes. Baroness Cox remarked, "Where
in Bristol could you get back on the road after 20 minutes if the
wheel bearings had gone?"

This is another fairly typical guardian angel story. The trav-
ellers had received a truly miraculous answer to prayer! Probably we shouldn't try to analyse these sorts of experiences!
God's sovereign hand was clearly at work. But it is interesting

to consider which is the most probable explanation – the natural one that a small local boy arrived with exactly the right wheel bearings for a sophisticated car, or the alternative that the intervention was literally that of a guardian angel? There is the more profound problem raised implicitly in the sermon – where were the angels (or indeed the human support) to help the persecuted Christians in the various situations which she described so eloquently? The main thrust of her sermon, and in the book about some of her work,[14] was of the amazing grace given to the beleaguered Christians in so many different situations. She also believes (and there is much in Scripture to support this, particularly in the searching parable of the sheep and the goats, Matthew 25:31–46) that God expects his church in the comfortable West to do far more by prayer, and by practical and political action, to support their brothers and sisters in adversity.

Angels bring comfort

Several of my parishioners have related experiences which point to angelic help. One old lady, who had a very simple Christian faith, and lived very much in a world of her own, often used to tell me that she could see angels around her small house. When she was in hospital, near death, she was obviously aware of spiritual beings all around her. I was rather inexperienced at the time, and somewhat uncertain about angelic visitations, but I couldn't help noticing that she was very calm. After her funeral, I mentioned her experiences to her relatives. I hoped, rather naïvely, that this might open the way to some serious spiritual conversation. The relatives, who were all very fond of the old lady, were profoundly unmoved. They clearly regarded angels as just another of her many eccentricities.

Ginnie, another parishioner, told me of a strange experience of waking up one night and seeing a tall man standing at the foot of her bed. She wasn't frightened, and her husband slumbered peacefully on. She remembered that he was wearing a trilby hat, and a raincoat. Despite the strange circumstances, and lack of any obvious communication, she felt a deep peace. Her natural reaction would have been to panic at such a visitation. Some years later, she was in hospital for cancer treatment. Naturally, she was quite fearful. One night, when everyone else in the ward was fast asleep, she woke up to see the same man, in identical dress, at the foot of her bed. He smiled, looked down, and said, "Don't worry – everything will be fine from now on." She felt a beautiful sense of peace, soon fell asleep, and all was well. She made an excellent recovery.

Marjorie told me about her first husband's death. She was quite young, and the day of the funeral had been exhausting and emotional. In the afternoon while the funeral gathering was taking place in her house, she was struck down by a terrible migraine. Exhausted and shaken, she retired to bed. Quite suddenly in the corner of her bedroom, she saw a wonderfully bright light, she felt that angels were present, and she remembered one of her favourite hymns[15] whose last verse runs as follows:

> Great Father of glory, pure Father of Light,
> Thine angels adore Thee, all veiling their sight;
> All laud we would render; O help us to see
> 'tis only the splendour of light hideth Thee.

Years later, on Pentecost Sunday 1994, we had a particularly powerful time of worship. After the sermon, the preacher prayed for the Holy Spirit to touch people – inviting them to stand, kneel, or sit, as they felt appropriate. Marjorie, sitting in the choir stalls, had an overwhelming sense of God's presence; and again she was aware of being enveloped in bright light. She found this very moving at the time; and very comforting, especially at times of serious illness, in subsequent years.

Angels and children

As we have seen, theologians have argued about the extent that guardian angels are available.

St Thomas Aquinas (c. 1225–74) wrote a huge treatise on the subject. But at the end of his life, after a mystical experience of Christ's presence, he said that this was worth far more than all his writings.

Experience suggests, and this seems to accord with Jesus' teaching, that children are particularly aware of angels. Here are two examples:

We have always enjoyed stories about angels in the family and have prayed for their protection on many occasions. When my eldest daughter, aged about four at the time, was experiencing fears associated with the dark and worrying about what was behind the door of a long wardrobe in her bedroom, we prayed together about it. One day shortly after, she remarked to me that she had dreamt there was a shining lady at the end of the wardrobe and that she was no longer afraid – only she wished that the lady could be there all the time. A year or so later when she had started school she was persistently asking me about how one could see an angel and, more particularly, if she could see an angel. I told her that God would send angels as messengers when He needed to. I told her to pray that night that He would send an angel to her one day too. The next morning, she awoke with an account of a vivid dream of angels, in the playground at school with children gathered round. We used this image to help her through all manner of playground and school problems that cropped up in the early years. The moments remain in our memories very clearly, in the same way that other times when the Lord has spoken to me very directly have too. A sort of gift of an imprint to remain for future reassurance and comfort.

Looking back on her short life to date, I realise that the Lord has blessed her so richly with signs and gifts and now, at almost thirteen, she has a profound faith that shines out to those closely associated with her. In her gentle way she has been instrumental in bringing several of her friends to a deeper understanding of Jesus, and this has come about in the simplest of ways – a question, friendship, generosity, concern and probably many others of the ways she sets me an example of being Christlike!

That story came from a former parishioner; here is one from a new friend. A lady, from a different faith, who has had a very tragic life, shared a story about her son.

When he was eight, he fell into a canal. He couldn't swim, and he cried out to God for help. He saw a bright light, and then felt himself pulled out of the water by a man, who promptly disappeared. He walked home dripping wet, and some while later told me the story of his remarkable rescue.

Christ's light and love seem to be touching this family, but the story of her son's rescue suggests that guardian angels do not confine themselves to Christians.

Angels and non-Christians

What are we to say about angelic appearances to non-Christians? It is far too simple to dismiss them all as demonic "angel of light" type of appearances. The crucial factor as in all spiritual matters, is to examine the fruit of the experience.

Some angelic experiences, as we shall see in the next two chapters, are almost certainly demonic – that shouldn't surprise any serious reader of Scripture. Jesus (Matthew 24:11 and elsewhere) warned his hearers of this possibility. Paul, similarly wrote, "The coming of the lawless one will be in accordance with the work of Satan displayed in all kinds of counterfeit miracles, signs and wonders, and in every sort of evil that deceives those who are perishing." (2 Thessalonians 2:9–10) Significantly, both Paul and Jesus taught that there will be an increase in false signs as the Second Coming approaches.

Some angelic appearances, and we've cited a number, appear to be God-given and to have borne fruit in changing and deepening people's commitment to Jesus.

But that leaves a huge grey area. Many people, not of a

committed Christian persuasion, or from other faiths have, *unsought*, experienced angelic protection, and have had near-death experiences, or other strong experiences. Such experiences, like many more normal ones, can be used for good or ill. For some, they will be a turning point, the beginning of a new awareness of God, and the start of a more serious spiritual quest. For others, they will lead to an increasingly bizarre search into the unknown, leading to a sense of great power, or false peace (see, for instance, Jeremiah 8:10–11). For some, they will be used for easy financial gain,[16] and the results will be spiritually very destructive.

Not surprisingly, angels are newsworthy. Many books have been published, and some TV programmes devoted to a fairly uncritical study of people's experiences. A typical example was the well-researched programme in the Everyman series, put out on BBC 1 early in the year 2000. Most of the programme was based on the careful research of a young PhD student called Emma Heathcote-James. Very wisely, she neither put forward her own views, nor much analysis of people's experiences. She was clearly moved by people's stories, and accepted that, in most cases, something strange had happened to them. She had received over 600 stories. They came from a wide range of faiths, and included some from agnostics and atheists. All believed that they, or their relatives had seen, and been helped by, angels. The majority of the stories did not come from practising Christians. However, a number of those who were featured in the programme had been encouraged by Christians (or at least by those with Christian sympathies).

One of the most powerful stories was shared by a blind lady who told of a tearful journey by train from Birmingham to London, shortly after her father's death. She spoke of having a vision of angels taking her father to heaven. The angels (as in Luke 15:10) were rejoicing. To her, what was particularly beautiful, as one blind from birth, was that she was able to *see* the angels, and to understand what joy looked like.

Many of the other experiences were similar to ones that I

have recorded – a man being rescued from probable death when surfing; a woman moved out of the way when a car was about to crash into the wall by her shop where she was standing; a man being comforted by an angel in hospital after a severe illness; and people seeing angels just before a close relative died.

One of the most interesting stories was provided by a woman whose father had told her about his sight of the Angel of Mons during the First World War (see p. 116, note 11). Her father had won the Military Cross, but like many others who survived the horrors of the trenches, declined to speak about his heroics. He did tell his daughter about the time that the Allies were facing a complete rout at Mons. They had already lost nearly half of an army of 60,000, mainly because of superior German firepower. He and his comrades were amazed to see the enemy suddenly turn round and flee. They looked up, and saw the white cavalry in the sky. His reaction, after the war, was to tell his family always to trust Jesus Christ who had delivered the British army from certain defeat. He also commented that many people saw the angels, some of whom were religious adherents, some not.

Not all the information came from the British side. Dr Moolenburgh[17] records receiving a letter from a German woman who had been an intelligence officer in the Luftwaffe in the Second World War. Her father had told her how he and other German soldiers had been temporarily blinded by angels at Yprès, in the First World War.

All of these examples clearly helped people, and strengthened their faith in God, and in many cases pointed them towards Jesus. Intermingled with these testimonies were a number of examples from people whom I would call professional angel watchers. These people, who appeared to have various psychic properties, saw angels everywhere – one woman claimed to be able to travel on a bus and sense that it was completely overcrowded, because most of the passengers had angels attached to them. Others appeared to be making a living from selling angel clothes and trinkets, while others were encouraging people on psychic journeys where they would be able to visualise their angels. "I can bring people in touch with their angels", was a fairly typical claim.

The programme included comments by a psychologist who made a number of carefully scripted negative comments. "Fashions come and go – today it's angels, a few years ago it was out of body experiences." "Such experiences are always accompanied with a sense of very bright light – a hyperactive force in the visual cortex." "Stress and fear induce these sorts of experiences." By contrast, the young researcher, who was obviously surprised by the results of her research, remarked that in her experience only about 20 per cent of the testimonies were in stress related situations. We, too, shall look at some "angel" experiences rather more critically in the next two chapters.

There is plenty of Scriptural evidence of angels appearing to non-believers, and even to opponents of God. Twice in Genesis the unfortunate Hagar, maltreated by Abraham and Sarah, is comforted by an angel (Genesis 16:7ff and Genesis 21:17ff); the false prophet Balaam, and his somewhat wiser donkey, have a celebrated encounter with an angel (Numbers 22:21ff); and the tyrannical Nebuchadnezzar was astonished to see a fourth person in the fiery furnace into which he had just thrown Shadrach, Meshach and Abednego. He cried out, "Look! I see four men walking around in the fire, unbound and unharmed, and the fourth looks like a son of the gods." (Daniel 3:25) When they came out of the fire, the King acknowledged that they had been rescued by an angel. In the New Testament, the shepherds who saw, and heard, the angels were not exactly numbered amongst the religious in Judea. The guards at the tomb of Jesus who were overwhelmed by angels on the first Easter Day (Matthew 28:2–4); the soldiers who arrested Jesus and fell to the ground, awestruck by his presence (John 18:6), were other examples of ordinary people who, when doing their duty, experienced a supernatural presence. As we noted in Chapter 5, both the Ethiopian eunuch and Cornelius were converted directly, or indirectly, as a result of angelic intervention.

Christians have no warrant for claiming a monopoly on angelic experiences, but they have every right to ask that these experiences are tested, and to note what fruit came from them. One of the oldest Christian books, the Didache (written perhaps as early as AD90) has some shrewd advice: If a charismatist, speaking in a trance, says "Give me money", do not listen to him.[18] Wise instructions! A similar test to those who charge money in exchange for providing angelic experiences might save a lot of spiritual deception.

We conclude this chapter with some experiences of angels at worship – which appears to be their principal function in the Courts of Heaven (Revelation 7:11f etc.).

Angels at worship

> Angel voices ever singing
> round Thy throne of light
> angel harps forever ringing,
> rest not day nor night;
> thousands only live to bless Thee,
> and confess Thee Lord of might.

Francis Pott's beautiful hymn captures an experience that many people claim to have had.[19] One of the most interesting experiences occurred in rural China in 1995. This testimony comes from a reliable Christian website.[20]

Angels discovered singing end-time song in rural Chinese worship service!

In May 1995, I received this most electrifying report from a friend who has been a missionary in China for several years. To protect him and his contacts in China, I must not reveal his name. But for you to better understand his credibility, let me explain that I have known him for many years. He is a graduate of a prestigious theological seminary and is a former pastor.

My friend is an intelligent and balanced servant of God. He is not given to sensationalism. The following is a summary of his recent report to me.

The whole province of Shandong, in eastern China (population 57 million), is in the midst of a sweeping revival. For fear of arrest, believers meet secretly in house churches, often by candlelight. At a 1995 meeting in Shandong, everyone was singing "in the Spirit" together (1 Corinthians 14:15), not in their own language, but "as the Spirit gave them utterance", all in harmony, but all singing different words. Someone audiotaped the meeting. Later, when they played back the cassette, they were shocked! What they heard was not what had happened there at all – but the sound of angels singing in Mandarin – a song they had never heard before, and with a musical accompaniment that had not been there! When my friend first heard the tape, before anyone told him what it was, he exclaimed, "Those are angels!" Actually, there was no other explanation. A Chinese Christian co-worker translated the tape. Below are the actual words sung by the angels! Note that the words express ideas with which these rural Chinese peasants were not familiar. (The original Chinese version is also available.)

"The end is near: rescue souls"
The famine is becoming more and more critical.
There are more and more earthquakes.
The situation is becoming more and more sinister.
People are fighting against each other, nation against nation.
Disasters are more and more severe.

The whole environment is deteriorating.
Disasters are more and more severe.

People's hearts are wicked, and they do not worship the true
     God.
Disasters are more and more severe.

Floods and droughts are more and more frequent.
There is more and more homosexuality and incurable
   diseases.
Disasters are more and more severe.

The climates are becoming more and more abnormal.
The earth is more and more restless.
The skies have been broken. The atmosphere is distorted.
Disasters are more and more severe.

Chorus:
The end is near. The revelation of love has been manifested.
Rise up, rise up, rescue souls.
The end is near.
Rise up, rise up, rescue souls.

The text was translated by two native Chinese Christians in Beijing who have personal knowledge of the church, and the pastor, where the incident happened.

This unusual event is, at the very least, a powerful *cri de coeur* from the angels to take seriously the great command (Matthew 28:19–20) and to fulfil one of the conditions necessary before Christ returns:

And this gospel of the kingdom will be preached in the whole world as a testimony to all nations, and then the end will come. (Matthew 24:14)

A second story comes from Surabayam in Indonesia in the summer of 2002. A large Christian convention was taking place, with many well-known speakers including Pastor Yonggi Cho. A photographer, called Jimmy, took a photograph of the worship. He was standing at the back of a stage, where the worship group was situated. He expected his picture to show an empty stage and many rows of worshippers. When it was developed, to his astonishment there were seven brilliant white angelic figures, with arms raised, worshipping on the empty stage. Although a number of people claim to have had angelic encounters during the conference, none were seen that night. The picture is very clear, although as we might expect, the faces of the angels are blurred. There are only two explanations for this photograph – either it is a skilful forgery (obviously possible with modern photographic techniques) or it is genuine.

About the same time, I received a strange photograph with a story from the 1980s. An aeroplane flying across the Tasman Sea, flew into an electric storm. The plane was severely buffeted, and the passengers were very frightened. The pilot spoke to the passengers on the intercom. He made an unusual request, "We are in danger – is there anyone who can pray?" One of the passengers prayed out loud, and the plane flew more normally, although the storm continued. A woman sitting by a window took a photograph of the storm. When she arrived home in South Africa, she had the film developed. The developer came to see her – to ask for an explanation of the photograph. The photograph (a copy of which I have in front of me as I write) appeared to show Jesus, standing in a long white tunic, amid the storm. His face is hidden, but somehow his body seems clearly recognisable. Anyway, the man who developed the photograph was convinced. He and his family became Christians!

In this chapter, we have looked at various examples where people have been convinced that there has been angelic intervention, now we turn to an even more critical life-stage, where people have experienced unexpected visions around the time of death, or after apparent death.

Notes

(1) Michael Green, *Matthew for Today*, Hodder & Stoughton, 1988, p. 172.

(2) Rosemary Guiley, *Encyclopaedia of Angels*, Facts on File, 1996, p.77.

(3) Martin Luther, *Table Talk* translated by William Hazlitt (1921). Reprinted by HarperCollins, 1995.

(4) Calvin, *Christian Religion* (XIV, 6).

(5) Calvin, *Christian Religion* (XIV, 7).

(6) See, for instance, *Pseudo Dionysius*, an influential book which speculated that the angelic kingdom could be found on nine levels. This influential book has very little biblical base, and was rejected by Protestants.

(7) Calvin, *Institutes* (XIV, 10).

(8) Jack Winslow, *Modern Miracles*, Hodder & Stoughton, 1968, Chapter 5.

(9) John Paton, *Missionary to the New Hebrides*, Hodder & Stoughton, 1893. See also John Woolmer, *Thinking Clearly about Prayer*, Monarch, 1997, p. 124, for an earlier example of protection of Mr Paton's mission. There are many similar stories of protection, from the mission field. See, for instance, Patricia St John, *Would You Believe It?*

(10) Wallace and Mary Brown, *Angels on the Walls*, Kingsway, 2000, Chapter 4.

(11) Joan Anderson, *Where Angels Walk*, Hodder & Stoughton, 1992, Chapter 1.

(12) The Revd Liz Smith, now Rector at St Peter & St Paul, Shepton Mallet.

(13) Baroness Cox is a well-known member of the House of Lords, who campaigns fearlessly on behalf of many third world, and other Christian causes. I am grateful to two of my children who heard the sermon for drawing my attention to it!

(14) Andrew Boyd, *Baroness Cox – A voice for the voiceless*, Lion, 1998.

(15) "Immortal, Invisible", Ancient & Modern Revised, 372 verse 4.

(16) Dr John Drane, *What is the New Age Still Saying to the Church?* Marshall Pickering, 1999, p. 84 and elsewhere.

(17) Dr H. C. Moolenburgh, *op. cit.* p. 143.

(18) *Early Christian Writings – The Apostolic Fathers*, Penguin, 1968, p. 233.
(19) See Hope Price, *Angels*, Macmillan, 1993, p. 7ff.
(20) Jim Bramlett. Photo at
http://www.geocities.com/bramlett2000/angelsindonesia

7

Angels at the Gates of Eternity

In this chapter, we look at the testimonies of people who have had encounters with God at the point of apparent death, and the way that this has influenced the rest of their lives.

Angels at the Gates of Eternity

"The last enemy to be destroyed is death" (1 Corinthians 15:26). This confident statement comes in the middle of St Paul's great chapter on the evidence for the Resurrection of Jesus, with its profound implications for all his readers. But what happens beyond death? Over the centuries, people of different faiths, and of none, have struggled with this question. Fascination with the afterlife has led many to seek solace in spiritualism; others have been comforted with beliefs in various forms of reincarnation; many have been driven to reject any belief in God (sometimes on the grounds that the afterlife sounds impossibly boring); a minority, recognising the seriousness of God's call, have been inspired to evangelise the lost, sometimes in inhospitable distant quarters of the earth and sometimes in their own backyard.

All sorts of different theories exist, and Christians of different traditions[1] have offered rival explanations of key passages of Scripture. Throughout time, Christians and others have had visions, experiences at the point of death, out of body experiences during serious operations, and a few have even returned to life after apparent death. Much of the interpretation is mere speculation, which lies far outside the scope of this book. Nevertheless, I would like to record a few of the most

well-documented experiences from both distant and recent
Christian history.

Biblical visions

The Bible contains many visions and deep spiritual experiences. Of these the ones that are most relevant to our subject
are Paul's great vision of Paradise, and the Book of Revelation.
Paul's vision (see earlier, p 81) he describes using the words
"whether in the body or apart from the body I do not know, but
God knows", and gives us a glimpse of the wonder and beauty
of Paradise. Paul didn't write much, saying that he "heard inexpressible things, things that man is not permitted to tell" (see 2
Corinthians 12:1–10).

The Book of Revelation which, as I said in the introduction,
is largely outside the scope of this short book, is an extended
vision given to the writer who "on the Lord's Day was in the
Spirit" (Revelation 1:10). Amongst many other things, this
mysterious, and often misinterpreted, book gives us a wonderful picture of the worship of angels, and saints, in heaven (see
Chapters 4 and 5, especially), a description of the intense battle
in the heavenly realms (Chapter 12 and elsewhere), and a grim
view of the second death and the lake of fire (Chapter 20). It
finishes with an electrifying vista of the radiance of the new
Jerusalem, with the crystal clear river of life, and the trees
whose leaves are "for the healing of the nations" (see Revelation 22:1–6).

Death and the early church

In the early church, martyrdom was the expected end for the
most fervent believers. Stephen's death, recorded at the end of
Acts Chapter 7, as we have seen, had a profound effect on Saul
of Tarsus (see p 76). It was also a model for much later Christian experience, expectation, and endurance.

But Stephen, full of the Holy Spirit, looked up to heaven and saw
the glory of God, and Jesus standing at the right hand of God.
"Look," he said, "I see heaven open and the Son of Man standing
at the right hand of God." (Acts 7:55–56)

Just over a century later, probably in AD155, Polycarp, Bishop
of Smyrna, was martyred. He was one of the most famous of
his generation of Christians, a venerable old man who said he
had "served the Lord for 86 years". He also taught Irenaeus of
Lyons, who was one of the most attractive theologians and
leaders of the next generation. The accounts of Polycarp's
martyrdom[2] are widely accepted as authentic. Irenaeus tells
us that the youthful Polycarp had been "instructed by the
Apostles, and had familiar intercourse with many who had
seen Christ". The account of his martyrdom is deeply moving.
The old man had foreseen it in an earlier vision. He faced his
ordeal before the Roman Governor, and a howling mob, with
immense courage. He prayed to the "God of angels and
powers", and refused to be nailed to the stake, saying, "Let me
be; He who gives me strength to endure the flames will give
strength not to flinch at the stake, without you making sure of it
with nails." When he finished a lengthy prayer with a
triumphant, "Amen", the men set light to the fire. The eye-
witness continues:

And then we who were privileged to witness it saw a wondrous
sight; and we have been spared to tell it to the rest of you. The fire
took on the shape of a hollow chamber, like a ship's sail when the
wind fills it, and formed a wall round about the martyr, and there
was he in the centre of it, not like a human being in flames, but like
a loaf baking in the oven, or like a gold or silver ingot being
refined in the furnace. And we became aware of a delicious
fragrance like the odour of incense.

Polycarp was eventually stabbed to death, and his body was
retained by the authorities "in case they should forsake the

Crucified and take to worshipping this fellow instead".

A generation later, the martyrdom of Perpetua and others, in AD203, was written up in great detail by Tertullian, who was living at the time. Perpetua was granted wonderful visions of the afterlife shortly before her own martyrdom.[3]

St Martin's testimony

We have much information about St Martin of Tours, who died in 397, from a biography from his friend Sulpicius Severus.[4] He records a number of incidents involving healing, deliverance, power encounters, and angelic visitations. One of the most dramatic occurred soon after Martin arrived, c. AD360, and set up his headquarters in a large cavern near Poitiers in France. A group of people, desirous of baptism and wanting instruction in discipleship, joined him.[5]

One of a group, when Martin was away, was taken ill with a violent fever. When Martin returned, the catechumen (as such enquirers were called) had died, without having been baptised. His body had been laid out for burial by his fellow catechumens, with many tears and much sorrow. Martin, moved by the Holy Spirit, ordered all the mourners to leave the cell where the body had been laid out. He bolted the door, and stretched himself out at full length over his dead brother. After praying for some time, and feeling confident in the presence of the Holy Spirit, he waited quietly for two hours beside the body of his friend. Then he saw the body begin to move, and the eyes began to open. Soon afterwards, the brother, who had been dead, started to praise the Lord. His friends, who had been waiting outside his cell, rushed in, and were amazed to find that the man they had left for dead, was now alive and praising God. He was immediately baptised, and lived for many more years. He became a powerful witness to the grace of God, and the faithful prayer of Martin. Part of his testimony, which is particularly relevant to this chapter, concerned his experience after death. He would tell how he was brought before the tribunal of the

Judge, and was given a severe sentence – assigned to gloomy regions and vulgar crowds. However, two angels testified that he was a man for whom Martin was praying most earnestly. As a result, he was released, and restored to life. Martin's reputation was greatly enhanced by this miracle, which was regarded as truly apostolic.

This account which is very much in the literary genre of the time has some features which don't seem to square with scripture. What is certain is that the restored catechumen was baptised, became a faithful disciple of Jesus, and follower of Martin. He was well able to "give the reason for the hope that he had" (see 1 Peter 3:15). He was living testimony to the grace of God, and an effective support to the ministry of one of Christendom's most lovely saints.

St Augustine's testimony

Another interesting account is found in St Augustine's *De Cura Pro Mortius*.[6] He writes at some length, in an answer to a pastoral question, as to whether there is any benefit "in someone being buried at the memorial of a Saint". There was a sense, in the early church, that being buried in, or near, the sepulchre of a martyr would help the deceased's pilgrimage in the next world. Augustine is not very sympathetic to this idea, but discusses the matters of reverent burial, the afterlife, and contact (or lack of it) between the two worlds.

In this context, he produces an extraordinary testimony of an event which, unwittingly, he became involved in. He tells the story of a man called Curma of the Curia (a minor official), who lay for some days "all but dead . . . not a limb did he stir, nothing did he take in the way of sustenance, neither in the eyes, nor in any other bodily sense was he sensible of any annoyance that impinged upon them. Yet he was seeing many things like as in a dream. . . ." In particular, he had seen a vision of the place of the dead. He was then told that it was one Curma the Smith who was ordered to the place of the dead. He then described how he saw himself being baptised in Hippo by Augustine. He was then dismissed from Paradise to return to his family with the words "Go, be baptised, if thou wilt be in this place of the blessed". He then woke up, he said "Let someone go to the house of Curma the Smith, and see what is doing there." Curma the Smith was discovered to have died at the precise moment that the other Curma woke up, revived from the point of apparent death. Curma of the Curia was surprised to discover that in reality he had *not yet* been baptised. The following Easter he was baptised in Hippo by Augustine, in circumstances which were exactly the same as in his earlier vision. Augustine knew nothing of this until some two years later, he heard about the story and interviewed Curma.

Augustine's main point in telling this story is that he, as a living person, had experienced nothing of Curma's vision and that, likewise, dead people may appear in visions whilst being unaware of what is happening. He is very cautious about contact between the two worlds, citing angels as the beings who "could be present in places both of the living and the dead". He discusses some of the well-known scriptural difficulties, such as the strange story of Saul visiting the witch of Endor (1 Samuel 28:7–25). Augustine, like others, is puzzled by the whole incident. He is uncertain whether the apparition is that of Samuel, or some spirit, which is set up for an evil task and resembled him. He acknowledges the presence of Moses and Elijah at the Mount of Transfiguration, and cites the appearance of the "Confessor Felix" who strengthened the believer when under attack by barbarians at Nola.

However, Augustine is clear that such events are highly unusual – just as the turning of water into wine, and the raising of Lazarus were untypical. Consequently, he taught that we were not to expect the dead to be regularly raised up by the living.

In this respect, he regards King Josiah as particularly blessed, because God said to him,

Tell the king of Judah who sent you to enquire of the Lord, "This is what the Lord, the God of Israel, says concerning the words you heard: Because your heart was responsive and you humbled yourself before the Lord when you heard what I have spoken against this place and its people, that they would become accursed and laid waste, and because you tore your robes and wept in my presence, I have heard you, declares the Lord. Therefore I will gather you to your fathers, and you will be buried in peace. Your eyes will not see all the disaster I am going to bring on this place." (2 Kings 22:18–20)

In other words, his blessed state, in death, would not be marred by seeing the future disasters that would overtake his kingdom.

Augustine writes movingly about his mother, Monica (see p 120ff), and concludes that if the souls of the dead took part in the affairs of the living, she would have surely visited him!

I have quoted Augustine at length, partly because of the strange story of Curma, of which he had first hand experience. (Gregory the Great also quotes this story.[7]) Augustine is a sober witness of these matters, and displays a reverent caution in these matters. In a later chapter (see p 221), we shall see how a modern book quotes from these pages of Augustine's writings, distorts them, and uses them to advance the case for spiritualism – something utterly abhorrent to Augustine.

The vision of Drycthelm

Our next testimony, which was widely read and influential in the Middle Ages, was obtained by the Venerable Bede (673–735),[8] near the end of the 7th century. Drycthelm, a devout man, who was the head of a large household in Northumbria, fell ill. He grew steadily worse, and surrounded by his family and household, died in the early hours of the night. At daybreak, to the great alarm of those who were weeping around his body, he suddenly sat up. Everyone except his wife ran away. Drycthelm said to her, "Do not be frightened; for I have truly risen from the grasp of death, and I am allowed to live among men again, but henceforward I must not live as I used to, and must adopt a very different way of life."

Bede, who received this account from a monk who lived in the vicinity of the monastic cell to which Drycthelm withdrew, wrote it up in great detail. His vision presents us with a considerable dilemma. I have summarised it as follows:

He was led away by a handsome man in a shining robe, and they walked in silence, and eventually came to a valley, which was both very broad and very deep. On the left there were dreadful flames, and on the right, raging hail and bitter snow. On both sides were men's souls, who seemed to be hurled from one side to the other. The guide said, "Do not think that this is Hell." Eventually, he was taken to an even worse place, which he described in some detail. His guide seemed to disappear. In a terrible chasm, he felt himself attacked by evil spirits who tried to drag him away from an approaching bright light. The light was brought by his earlier guide, who led him out of the darkness, up an apparently impassable wall into a bright meadow full of flowers and companies of people in white robes. His guide told him, "No, this is not the Kingdom of Heaven as you imagine it." Eventually, he saw an even more lovely light, and glimpsed the Kingdom of Heaven itself. His guide explained the four places – the first was for those who had only been penitent at the last moment; the second was the very mouth of Hell from which there was no escape; the third was for people who have done good, but did not yet merit entry into the Kingdom of Heaven, and the fourth was the Heaven itself from where he had heard the sound of glorious singing.

Each of these early visions, of St Martin's catechumen, St Augustine's baptismal candidate, and Drycthelm who became a monk, present us with serious theological problems. The stories are fascinating, the evidence for their truthfulness is strong, but they don't sit comfortably with Scripture. Why was the catechumen, who was apparently in the process of turning to Jesus "assigned to the gloomy regions", only to be rescued by the prayer of the Saint? The angelic change of mind is reminiscent

of Isaiah's two different messages to the ailing King Hezekiah
(see 2 Kings 20:1–11). The main difference seems to be that
while Hezekiah went downhill spiritually, Martin's catechumen
flowered. Curma's story presents the theological problem of the
angels summoning the wrong man. Neither Augustine, nor
Pope Gregory the Great who also told the story, seemed to find
this a problem! Drycthelm's vision was very influential in the
formulation of the doctrine of Purgatory, something for which
there appears to be no scriptural justification, and which
contributed to many of the worst clerical abuses in the Middle
Ages.

There is some evidence that early writers, like Bede and
Sulpicius Severus, wrote to conform to accepted literary and
theological forms. It would be very foolish to draw any doctrinal conclusions from these accounts, but they are certainly
based on true stories that occurred during, or only a few years
before each of the writer's lifetimes. Augustine's account has a
considerable stamp of literal truth, as he clearly met and talked
with Curma. We should receive these stories as support for the
existence of the future life, and angelic involvement in judgment, both of which are Scriptural – see, for instance, the Parable of the Wheat and the Tares (Matthew 13:41). On the other
hand, we would be unwise to press the details too far.

Experience of God at the point of death

James Durham[9] died in 1658. He was a godly Puritan preacher,
whose ministry was blessed and useful. He would, of course,
have expounded, and have believed the doctrine of Election
(Ephesians 1:4, etc.). The Puritans had a great sense of God's
choice, and also believed that once converted, a true believer
couldn't fall away. Yet despite this, on his deathbed, James was
doubtful. He confided to a colleague, "Brother, for all that I
have preached and written, there is but one Scripture I can
remember, or dare grip unto; tell me if I dare lay the weight of
my salvation upon it. It is 'him that cometh to me, I will in

nowise cast out.'" (John 6:37 – AV). "You may depend upon it," said the other, "though you had a thousand salvations to hazard." Shortly afterwards, Durham cried out, "He is come; He is come. All was well."

This experience is quite typical of the Puritan saints who, despite believing in the doctrine of the "Final Perseverance of the Saints", often experienced both uncertainty and a great comfort in the hour of their deaths.

I remember a bishop preaching in the church where I was curate. He had been through a testing time, particularly because of the early death of his much-loved wife. He told a story, which I think gave him great comfort, of his visit to an old lady. As he walked into her bedroom, and came beside her bed, she sat up, looked straight ahead, and cried out "My God", and instantly lay back, and died. He believed that she had received a vision at the point of death.

Dorothy Kerin's experience

In February 1911, Dorothy Kerin,[10] aged 22, was blind and apparently dying. Her well-documented illness had been diagnosed as an advanced state of tuberculosis and diabetes. She was in great pain, and very emaciated through lack of food.

Dorothy Kerin, and all within the walls of 204 Milkwood Road, Herne Hill, London, will never forget Sunday eve, 18th February. Friends and neighbours were then gathered together to see the last of Dorothy. The doctor had said she could not live until the morning. He had kept her alive for six weeks by means of brandy and opium and starch. During the last fortnight she had lain like a log of wood and never moved her position in the bed, and was now *blind* and *deaf*, and for the most part unconscious. She had been attended by eight-and-twenty doctors, and had been sent home in an ambulance from a Home for Incurables, with only a week to live. She had been five years confined to her bed, and had been turned out of five hospitals – incurable.

Such was her condition, and now the end had come. About half-past nine on Sunday evening, as mother and friends stood watching, she seemed to breathe her last. Anyhow, for eight minutes her lungs ceased to breathe, and her heart ceased to beat, and they deemed her dead. But just at this juncture, Dorothy tells us *someone* called her by name, three times distinctly, and she replied, "Yes, I am listening, who is it?" and he said, "Listen!" and she felt two warm hands take hold of hers. A beautiful Light then flashed over the screen and came right over the bed. In the midst of the Light stood the Angel of the Lord, who, still holding her hands in his and lifting up to her eyes, and touching her ears, said "Dorothy, your sufferings are over, get up and walk."

She then opened her eyes and sat up, greatly wondering to see so many friends around her bed, to whom she said, "I am well now! I want my dressing-gown. I want to walk." Of course, her request was unheeded, and she began to get up without it, when her mother came and held her down, saying, "No, Dorothy, you will fall, you must not get up!" While thus held, the angel again the second time said, "Get up and walk!" Dorothy then appealed to her mother asking her if she did not hear, on which she then relaxed her hold on her, and someone suggested that the dressing-gown should be given her just to gratify her, and convince her that she could not walk.

Just then a part of the beautiful Light, seen only by Dorothy, came and stood at the right-hand side of her bed. Then, with eyes and ears opened, and strength imparted to every limb, she threw off the bedclothes from her, and stepped on to the floor, placing her hand upon the Light that was to lead her.

The Light then moved forward, and she followed, saying to her friends, "I am following the Light." It led her straight out of the room, through a passage into a room where she expected to find her stepfather who, however, was not there. The Light then led her into another room, where she found him, and in the joy of her restoration she threw her arms around his neck and kissed him.

The Light then led her back again to her own room, where she found the whole company shaking and trembling with fear! Her stepfather, who was following her, then fell upon the floor, and began to cry – in the attitude of prayer.

The account concludes with Dorothy's request for a full meal, and the general amazement and awe of all her friends. She had a perfect night's sleep, and the doctor, who had been expecting a request for a death certificate, was completely amazed. He kept saying, "What does it all mean?" For Dorothy, the meaning became quite clear. After many years of preparation and spiritual battles, she was able to open the famous house of healing at Burrswood, in Kent. When God grants such experiences, he expects people to put them to good effect!

A glimpse of eternity

Ian McCormack's story is, by any standard, remarkable.[11] Ian's testimony begins with his disillusionment at his Confirmation Service in New Zealand in the 1970s. At the age of 14, he expected to hear God speak to him. He embarrassed his father, his parish priest, and his mother, with his questions. He walked away, announcing that he would never come back to church. As he stamped off to the family car, his mother, uncharacteristically, yelled at him, "Son, if I can teach you nothing else – remember one thing – however far you find yourself from God, if you cry to God from your heart, he will hear you and forgive you."

For ten years, Ian lived a carefree life. He sought pleasure in sport, travelling, surfing, and especially in scuba diving. Visiting the island of Mauritius in 1982, he enjoyed some magnificent scuba diving, catching huge lobsters, avoiding sharks . . . All went well until one night when his torch picked up an interesting looking box-shaped jellyfish. He squeezed it with his leather gloves. Unlike the others in his party, he wasn't fully protected, and in return for his inquisitiveness, he received four stings from the deadliest jellyfish known to man – known as "the invisible one" to the locals. One sting can kill a man in ten minutes. By the time a terrified teenager got him to the shore, he was already paralysed on one side. The boy panicked and left him. He crawled into the middle of a road at 11 p.m. without much prospect of a rescue. The poison made him sleepy.

He heard a voice saying, "Son, if you close your eyes you shall never awake again." Moments later he crawled around a bend and found three taxi drivers. He heard the voice say, "Son, are you willing to beg for your life?" Ian begged the taxi drivers to rescue him and to trust him to pay them later. Two laughed and walked away, the third agreed (with the promise of $50) to drive him to hospital. The third driver took him to a tourist hotel, decided that he would never pay his fare, and physically pushed him out of the taxi. At the hotel he met a friend, Daniel, who couldn't believe that he'd been stung by "the invisible" and wasn't yet dead. Three Chinese proprietors of the hotel wouldn't take him to hospital. He could feel the coldness of death creeping up his body, he knew enough veterinary science to know exactly what was happening to him.

Eventually, an ambulance arrived, because his Creole friend Daniel had phoned the hospital. On the way to the hospital his whole life flashed before him. He knew that he was going to die. Then he saw his mother, in a clear vision, praying for him in the ambulance . . . she began to share the same words with him that she had spoken after his confirmation. He didn't know which God to pray to, but decided that as his mother would pray to Jesus he'd better try that. He tried to remember the Lord's Prayer. In a jumbled fashion, it came back to him. "Forgive us our sins." Ian tried to list his sins, but settled for admitting his hypocrisy, particularly his desperation in turning to God at such a time. The next phrase that came to him was, "Forgive those who have sinned against you." He didn't feel there were many people that he needed to forgive. Then he saw the face of the Indian taxi driver who had pushed him out of the car. "Will you forgive him?" "I wasn't planning to!" Then he saw the Chinese who had refused to take him to hospital. "Will you forgive him?" Suddenly he realised that, to use a New Zealand expression, this was where "the rubber meets the road". Either he forgave these people, or he couldn't be forgiven. He prayed, "If you can forgive me, I will forgive them." The third phrase of the Lord's Prayer that he remembered was "Thy will be done, on earth as it is in heaven." He submitted to God's will, admitted that he'd been rebellious and wrong for 26 years, and promised to follow God for the rest of his life. He then remembered the whole prayer, and received a great sense of peace. After arriving at the hospital, every emergency treatment was tried – without success. After about ten minutes, a doctor said kindly, but clearly, "Son, I'm afraid we've done all we can for you."

His eyes closed, he gave a great sigh of relief, and he found himself wide awake in a pitch black void. He had a huge sense of terror, he realised that he was "out of his body", yet conscious. He said, "Where am I?" Two voices spoke in the darkness. The first said, "Shut up," and the second, "You deserve to be here, shut up." Then one of the voices said, "You're in Hell – shut up!" and Ian heard the voice that he had heard when lying on the road saying, "If you hadn't prayed that death bed prayer in the ambulance that's where you would have stayed." Then he saw a brilliant light, and he was lifted up into the presence of an incredibly brilliant, but distant light. Waves came from the brightest source and filled his body with warmth, comfort, peace, and joy. He was drawn closer to the source of the light which was as radiant as a mountain of diamonds. He wasn't sure whether the source was personal or impersonal. Then the voice spoke again, "Ian, if you return, you must see in a new light."

He remembered words on a Christmas card that he had received, "God is Light, and in him there is no darkness at all". (He didn't know that this was a biblical text – 1 John 1:5.)

Ian felt completely unworthy, but wave after wave of light touched him, filling him with love and more love. Weeping, he cried out, "I want to see you." He felt a great healing radiance, and saw a man's feet, but where the face should have been there was a brilliant, dazzling light. (Afterwards Ian read Revelation 1:13–18 and recognised what he had seen as corresponding to the vision of St John.) He was able to see behind the form of Jesus, and was shown a vision of Paradise, with green pastures, mountains, blue sky, trees, and a crystal clear stream (again, afterwards, Ian read Revelation Chapter 22 and 2 Peter 3:10–18 and recognised much of what he had seen). He remembered that he had travelled the world looking for such a place, and asked, "Why wasn't I born here?" The voice replied, "You've got to be born again, Ian now that you've seen, do you want to step in or return?"

He wanted to say goodbye to the sick, tired world. No one would miss him. He had no debts. Then he remembered his mother. If he entered Paradise, she would assume that her prayers had been unanswered, and that he had entered a lost eternity. He saw that Jesus was the door to Paradise, leading on to green pastures (again, afterwards, he read John 10:7–9). He knew that he must speak to others to give them the same chance that he had been given, and he chose to go back.

The voice said, "Tilt your head", and he woke up to see a terrified Indian doctor who was prodding his feet. He tilted his head the other way and saw the look of blank horror on the faces of the nurses and orderlies in the doorway of the room where he had been laid out – apparently dead for fifteen minutes.

For a moment he thought he had returned as a quadriplegic. He prayed, "Lord, if you can't heal me . . ." Ian then felt an extraordinary warmth which lasted four hours, then he knew that he was completely healed. He walked out of the hospital the next day. None of the locals could face him. They thought he was a spirit who had returned, and they were terrified of him (a reaction not unlike those who prayed for Peter's release from prison!).

Ian, in his account, says quite humbly that he believes he "died", but that others may prefer to interpret his experience in line with Paul's vision recorded in 2 Corinthians 12:2–4, and discussed earlier (see p 81).

Perhaps the most amazing part of his testimony was the experience of his mother, who, exactly when this drama was happening, woke up hearing a voice, "Your son is nearly dead – pray for him." Ian McCormack is not the first person, nor the last, to owe his salvation, humanly, to a godly, praying mother! St Augustine (see p 120f) was another!

A Nigerian pastor

On Easter Day 2002, I watched a video clip of an account of a Nigerian pastor[12] who had suffered, in the previous November, an apparently fatal car accident. His wife had taken him to a hospital in Ouitsa, where he was in a critical condition. He had woken up, and commended his wife to remove him to the hospital near his home in Owerri. Against all medical advice, she obeyed. During the journey, he told her how to carry on his ministry, and care for their children, and then appeared to die. On his arrival at Owerri, he was given a thorough examination by a doctor, pronounced dead, and placed in the mortuary. Both the doctor and the mortuary attendant testified in the video that he was dead. The doctor said, "No breathing, no heartbeat, no pulse . . ."

On the third day after his arrival in Owerri, the German evangelist, Reinhard Bonnke was opening a new church. A huge congregation had gathered. The pastor's wife believed that God had promised to raise her husband. In particular, she had received the text "women received back their dead, raised to life again" (Hebrews 11:35a). She, and the pastor's father, took his corpse out of the mortuary and went to the new church. She believed that the anointing at Bonnke's meeting would be such that such a miracle would be possible. Her amazing faith and courage were rewarded!

When they arrived, the evangelist was preaching. The body was laid out in a side room. After the sermon, Bonnke started to pray for the sick. About that time, those watching the pastor's body saw that it had started to breathe. They told the church congregation, adding that his body was still stiff and frozen. At this stage, a crowd gathered to pray and praise God. Someone had brought a video camera to the meeting (not unusual in Africa) and started to film what was happening.

Gradually, life returned. For a while, one of the watchers massaged the pastor's neck. Suddenly he stood up. He immediately demanded to know, "Where is my file?"

Gradually he explained that he had a vision of the next world. As he was dying, during the car journey to Owerri, he had been aware of two angels. They allowed him to give his wife instructions about his house, his children, and his congregation, but *not* to reveal their presence. He was given a file in which to record his experiences. He was then taken on a journey to a celestial city, which was far too beautiful to describe (cf 2 Corinthians 12:2–4). He had then been given a glimpse of Hell. Here, a pastor who had been a habitual thief hailed him and told him to report that the "prayer of the rich man had been granted". He noted this in his file, but was puzzled as to what it meant. In passing, we might remember that St John was puzzled by part of his vision and reduced to tears (see Revelation 5:4).

When he arose from his experience of death, he immediately asked for his file. Later he realised that the strange reference to the rich man referred to Luke 16:19–31, where the rich man asks Abraham to send Lazarus to warn his brothers of their need to repent. He believed that he had been sent back to give this generation a final warning.

This extraordinary story was told with remarkable restraint, and considerable corroboration from the doctor, the mortuary attendant, and those who saw the pastor come back to life.

A Tanzanian newspaper covering Bonnke's crusade in Arusha in July 2002, remarked with biting cynicism, "How come that there was a video camera available?" There is however no way that the film could have been faked, the actual video evidence came near the end of the story, and anyone who travels in Africa knows that in the more wealthy parts of Africa, electronic equipment is quite common.

In the television programme, Bonnke is very careful to disclaim any involvement in the miracle. He sees the event as a very powerful sign to an unbelieving world performed by a *sovereign act* of God in response to the faithful prayer and action of the pastor's wife.

Conclusions

The experiences cited in this chapter are by any yardstick unusual. Many different conclusions might be drawn. One serious researcher, Dr Maurice Rawlings, a cardiologist,[13] was so shaken by some of his patients' accounts of "out of body", and "near death" experiences, that he conducted serious research, both into people's experiences and into the teaching of the major religions about the afterlife. This was his conclusion:

> After a laborious study of comparative theology in the sacred books of many religions, including the Torah and Talmud of Judaism; the Koran; the Vedas, Upanishads, Brahmanas of Hinduism; the Avesta of Zoroastrianism; the sayings of Confucius; the Agamas of Jainism; the Tripitake of Buddhism; the Kojiki of Shintoism; the Tao-te-ching of Taoism; and the Analects, I have discovered that the one book that is the most descriptive of the after-death experiences of resuscitated patients is the Christian Bible.

He was also increasingly concerned by the "bright light" phenomena which suggests that "all would be well" in the afterlife – irrespective of previous lifestyle. One of his most seminal experiences[14] was when he talked to a young man, aged 21, who was recovering from three serious gunshot wounds.

His patient told him that he had an out-of-body experience, and had felt surrounded by a heavenly light which was "understanding". He felt no rejection. There was no examination of his past life. "Peace and Love" were communicated. The young man was surprised, and told the doctor of his past life. It was not a pleasant tale – involving a double murder during a robbery three years earlier, and a dance in a bar with a "woman" who turned out to be a cross-dressing homosexual man. He attacked his dance partner, and for his pains, he got shot three times in the chest.

Not surprisingly, he felt his experience of the accepting light was distinctly odd. He concluded by asking a question, "Doc, does God ever make mistakes?"

Dr Rawlings concluded that this was a clear example of Satan masquerading as an "angel of light". Ian McCormack (see above) agrees. One questioner asked him how he accounted for near-death experiences where people experienced neither Hell nor Jesus. He replied robustly that these experiences were deceptions because the true God requires repentance. Certainly, experiences of the "all will be well" type, and which lead to no discernible change of lifestyle or belief, would seem to be misleading.

Dr Alison Morgan, in her powerful book, *What Happens When We Die?* looked at various hypotheses about these experiences, She writes:[15]

Are there any natural explanations of the near-death experience?

Most researchers into the near-death experience have not limited themselves to the mere collecting of data. They have sought in a great variety of ways to find a hypothesis which would explain those data, and all kinds of theories have been put forward to explain the NDE in purely naturalistic terms. Such theories fall into three groups.

1. The NDE is caused by medical or physiological factors such as oxygen deprivation, the effect of pain-killing or other drugs, the malfunctioning of the central nervous system, fever and biochemical reactions in the brain.
2. The NDE is caused by psychological factors such as unconscious wishful thinking, hallucination, and self-protective devices.
3. The NDE is caused by religious or cultural factors; people experience what they expect to experience.

The problem with these hypotheses is that none of them success-fully accounts for all the documented instances of the near-death experience; examples can be found to disprove each one. The find-ings of parapsychologists Karlis Osis and Erlendur Haraldsson are particularly important in this regard. Osis and Haraldsson sent questionnaires on the experiences of the dying to over 2,000 doctors and nurses in both America and India, and conducted a detailed computer analysis of the returns. They found that there was no correlation whatsoever between medical, psychological or religious factors and the occurrence or nature of a near-death expe-rience. So, for example, patients treated with sedatives or drugs, and those suffering from illnesses normally associated with the presence of hallucinations were in fact less likely, not more likely, to have an NDE than other patients. And those who hallucinated while suffering from a particular medical condition reported seeing living persons, whereas near-death visions were invariably of deceased persons. Oxygen deprivation, stress, expectations of death or recovery, the presence of particular psychological states, adherence to Christianity or Hinduism, and other possible factors appear to have had no influence on either the occurrence or the non-occurrence of the NDE. The researchers were forced to conclude that there is no naturalistic explanation currently avail-able to us which can account satisfactorily for the near-death expe-rience.

We cannot draw many conclusions from the small number of stories that I have cited. However, it is worth noting that in almost every case, the survivors were *surprised* by their theo-logical discoveries, and led fruitful Christian lives as a result. St Martin's catechumen was duly baptised, and became an effective disciple well able to testify to the reality of the future world. Curma, the minor town official, who presumably knew little about Christianity before his miraculous recovery, duly found his way to Hippo, and was baptised by Augustine. We know nothing of his subsequent discipleship, but the fact that some two years later Augustine found him and heard his unusual story suggests at the very least he was living as a faith-ful disciple. Drycthelm, who was already a Christian, lived an exceptionally devout life. His vision, which curiously included four states of the afterlife – a valley of fire and snow, which Bede understood as purgative, Hell, an Earthly Paradise, and finally Heaven itself – was very influential on medieval theology (not always helpfully, it must be admitted). He was very reluctant to talk about it, but inevitably, as people came to hear of it, there was great interest. His story influenced a future king, a future bishop, and a monk who told the story directly to Bede.

Dorothy Kerin had been unwell for many years, probably since the death of her father when she was only twelve. Brought up in a Christian home, her vision and healing led to a lifetime of service. By contrast, Ian McCormack had no expectation of a future life, and was very startled by his encounters – experiencing both a little of the terrors of eternal darkness, and a great deal of the light of Christ and the beauty of Paradise. He has used his new life to bear witness to the saving power of Jesus, and to warn people of the dangers of living as he had done previously. The Nigerian pastor's vision of the future life was very much in accordance with what he already believed, though obviously he and all those who witnessed it were given a much greater urgency to proclaim the full message of the Gospel.

In every case, the fruits of these experiences were beneficial, both to the individuals and to those around them. The fact that some of their spiritual visions do not entirely square with the Scripture, as we may interpret it, is a real difficulty. Some will want to discard their testimonies, others to draw dangerous doctrinal conclusions from them. It would be wrong to build doctrines either of the fires of Hell, or of some sort of medieval purgatory from these accounts. We cannot build a theology from anecdotes, however powerful. But each story does bear witness to the power of the Risen Lord, the place of angels in the world to come, and the dangers of impenitence, and for these reasons I am happy to include them, even if they do not fit into a neat, tidy theological package.

We leave this chapter with two other short stories. The Dean of Chester Cathedral, Dr Gordon McPhate, interviewed in the *Church Times* in October 2002 tells how, at the age of 18, he was already intent on a medical career. He then talked about the event that took him beyond the limits of scientific understanding.

> I was in a car crash, and had an out-of-body experience during a cardiac arrest. It was only when I read the prologue from St John's Gospel in the Gideon Bible at my hospital bedside that I properly understood what had happened to me. Science alone could not make sense of my being outside my body, watching my self being resuscitated by paramedics. While outside my body, I had an encounter with a person. It was so loving that I did not want to leave. But somehow, it was communicated that I was to come back to fulfil a purpose. I still don't know fully what that purpose is. It unfolds as I go along.

So far, it has meant a life devoted to academic medicine, and ordination – quite an unusual combination! Dr McPhate's experience was certainly unexpected, and theologically transforming.

My second story was told to me by a distinguished Catholic lady, with whom I have often stayed in the South of France. It concerned a man whose wife had left him to set up home with his best friend. In despair, he attempted to hang himself. He was surprised to find himself on his bed, some distance from the rope, with his neck marked by the rope. He heard a voice saying, "Don't do that again." Not surprisingly, he became a believer, and is an active member of a prayer group in the region.

What is God saying to us? Many see these events as signs of the imminent return of Christ. I think that we should be *very cautious* about this. The times are unknown to the angels, and will be *unexpected* even to believers (see Matthew 24:42ff). These experiences can be a great boost to our fragile faith, but should also act as a solemn warning against tampering in forbidden fields. Satan has a field day when we wander, uncritically, into these pathways. To this matter we now turn.

Notes

(1) Dr Alison Morgan, *What Happens When We Die?* Kingsway, 1995, p. 54ff and elsewhere.

(2) Penguin Classics, *Early Christian Writings*, 1968, p. 153ff.

(3) Dr Alison Morgan, *Dante and the Medieval Other World*, CUP, 1990, p. 206ff.

(4) Sulpicius Severus (363–c.425), a lawyer who became a hermit and follower of St Martin, wrote a contemporary biography of St Martin.

(5) Christopher Donaldson, *Martin of Tours*, Routledge and Kegan Paul, 1980 p. 60ff, mainly a translation from Sulpicius.

(6) *Nicene & Post Nicene Fathers* – Augustine 'On Care of the Dead', 1st Series, Volume 3, Hendrickson, 1995, p. 535ff.

(7) Dr Alison Morgan, *op. cit.* p. 229. Gregory the Great clearly knew the story, although he renames the characters, calling Curma, Stephen.

(8) Michael Mitton, *Restoring the Woven Cord*, Darton, Longman and Todd, 1995, p. 73.

(9) The *Free Presbyterian Magazine*, November 2001, p. 323. In *Healing & Deliverance*, March, 1999 (p. 178f), I quoted the remarkable story of the apparent raising from the dead of Lord Ochiltree (c.1600) through the prayers of an eminent Puritan, John Welch. Mr Welch prayed for over two days! Lord Ochiltree woke up, completely well, except for the places where physicians had pinched his body. He had apparently no visions of the future life to share.

(10) Dorothy Arnold, *Dorothy Kerin, Called by Christ to Heal*, Hodder & Stoughton, 1965, p. 9.

(11) Ian McCormack, *A Glimpse of Eternity*, Kingdom Power

Trust Video, from St Andrew's Church, Chorleywood.

(12) Broadcast on Cable TV, 21st March 2002, interview with Reinhard Bonnke.

(13) Dr Alison Morgan, *op. cit.* p. 80.

(14) Maurice Rawlings, M. D. *To Hell and Back*, Nelson, Nashville, 1993.

(15) Dr Alison Morgan, *op. cit.* p. 80–81 from "Deathbed Observations by Physicians & Nurses", *Journal of American Society for Psychical Research* 71, July 1977, p. 237ff.

8

Angels in Opposition

In this chapter, we see that Jesus had clear convictions about the existence and origin of evil. We look at various stratagems of Satan, and argue that it is pastorally and theologically absurd to deny the existence of spiritual opposition. We look at the twin dangers of denying the existence of the Devil, and of exaggerating his influence. Our central thesis is that God is in control and that the Devil's power, although real, is limited.

Angels in Opposition

Scripture is strangely silent about the origin of Satan. After the serpent slithers off the stage, Satan seldom appears in the Old Testament. By contrast, Jesus' ministry initiates a clear conflict between light and darkness, the Kingdom of God, and the kingdom of Satan. Likewise, the epistles have a number of classic passages about spiritual warfare, and the final book of the Bible, the Revelation of St John, paints a vivid picture of heavenly battles – past, present, and future.

Jesus and Satan

The conflict which begins in the wilderness (see p 62f), explodes in Jesus' first recorded day of ministry.

> They went to Capernaum, and when the Sabbath came, Jesus went into the synagogue and began to teach. The people were amazed at his teaching, because he taught them as one who had authority, not as the teachers of the law. Just then a man in their synagogue who was possessed by an evil spirit cried out, "What do you want with us, Jesus of Nazareth? Have you come to destroy us? I know who you are – the Holy One of God!"
> "Be quiet!" said Jesus sternly. "Come out of him!" The evil

spirit shook the man violently and came out of him with a shriek.

The people were all so amazed that they asked each other, "What is this? A new teaching – and with authority! He even gives orders to evil spirits and they obey him." News about him spread quickly over the whole region of Galilee. (Mark 1:21–28)

The conflict continues throughout his ministry of healing and deliverance – for instance Jesus heals a crippled woman "whom Satan had bound for eighteen long years" (Luke 13:11). It draws to its climax in Gethsemane and on Calvary. Just before this, Jesus sees Satan entering the unfortunate Judas Iscariot (Luke 22:3 and John 13:27).

In John's Gospel, three times Jesus describes Satan as "the prince of this world".

"Now is the time for judgment on this world; now the prince of this world will be driven out." (John 12:31)

"I will not speak with you much longer, for the prince of this world is coming. He has no hold on me, but the world must learn that I love the Father and that I do exactly what my Father has commanded me." (John 14:30–31)

". . . and in regard to judgment, because the prince of this world now stands condemned." (John 16:11)

In the first, Jesus foresees the ultimate victory of his Kingdom over the forces of evil; in the second, he announces the beginning of the conflict in the Garden of Gethsemane and on the hill of Calvary; in the third, he declares that Satan now stands condemned.

The mission of the 72 (Luke 10:1–23) is particularly revealing about Jesus' strategy and understanding of Satan. He gives his workers authority to proclaim that "the kingdom of God is near you" (v. 9). When they return in triumph, they declare "Lord, even the demons submit to us in your name." (v. 17).

Jesus replied, "I saw Satan fall like lightning from heaven. I
have given you authority to trample on snakes and scorpions
and to overcome all the power of the enemy; nothing will harm
you" (v. 18–19).

What did Jesus mean when he declared that he had seen
"Satan fall like lightning from heaven"? Clearly Jesus knew
where Satan had come from, and where his current sphere of
activity lay. Probably two relatively unknown Old Testament
passages lay behind Jesus' teaching.

> How you have fallen from heaven, O morning star, son of the
> dawn! You have been cast down to the earth, you who once laid
> low the nations! You said in your heart, "I will ascend to heaven; I
> will raise my throne above the stars of God; I will sit enthroned on
> the mount of assembly, on the utmost heights of the sacred moun-
> tain. I will ascend above the tops of the clouds; I will make myself
> like the Most High." But you are brought down to the grave, to the
> depths of the pit. (Isaiah 14:12–15)

> The word of the Lord came to me: "Son of man, take up a lament
> concerning the king of Tyre and say to him: 'This is what the
> sovereign Lord says: You were the model of perfection, full of
> wisdom and perfect in beauty. You were in Eden, the garden of
> God; every precious stone adorned you: ruby, topaz and emerald,
> chrysolite, onyx and jasper, sapphire, turquoise and beryl. Your
> settings and mountings were made of gold; on the day you were
> created they were prepared. You were anointed as a guardian
> cherub, for so I ordained you. You were on the holy mount of God;
> you walked among the fiery stones. You were blameless in your
> ways from the day you were created till wickedness was found in
> you. Through your widespread trade you were filled with violence,
> and you sinned. So I drove you in disgrace from the mount of God,
> and I expelled you, O guardian cherub, from among the fiery
> stones. Your heart became proud on account of your beauty, and
> you corrupted your wisdom because of your splendour. So I threw
> you to the earth; I made a spectacle of you before kings. By your
> many sins and dishonest trade you have desecrated your sanctuar-
> ies. So I made a fire come out from you, and it consumed you, and

I reduced you to ashes on the ground in the sight of all who were watching. All the nations who knew you are appalled at you; you have come to a horrible end and will be no more.'" (Ezekiel 28:11–19)

Both are controversial. The Isaiah text is about the King of Babylon, and the Ezekiel one about the King of Tyre. Old Testament prophecy often needs to be read, and understood, at several levels. These two texts may well refer to historic rulers, but the language is such that they also point to a deeper meaning. In Isaiah, we discover "a fallen morning star who had tried to ascend above the stars of God"; and in Ezekiel "a model of perfection thrown out of Eden". Ambition and pride seem to have been the root causes of this terrible fall: a point, incidentally, understood by Shakespeare in Cardinal Wolsey's fall from grace.

> Mark but my fall, and that that ruin'd me
> Cromwell, I charge thee, fling away ambition:
> By that sin fell the angels: but can man then,
> The image of his Maker, hope to win by't?
> Love thyself last: cherish those hearts that hate thee:
> Corruption wins not more than honesty.
> *King Henry VIII*, Act III, Scene II (lines 440–445)

The Scripture texts point to a primeval depth of dark disobedience amongst the ranks of the angels. Scripture may be somewhat opaque about the origins of evil, and the precise nature of Satan's rebellion, but it is crystal clear about his existence, and full of warnings about his strategies.

Satanic strategies

"We are not unaware of his schemes" (2 Corinthians 2:11). St Paul writes with characteristic confidence. He knows that he can read, and understand, the stratagems of Satan. The modern church, however, behaves and thinks somewhat differently. On one side, liberal theologies dismiss as medieval superstition, all talk of the Devil and demons. From the opposite side, some contemporary exorcists appear to see demons in every emotional problem which is not fully under control, and in any illnesses which do not respond to treatment. From a third direction, post-modern New Age followers confidently call up spirit guides, and follow a path of benign acceptance of almost everything out of the ordinary. (We shall consider this in the next chapter.)

According to Scripture, and throughout Christian history, Satan appears to have had a number of prime strategies – to encourage clever people to deny his existence; to swamp over-enthusiastic exorcists by encouraging them to see his hand everywhere; to spread false guilt in the souls of true believers; to promote false living, especially by Christian leaders; to promote false doctrines – especially the denial of the divinity of Jesus, the efficacy of the Atonement and the historicity of the Resur-rection; to encourage the practice of "white magic" – particu-larly the widely held view that such practices are harmless, or even beneficial; and finally, behind all of this, Satan has a small number of people, well hidden, who have been snared into delv-ing deeply into, and practising, the dark arts. (We shall look at the first five in this chapter, and the last two in the next.)

The Devil denied

Some years ago, I was invited to preach in a cathedral. A member of the cathedral staff, a very interesting and compas-sionate theologian, had stated, publicly, that he didn't believe in the Devil. Perhaps foolishly, I decided to put a different view-point. The set readings for the service included some instruc-tions of Jesus to the disciples.

Calling the twelve to him, he sent them out two by two and gave them authority over evil spirits (Mark 6:7).

I included various stories about the reality of evil powers, and of the interest of the public in white witchcraft and related matters – as illustrated by the shelves of major booksellers, and current articles in *The Times*.

The reaction to the sermon was interesting. Many people, including one senior clergyman, thanked me profusely, the theologian smiled quizzically, and one or two people pressed me on the details of some of the material that I had included. Some local pagans, justifiably upset by an anecdote that was unintentionally identifiable, demanded a "pistols-at-dawn" confrontation. Honour was satisfied with a Channel 4 television programme called "The Good, the Bad, and the Pagans". The "good", I suppose, were represented by myself and a young woman[1] who had had a dramatic conversion from Shamanism (a form of white magic) to Christianity. The "bad" was represented by a very sad woman, deep into black magic, who openly talked about her out-of-body sexual exploits, and clearly believed that she was living under a curse which would kill her in a few years time. The pagans danced cheerfully around spring fires, prayed in circles with strange incantations in tongues unknown to me, and portrayed themselves as pleasantly harmless.

In this chaos, the forces of darkness must allow themselves an evil cackle. Disbelieving in the Devil may be theologically fashionable, but it is *pastorally absurd*. Consider what happens when a church leader is approached by someone who is living in what they believe to be a disturbed building, or who believes that they themselves may be affected in some way by evil powers. A pastor who believes in the *possibility* that such problems could be real, is well placed to exercise the gift of discernment (1 Corinthians 12:10). He can then minister, with others as appropriate, in an effective way. His diagnosis, which may sometimes be negative on the question of direct demonic involvement, is likely to be accepted. His ministry will give the distressed person confidence. People need reassuring of the reality of their situation (most people encountering strange phenomena in their houses assume that they have taken leave of their senses!) and thus need quiet, authoritative, ministry.

On the other hand, a pastor who regards such problems as medical, imagined, or signs of derangement, will face serious difficulties. If he is sensible, he will seek help from those who understand these matters. But often, pastors try to manage without outside help. Then, either he (or she) will be brutally honest and say that he can't accept this sort of worldview, or he will put on his robes and go through some sort of prescribed ritual in which he has little confidence. In the first case, the distressed person will look elsewhere. Usually they will consult a believer in spiritualism. The result will usually be expensive, the problem may get worse (see Luke 11:24–26), and there may be considerable pastoral confusion. In the second case, the ministry will usually be ineffective. Occasionally the pastor, like the sons of Sceva (see Acts 19:13–16) may get a considerable surprise. God is gracious. I know from personal experience, and from the reaction of others, the incredible surprise when, for the first time, you realise that demonic problems and powers exist in practice as well as theory!

Theologically, if there is no spiritual opposition, no fallen angels, then God stands accused of having made an appalling world. Recently, I watched a TV programme on the Congo, in which there was a long section on the behaviour of gorillas. For the most part, they seemed much more pleasant, and far more caring, than many human beings. My reaction was somewhat confirmed by watching, a few days later, a horrific documentary on the extermination of the Jews in the Second World War, and the part played by the outwardly charming Adolf Eichmann. If there is no spiritual opposition, then the mess that mankind is in has to be put down almost entirely to human greed, selfishness, and sexual desires. Of course, Jesus spoke about this (see Mark 7:1–23) when disputing with the Pharisees about what was clean and unclean. He quotes Isaiah:

> These people honour me with their lips, but their hearts are far from me. They worship me in vain; their teachings are but rules taught by men. (Mark 7:6–7, quoting Isaiah 29:13)

But he also taught that the problem was deeper than human sin; it was due to a longstanding spiritual rebellion. When Jesus accused the Pharisees of travelling "over land and sea to wine a single convert" he added that such a convert would be "twice as much a son of hell" as they were. Jesus taught that behind human sin, behind the fall, the power of Satan lurked.

If there is no spiritual opposition, then many statements and actions attributed to Jesus by the Gospel writers are wrong. If there is no spiritual opposition, then people today who are healed by prayers of deliverance and whose disturbed buildings are quietened by Christian prayers, are being helped by misguided, albeit well-meaning mumbo-jumbo. If there is no spiritual opposition, then Eichmann and his Nazi superiors were entirely governed by racial hatred and the lust for power, whereas there is some evidence that some of them looked to dark powers for their evil inspiration.

The victory of Christ

In the light of all this, it is important to read Paul's great statement:

> Having cancelled the written code, with its regulations, that was against us and that stood opposed to us; he took it away, nailing it to the cross. And having disarmed the powers and authorities, he made a public spectacle of them, triumphing over them by the cross. (Colossians 2:14–15)

Herein lies the theological basis of Christ's victory. Through the Cross, the possibility of extraordinary conversions (and in a real sense all conversions are extraordinary – but some like those recorded in Chapter 5 seem more unlikely), and the reality of the routing of dark powers from people's lives, troubled buildings and even territories, become possible. God's saving sovereign grace, released to us through Jesus' sacrifice on the Cross, reaches both the darkest recesses of the human soul and

the most troubled places. This does not release humanity from
its terrible collective, and individual, guilt in matters like the
Holocaust; but it may help to explain the depth of human
wickedness.

The problem with this sort of theology to many Christians is
not only that it appears medieval and outdated. Doesn't modern
psychology dispose of the Devil? Actually, no! My very
subjective impression is that more psychiatrists than clergy
believe in the Devil. Such theology can appear to be dualistic.
In simple words, are God and Satan equal and opposite forces
fighting over our fallen world?

It is worth repeating Cullmann's wise words (see p 111).

> The devil is bound to a line which can be lengthened even to the
> point that for a while Satan can make himself independent and has
> to be fought against by God. Going slightly beyond the Revelation
> of St John, this means that the whole fearful character is to be
> attributed to the evil, which temporarily looses itself from these
> bonds. If this event is taking place within the divine plan, then God
> himself has limited his omnipotence for this interim period. Evil
> cannot ultimately prevail, but we can choose evil and greatly
> hinder God's purpose.[2]

What this means is that God enjoins our help – our prayers – in
the battle against evil. The ultimate victory is assured, but the
intensity of the battle may vary as we pray.

This makes perfect pastoral sense. It makes sense when
faced with people genuinely troubled by evil spirits.[3] When you
meet a spirit in a Zambian lady in a very rural area speaking
perfect Oxbridge English, or another speaking French, it is
much simpler to believe that you are dealing with a situation
somewhat similar to that faced by Jesus in the synagogue in
Capernaum (Mark 1:21–28), than that there is a "split personality psychiatric" explanation. Of course, the insights of psychiatry are valuable. Many people do have personality disorders
which are not caused, or primarily caused, by evil spirits.

Cullmann's theology also makes sense when dealing with troubled houses, and with dark areas. Countless examples could be given, but Christians would be wise to realise there are exceptional places where Satan appears to have an almost free hand. The Transformations Videos[4] show how God has brought amazing revivals in Cali, a town in Colombia, in Guatemala, in a township in Kenya, and above all in Uganda. They bear witness in each case to the power of active occult practitioners which had to be broken through prayer, before the grace of God was seen to take effect.

Devils everywhere

If denying the existence of Satan undermines both the witness of Scripture and the doctrine of the goodness of God, seeing demons everywhere is equally contrary to Scripture, and highly dishonouring to God.

I listened to a famous speaker expounding Luke 17:37. "Where, Lord?" they asked. He replied, "Where there is a dead body, there the vultures will gather." His talk ran along the lines "Vultures gather round dead bodies." We were all dead before we came to Christ (Ephesians 2:1, etc.). The vultures represent evil spirits. In the wild, it is *normal* for vultures to descend upon, and feed off, dead carcases; so it is *normal* for demons to have invaded people before they are converted.

This theology would be laughable, but for the melancholy fact that it is the accepted basis of some healing groups when at prayer. It may be expressed differently, it may be denied strenuously (we don't believe everyone is demonised!); but, in practice, many people are left bewildered, vulnerable, and highly dependent on their counsellors, after prayer ministry which attempts to cast out endless demons of anger, lust, . . . Many people are told that they need more ministry, and they return, over and over again, for apparently unending prayer sessions which are both demoralising and demanding.

The problem with seeing non-existent demons in every

headache, character defect, signs of depression, or unusual behaviour, is that it makes ministry to people with genuine problems *much more* difficult.

If Satan's primary strategy is to get people to deny that he exists, his secondary strategy is to get Christians so excited at the prospect of casting out demons that they take their eyes off the Lord, and cause chaos as they tilt at non-existent spiritual windmills.

I have written at length elsewhere[5] of the main reasons why people can be demonised, and of genuine situations where people and buildings have been cleansed and set free. In brief, the main reasons for demonic problems seem to be some form of occult involvement, psychic qualities inherited – often from grandparents, (see Exodus 20:5), living in a building which is either built on disturbed ground, or in which unpleasant things have happened, or from extreme character flaws.

> Who is wise and understanding among you? Let him show it by his good life, by deeds done in the humility that comes from wisdom. But if you harbour bitter envy and selfish ambition in your hearts, do not boast about it or deny the truth. Such "wisdom" does not come down from heaven but is earthly, unspiritual, of the devil. For where you have envy and selfish ambition, there you find disorder and every evil practice. (James 3:13–16)

James seems to allow that bitter envy, selfish ambition, (and other serious character flaws) can bring complete disorder and chaos into people's lives. *Occasionally*, this may manifest itself in an evil spirit that needs removal at the name of Jesus. However, the normal New Testament approach is very restrained.

While Jesus dismisses demons at a word, and Paul recognises the spiritual battle in the heavenly places (Ephesians 6:10ff, etc.), Peter sees "The devil, as a roaring lion, [who] walketh about, seeking whom he may devour: Whom resist steadfast in the faith, knowing that the same afflictions are accomplished in your brethren that are in the world." (1 Peter

5:8b–9 KJV). But nowhere is it suggested that it is normal for people, or places, to be demonised. What is normal is for people to have a problem of the flesh (*sinful nature* in NIV). The flesh is not what English tabloid newspapers continually expose; but that part *of all of us* which is bitterly opposed to what God is calling us to do!

Paul's language is incredibly strong. His personal testimony in Romans 7:15–18,

> I do not understand what I do. For what I want to do I do not do, but what I hate I do. And if I do what I do not want to do, I agree that the law is good. As it is, it is no longer I myself who do it, but it is sin living in me. I know that nothing good lives in me, that is, in my sinful nature. For I have the desire to do what is good, but I cannot carry it out.

is backed by his comments elsewhere.

> If we have been united with him like this in his death, we will certainly also be united with him in his resurrection. For we know that our old self was crucified with him so that the body of sin might be done away with, that we should no longer be slaves to sin – because anyone who has died has been freed from sin. (Romans 6:5–7),

and,

> I have been crucified with Christ and I no longer live, but Christ lives in me. The life I live in the body, I live by faith in the Son of God, who loved me and gave himself for me. (Galatians 2:20)

For Paul, and the rest of the New Testament writers, the primary internal battle is within our sinful nature, and *not* with external demons.

Jesus (Mark 7:20–23), Paul (Galatians 5:16ff), and John (1 John 2:15–17), teach us very clearly about this universal

problem. If I have laboured this point, it is because I believe
that false theology here clouds our ability to understand the real
spiritual battle, and masks the subtlety of Satan's deceit.

Devilish accusations and devilish advice

Then I heard a loud voice in heaven say, "Now have come the
salvation and the power and the kingdom of our God, and the
authority of his Christ. For the accuser of our brothers who
accuses them before our God day and night, has been hurled
down." (Revelation 12:10)

False guilt and false accusations cause great difficulties to
many Christians. Many Christians are "driven" to work absurd
hours, to go to impossible lengths to serve aged relatives, feel
very uneasy after rightly confronting someone about a problem,
and are generally unable to think of themselves with what St
Paul described as "sober judgment" (Romans 12:3). Satan uses
many people, as well as our own insecure conscience, to load
us with false guilt. Seemingly wise people can come, deliberately or otherwise, loaded with false advice. The subtle advice
of Shemaiah (Nehemiah 6:10) designed to lure Nehemiah away
from actively defending the walls and into a spurious meeting
in the Temple, is a good example.

Satan also uses false accusations. I have known people in
senior positions in churches accused falsely. There are clear
examples from former Communist regimes, distressing ones in
some African situations, and subtle cases in the sophisticated
West. We should not be surprised. Jesus, Paul, Stephen and
others were accused falsely. Even Peter, after his declaration of
faith, temporarily became the mouthpiece of Satan:

"But what about you?" he asked. "Who do you say I am?" Simon
Peter answered, "You are the Christ, the Son of the living God."
Jesus replied, "Blessed are you, Simon son of Jonah, for this was
not revealed to you by man, but by my Father in heaven. And I tell
you that you are Peter, and on this rock I will build my church, and

the gates of Hades will not overcome it. I will give you the keys of the kingdom of heaven, whatever you bind on earth will be bound in heaven; and whatever you loose on earth will be loosed in heaven." Then he warned his disciples not to tell anyone that he was the Christ.

From that time on Jesus began to explain to his disciples that he must go to Jerusalem and suffer many things at the hands of the elders, chief priests and teachers of the law, and that he must be killed and on the third day be raised to life.

Peter took him aside and began to rebuke him. "Never, Lord!" he said. "This shall never happen to you!" Jesus turned and said to Peter, "Get behind me, Satan! You are a stumbling-block to me; you do not have in mind the things of God, but the things of men." (Matthew 16:15–23)

Devilish conduct

Jesus points to a sharp contrast between those within the professing church who produce good fruit, and those whose conduct is of the Devil.

In the Sermon on the Mount (Matthew Ch. 5–7), Jesus covers a wide range of subjects, including true blessedness, the call to be salt and light, the dangers of anger, adultery (even in thought), revenge, generous giving, prayer and the need to forgive, priorities in life, anxiety, judging others . . .

He sums it all up with these powerful words:

Watch out for false prophets. They come to you in sheep's clothing, but inwardly they are ferocious wolves. By their fruit you will recognise them. Do people pick grapes from thorn bushes, or figs from thistles? Likewise every good tree bears good fruit, but a bad tree bears bad fruit. A good tree cannot bear bad fruit, and a bad tree cannot bear good fruit. Every tree that does not bear good fruit is cut down and thrown into the fire. Thus, by their fruit you will recognise them.

Not everyone who says to me, "Lord, Lord," will enter the kingdom of heaven, but only he who does the will of my Father who is

in heaven. Many will say to me on that day, "Lord, Lord, did we
not prophesy in your name, and in your name drive out demons
and perform many miracles?" Then I will tell them plainly, "I
never knew you. Away from me, you evildoers!" (Matthew
7:15–23)

These words seem to be a particular warning to those in leadership, and those apparently displaying *spiritual power*. Financial
and sexual scandals seem to be amongst Satan's most effective
weapons for discrediting the church, and causing deep pastoral
hurt.

Paul illustrates this all too clearly, particularly with his
instructions for dealing with a case of deep sexual immorality
(see 1 Corinthians 5:1–5). This melancholy subject would be
outside our scope, were it not for the sad fact that some of the
worst cases occur amongst Christian leaders. When people
teach one thing and live in a completely different way, the
Devil's cause is well served. If Christian leaders abuse children, the scars are incredibly deep. If a prominent Christian
spends most of his ministry publicly, and very effectively,
preaching an orthodox biblical moral view, and then breaks up
his long standing marriage by setting up a homosexual partner-
ship, the despair and disbelief of his previous congregation is
very deep. If he then starts to justify it from a new understanding of the Bible, the result is chaos. If a Christian pastor admits
to an adulterous relationship, having preached for years about
the sanctity of marriage, the result is bewilderment. Paul refers
to false teachers as "angels of light" (2 Corinthians 11:14); and
that would seem to be a reasonable designation of those in
positions of leadership whose conduct falls far short of the
Gospel. Of course, every Christian minister is deeply aware of
the sinfulness of *his own* heart, but there do seem to be levels
of conduct which move from being "sins of the flesh" into the
realms of the demonic.

But thank God for Article XXVI of the Church of England!

"Of the Unworthiness of the Ministers, which hinders not the effect of the Sacrament".

Although in the visible Church the evil be ever mingled with the good, and sometimes the evil have chief authority in the Ministration of the Word and Sacraments, yet forasmuch as they do not the same in their own name, but in Christ's, and do minister by his commission and authority, we may use their Ministry, both in hearing the Word of God, and in the receiving of the Sacraments. Neither is the effect of Christ's ordinance taken away by their wickedness, nor the grace of God's gifts diminished from such as by faith and rightly do receive the Sacraments ministered unto them; which be effectual, because of Christ's institution and promise, although they be ministered by evil men.

Nevertheless, it appertaineth to the discipline of the Church, that enquiry be made of evil ministers, and that they be accused by those that have knowledge of their offences; and finally being found guilty, by just judgment be deposed.[6]

This rightly limits the damage that such people can do. God's grace can be ministered through unworthy hearts and lives. If that were not so, *none* of us could utter a word; if that were not so Judas Iscariot could not have performed miracles (see Mark 6:7–13 for instance).

All Christians are puzzled by the cases of Judas, Ananias and Sapphira (Acts 5:1–11), Simon Magus (Acts 8:9–24), Demas (2 Timothy 4:10), the incest at Corinth (1 Corinthians 5), and other scandals which disfigure the early church. They were serious blots on the spiritual landscape (Jude vv 3–16), but their overall effect was quite small. Provided we continue to look to Jesus, and set our minds on the things that are above, we will not be too disheartened by those that Satan snares. We shall be sad for them as individuals; and all are too well aware that if we "think we are standing firm, we should be careful that we don't fall" (1 Corinthians 10:12, pronouns altered).

Devilish doctrines and deceptions

"The Spirit clearly says that in later times some will abandon
the faith and follow deceiving spirits and things taught by
demons." (1 Timothy 4:1)

The Bible gives many examples of false doctrines. 1 Timothy 4, refers to false asceticism which was being preached by
Paul's opponents. In 2 Timothy 2:17, there is a blatantly false
doctrine of the Resurrection being pedalled by Hymenaeus and
Philetus. In Galatians 1:8, a false doctrine, replacing the grace
of God by justification by keeping the law, was being taught by
the followers of "James". Paul says that such a doctrine, even if
preached by himself or an *angel* should lead to eternal condem-
nation. Later, Paul, driven to exasperated bewilderment, writes:

> You foolish Galatians! Who has *bewitched* you? Before your very
> eyes Jesus Christ was clearly portrayed as crucified. I would like to
> learn just one thing from you: Did you receive the Spirit by observ-
> ing the law, or by believing what you heard? Are you so foolish?
> After beginning with the Spirit, are you now trying to attain your
> goal by human effort? Have you suffered so much for nothing – if
> it really was for nothing? Does God give you his Spirit and work
> miracles among you because you observe the law, or because you
> believe what you heard? (Galatians 3:1–5 – my italics)

In Mark 13:5, Jesus warns about deception concerning the
Second Coming. False miracles (Mark 13:22 and 2 Thessalonians 2:9), and false dating of the Second Coming (unknown to
the angels or to Jesus – Matthew 24:36) are particularly
common errors.

Dr Moolenburgh[7] is particularly strong on this point.

> In January 1991, a strange story was told. A Dutchman, driving his
> car along the motorway, picked up a hitchhiker. When the car was
> once again travelling at considerable speed, the hitchhiker

suddenly started to warn the driver in a serious tone that Jesus was on the point of returning. The driver looked round at him rather pityingly, and realised, to his intense shock, that he was in the car alone. The hitchhiker seemed to have vanished into thin air. Badly frightened, he parked his car on the hard shoulder, where a traffic policeman soon stopped to ask him what he was doing there. The policeman then helped the man, who was in a fairly distraught condition. The so-called "Angel on the motorway" was a great success in evangelical circles. There was a great deal of speculation about it from every quarter. A vicar spoke on the subject from the pulpit, articles appeared in magazines, and even radio and TV stations devoted some time to it. A sergeant from the traffic police inserted a message in the police newspaper, asking the policeman concerned to come forward. The strange thing is that this story was not new. Although it was described as having "just happened", the story was much older. In 1983, a similar rumour was circulating in Germany.

I, too, heard this sort of story back in the 1980s when there was a lot of hysteria about the date 1984.[8] Moolenburgh calls this "a monkey roll" story:

> The stories have one other thing in common: they cannot be verified. Everyone who tells the story has heard it second hand. No one knows anyone who was directly involved. This means that the whole affair can be categorised as what is known in my part of the Netherlands as a "monkey roll" story. In case the reader is not familiar with this sort of story, here is an example. My aunt has a cleaning lady whose niece told her that in Amsterdam there's a butcher who sells rolls with monkey's meat. It must be true, because the other day I heard it from a man whose brother's wife had been told so herself by the baker, whose eldest son had eaten a monkey roll.
>
> Everyone believes the monkey roll story, but no one knows exactly who was involved or where it took place.

He points out that the angel shouldn't have made the driver commit a serious traffic offence (picking up a hitchhiker on a motorway), the angel shouldn't have startled the driver by disappearing, and shouldn't have claimed to have knowledge that it was impossible for an angel to have (Mark 13:32)! In other words, the story was a none-too-subtle deception.

Far more blatant was the cult in Uganda which caused a hysterical mass suicide (or, perhaps, murder) when the new millennium didn't bring the return of Jesus. A pastor friend of mine was the first Christian on the scene; he spoke movingly, to me, of the horror of arriving at the burning buildings. The cult leaders appear to have escaped, with considerable proceeds, to nearby Congo. If this is true, the deception was criminal rather than demonic. The result was just as bad.

The clearest New Testament tests come in the First Epistle of John. We shall reinforce this view with an interesting "New Age" quote in the next chapter. Jesus knew that false spirits would always deny the Incarnation of Christ.

> But you have an anointing from the Holy One, and all of you know the truth. I do not write to you because you do not know the truth, but because you do know it and because no lie comes from the truth. Who is the liar? It is the man who denies that Jesus is the Christ. Such a man is the antichrist – he denies the Father and the Son. No-one who denies the Son has the Father; whoever acknowledges the Son has the Father also. (1 John 2:20–23)

It will become apparent that many "spiritual" experiences are, in scriptural terms, both false and dangerous. It is to those matters that we now turn.

Notes

(1) See Chapter 10 for her detailed testimony.
(2) Oscar Cullmann, *Prayer in the New Testament*, SCM, 1995 p. 141.
(3) For a more detailed discussion of these and other incidents see John Woolmer, *Thinking Clearly about Healing &*

Deliverance, Monarch, 1999.

(4) Transformations Videos I & II – distributed by Gateway Christian Media, PO 11905, London NW10 4ZQ.

(5) John Woolmer, *ibid*, especially p. 264ff.

(6) Book of Common Prayer, Article 26. The 39 Articles can be found at the back of all full editions of the BCP.

(7) Dr H. C. Moolenburgh, *Meetings with Angels*, C. W. Daniel, 1992, p. 1ff. He too applies Occam's razor (see page 90) to deduce that it is a "monkey roll" story rather than an angel causing chaos.

(8) Based on George Orwell's apocalyptic book entitled *Nineteen Eighty Four*.

9

Angels Can Deceive

In this chapter, we examine some of the confusion caused by some New Age teaching. We look at Satan's various strategies, and consider what our response should be.

Angels Can Deceive

Some years ago, a popular children's book called *The Dark is Rising* portrayed a new age when the ancient religions would flourish once again. In contrast, the Church was portrayed as kindly, bumbling, out of touch, and ineffectual.[1] Unfortunately, this is sometimes all too true!

All around the UK, especially around the ancient town of Glastonbury in Somerset, New Age activities flourish. Walk down Glastonbury High Street, enjoy the scent of smoked grass, have your tarot reading, buy a crystal, have your allergy tested by a pendulum, buy books on angels, healings, numerology, clairvoyance, white witchcraft, Wicca, . . . For the most part, it is all very amicable, very friendly; occasional conflicts break out with drunken wayfarers or destitute hippies, while kindly Christians in the parish church and other churches, and the atmosphere of the ruins of the ancient Abbey do their best to minister to people's spiritual and bodily needs. Here is a warning testimony:

A Glastonbury experience

Several years ago, I injured my neck following a road traffic accident and a judo injury. Despite seeing various GPs, physiotherapists and osteopaths, and taking various tablets, I was never free of pain. However, I endeavoured to keep fit and attended a leisure centre for several years. One day when talking to a gentleman, the conversation turned to my neck injury and the on-going pain. He told me that he and his partner were healers in Glastonbury and offered his help. He gave me his card which read "Healer and Counsellor", in case I wished to contact him. I said I would think about it. Eventually, as the pain continued, I phoned and made an appointment. I went to see him weekly for over a year. I wasn't told what type of healing it was despite asking how it worked. Initially, we had a discussion to discover anything I needed to talk about and, on each occasion, I would open up to him. I would then lie on the couch and he would go round my body with his hands just over me. This generally took between 1½–2 hours. I was asked to make a donation of whatever I could afford.

At this time I was involved in a relationship (not with the healer) which ended abruptly, and I found myself very low afterwards. The healer told me that healing would help, so I continued with it. I was given some "sayings" to repeat morning and evening. I can't remember them, but I now realise that they encouraged me to isolate myself from others. At one point I asked if this was a religious healing group, but he merely laughed and said, "I thought you would say that."

Gradually, I began to develop an interest in psychic things and was encouraged to go to a spiritualist church. Whilst there, I asked two healers if they thought I could heal. They told me to open my hands, and then said there was something there. I was encouraged by the Glastonbury healer to read widely about healing and started to read any books relating to healing and psychic issues. I was also receiving psychic mail.

I began to have premonitions, which increased my anxiety. One related to the Paddington rail disaster. When I told the healer, he said that I was discovering my psychic powers and that he would teach me to "cover up" and protect myself from this. He also said that being a nurse, I needed to protect myself when I went into the hospital by covering myself (mentally) with a white blanket. This was also important when treating patients. It took me nearly two years to move on and forget this strange idea.

During this time I went to France with my parents and son. I felt

strange at times, with a sense of déjà-vu. Once, on a beach, I saw a
figure in white which, I believe, was an angel, spirit, or apparition.
Strangely, when I got home I had a compulsion to search and read
about Camille Monet, (the wife of the Impressionist artist) who
had died in her early thirties. When I told the healer, he said it was
the work of the infinite spirit world.

I told my sister that I had psychic/healing powers and that various psychics had confirmed this ability. I tried to heal my sister,
but she was angry with me and told me I needed psychiatric help.
About this time I also began to get blinding headaches, and
became forgetful and often confused as to my whereabouts when
shopping, particularly in the supermarket. My GP prescribed anti-
depressants and anti-psychotics. I phoned the Glastonbury healer
and said I couldn't go any more, and that my family didn't agree
with what I was doing. He said this was absolute madness and he
told me to phone him anytime, any day, if I wanted to go back.

I was very afraid that these people would use their powers in a
telepathic form to encourage me to join them. I also felt that I had
been taken over, or possessed by something, and that I was losing
control of myself and this "something" was taking over. I began to
have severe panic attacks; my mother realised the danger and
asked John Woolmer to see me. My doctor also encouraged the
Church to get involved. John and another senior member of the
local church came to see me. They listened to my story, and prayed
very gently. Afterwards I felt safe, and no longer afraid. I also felt
that the dark presence had left.

My friend is not yet a worshipping Christian, but writes hoping
that her words will help others avoid the same sort of mistake.

Hypnotism causes confusion

About the same time as my meetings with the previous individual, a lovely old lady came to see me. She was a believing
Christian and enjoyed coming to church with her husband. She
was suffering from failing eyesight and her optician had
encouraged her to go and see a "nice hypnotist" in a nearby
village.

The result was considerable confusion. She felt unhappy under the hypnotist's power; she'd spent a lot of money on four expensive sessions, she no longer enjoyed coming to the church, and she was psychologically worse and physically no better!

With some difficulty, I persuaded her husband to cancel all future appointments with the hypnotist, and after some prayer, her peace was eventually restored.

Practitioners of white magic flaunt their wares. A child is publicly proclaimed as the youngest witch in the UK. Practitioners of Wicca, and even Satanists, insist that their practices are quite harmless. Once, recently, a local TV studio asked me to watch and then comment on a 45-minute video of a West Country Satanist. For the most part, the interview was a confused ramble full of repetitive statements, and very dull. Apparently, the Satanists didn't believe in the Devil, liked everyone – except those who crossed them. Vengeance was then in order, but otherwise Satanists were harmless.

About the same time, a gruesome murder trial in Germany attributed a horrible murder directly to the commands of the Devil. The perpetrators were Satanists. Of course, there is no obvious connection between a West Country eccentric who wants to practise his "harmless Satanism" and a vicious cult in Germany. Nevertheless, this cry of innocence is overdone, and we need to be aware of the subtle strategies of Satan – usually using people who are quite unaware that what they are doing is harmful to themselves and others, and inimical to the teachings of Scripture.

Stratagems for deception

Satan has many tactics. Some of the most obvious are:

1. Encourage the belief that white magic is *harmless.*
2. Insist that ghosts are nothing to worry about.
3. Infiltrate Christian organisations.

4. Encourage people to *develop* their psychic gifts.
5. Send false prophecy and visions.
6. Lure people into dark arts.

Strategem (1) "Harmless" practices

Obviously, it is possible for Christians to go to absurd lengths
condemning all sorts of practices. For instance, herbal medicine is often beneficial. Many of our modern drugs are based
on old herbal remedies. I well remember walking in a rain
forest in Kenya with a guide, who pointed out the medicinal
uses of many of the plants and trees. The problems arise when
such medicines are "prayed over" by people using "psychic
powers".

A hundred years ago, practices like table turning, automatic
writing, and even spiritualism were regarded as harmless occu-
pations – particularly for the leisured classes. My aunt who
lived to a great age, and who died in 1988, told me of one such
experience. She was the very essence of a respectable, God-
fearing, "Victorian" lady – someone of considerable spiritual
understanding and grace.

In about 1919, she went to play tennis at a famous house in
Yorkshire called Burton Agnes. The house was known to be
haunted. There was an old legend concerning a skull that
resided on the drawing room mantlepiece. A new owner
removed it, placing it behind a wall. It "screamed", until
returned to its rightful place. Be that as it may, it was certainly
a house which generated psychic presence and power (see,
perhaps, Luke 5:17 for the Christian equivalent). The weather
was terrible, tennis was impossible. The party tried "table turning" (an attempt to contact the dead which was fashionable
particularly after the First World War). Aunt Hilda was terrified
that they would attempt to contact her beloved brother Jim,
who had recently died of wounds sustained in the terrible battle
of the Somme. However, soon after they had started, proceed-
ings were abruptly terminated when, in my Aunt's words "The
table took off, crashed into a wall, and everyone was terrified".

Interestingly, my godmother, from very much the same generation, was troubled by disturbing dreams, and in her nineties asked me to pray for peace and calm. I think her family had been interested in table turning, and she certainly acknowledged both its dangers and its baleful effect.

Much of this seems harmless, but the effects are long lasting. Nowadays the ouija board, tarot cards, Shamanism and spirit guides are more in fashion. Modern writings often defend, indeed *encourage* such practices.

A fairly typical example (*Angels and Companions in Spirit*)[2] has a chapter answering people's questions. In the midst of this we find the following "In the Universe we never die" ; "human beings have fashioned the devil . . . in order to avoid taking responsibility for their own malicious attitudes and destructive behaviour". "Smoke only when the spirits tell you to" (Angelica as used by Californian Indians, cannabis, and varieties of mushrooms are amongst other things recommended). "The misuse of spirit guide information generates terrifying karma." "As a practising Quaker, I can report that my years of experience with spirit guide work have only served to deepen my faith. Many Saints and Biblical figures have *sought* and received the advice of angels [my italics]. The Laws in Deuteronomy and Leviticus have since been rephrased in the New Testament, or modified by Christian authorities and proponents of Reformed Judaism, or abandoned entirely."

All of which is pretty remarkable, and totally contrary to Scripture! A quick glance at Deuteronomy 18:9–13; Leviticus 19:13; Isaiah 47:8–15; Malachi 3:5; Acts 13:8; Acts 19:19; Revelation 22:15, not to mention Jesus' encounter with Satan (who also specialises in quoting Scripture for his own benefit – see Matthew 4:1–11), should convince anyone prepared to take the Bible seriously that the book, quoted above, is teaching dangerous things.

The book is full of encounters with angels and archangels. A spirit guide called White Eagle is linked with St John the Divine (read Revelation 13:13 and beware!).

The deception of reincarnation

It is easy to see why people chase after such experiences. In today's lonely, frenetic world many churches seem unfriendly, and unspiritual. By contrast, many New Age people are warm, welcoming, concerned about the environment, and very willing to help one another. Besides all this, there is the ultimate problem of death. Reincarnation points to a nice hopeful solution. It deals with failure, and offers peace and reassurance. The trouble is that it is completely wrong! Wrong, because it undermines the Cross of Christ: "You [an individual, unique, person] were bought at a price. Therefore honour God with your body" (1 Corinthians 6:20). Wrong, because there is no evidence for it. It is quite extraordinary how people's pre-incarnations are usually of famous people; and how intertwined and complicated "relationships" become. Wrong, because mankind isn't getting any better. If reincarnation were true, there would be clear evidence of progress in our attitudes, lifestyle, relationships. . . . Wrong, because it is mathematically impossible. A typical statement about reincarnation reads "I have had 30,000 previous incarnations". A statement that you never find in these books is "I am a first time incarnate soul". Curious, because mathematically it is quite impossible for all of us to be reincarnations of other humans – unless, of course, you believe in souls on other planets, etc.!

It is sometimes alleged that the Bible teaches reincarnation (the appearance of Moses and Elijah on the Mount of Transfiguration is cited, particularly with reference to Matthew 17:12, which is interpreted to identify John the Baptist with Elijah). Also it is suggested that Jesus taught reincarnation. Actually his teaching on the importance of *each* individual could hardly be clearer. See for instance, Matthew 18:13 – "And if he finds it, I tell you the truth, he is happier about that one sheep than about the ninety-nine that did not wander off."

Distorting Scripture and Christian writers

Satan is very skilful at distorting Scripture. We have already mentioned the Temptations of Jesus (see above and p 62f). We have seen how Satan twisted Scripture during the 40 day encounter. Some New Age books have a considerable veneer of Christian teaching, which, in my view, makes them *from a Christian perspective,* even more dangerous. An interesting example is called *Spirit Guides and Angel Guardians.*[3] The author quotes various Christian texts about guidance (e.g. Isaiah 65:24 and Philippians 4:13). He even gives the classic Colossian warning (see Chapter 2, p 35 and Colossians 2:18) about not worshipping angels, and tells the story of angel choirs singing near Lee Abbey.[4]

The opening chapters are quite scriptural. However, by page 27, things are beginning to change. Lucifer (Satan) is seen as responding to God's request for "a volunteer to go to Earth to *help* mankind" (my italics). The storytellers (the biblical writers) gradually forgot that "Lucifer was sent down by God to test humankind. Instead, he became regarded as a force for evil". By the middle of the book,[5] we have an extraordinary mishmash including a "quotation" from St Augustine of Hippo, enthusiasm for Native American Chiefs, Chinese sages, and Egyptian priests who "guide" spiritualist mediums. The ouija board "can be a useful instrument when used responsibly". After a brief warning about the possibility of encountering "negative spirits", there is a dramatic biblical quotation:

Dear friends, do not believe every spirit, but test the spirits to see whether they are from God, because many false prophets have gone out into the world. This is how you can recognise the Spirit of God: Every spirit that acknowledges that Jesus Christ has come in the flesh is from God, but every spirit that does not acknowledge Jesus is not from God. This is the spirit of the antichrist, which you have heard is coming and even now is already in the world. (1 John 4:1–3)

The Apostle John would be *astonished* to find his trenchant spiritual test misused as a user-friendly text to justify spirit guides and the use of the ouija board!

Augustine, too, would be surprised to find himself quoted as follows :

> St Augustine wrote in his "De Cura Pro Mortuis", "The spirits of the dead can be sent to the living and can unveil to them the future which they themselves have learned from other spirits or from angels, or by divine revelation".

I cannot find this quotation. It appears to be based on the following much more cautious passage:[6]

> It *may be*, that spirits of the dead do know something of the events on earth. The Spirit of God decides what they need to know, and who needs to know about things past, or present, or *even future*. The prophets knew some of these matters, *but only* those which the providence of God chose to reveal to them. Scripture testifies that some of the dead are sent to the living (just as Paul went from the living to Paradise). Samuel, who died, appeared to Saul, and predicted his death. Although some think that it wasn't Samuel "but some evil spirit purporting to be Samuel". In the Gospels, Moses, when dead, appeared to the living (at the Transfiguration).

As we mentioned above (p 121f), Augustine regards such events as unusual, and dearly as he would loved to have been contacted by his mother (in a dream, or a vision), he would never have initiated such contact! Augustine is content to leave these matters to *God's initiative*, and he would be horrified at the way his tentative speculations about difficult matters have been distorted.

Stratagem (2) Ghosts are nothing to worry about

This is a widely held view. Many people have told me about their "friendly" ghost. Others, however, are very frightened – both by the experience, and also by the anticipation that their partner would regard them as mad. Amongst numerous experiences,[7] I can remember a teenager terrified by a Roman soldier in her bedroom (they lived above a recently excavated site near the Fosse Way); a teenager who couldn't sleep because of playing with ouija boards; a house full of the smell of smoke (nobody smoked in the house, but the old farmer who had lived there was a heavy smoker and committed suicide); a woman who had a series of terrible experiences (many unexpected deaths in neighbouring houses including her own, a near-fatal rifle shot from outside her house, a horse which had bled to death just outside her house – her garden contained a well where there was an unexpected death about 50 years earlier); a family who heard footsteps and had other experiences (in Victorian times, the mother of the household had died, and her son had been locked up for exhuming her body from the local graveyard); a young mother who heard knocking on the walls and people walking up a non-existent staircase next door. She was somewhat relieved when she discovered that the next door neighbour was hearing the same thing, and so was her previously sceptical husband (no obvious explanation – probably some tragedy in the past when the house was a mill).

None of these experiences were benign, and all the occupants were grateful to be free from them. Some people had paid psychic healers who hadn't solved the situation; all were grateful for the free services of the Christian church.

A friend who is a diocesan exorcist told me the following story:

This incident took place in a nursing home that was converted from a seaside hotel just a few years ago. The problem first came to light because the staff identified one particular room as "dangerous" for patients. There appeared to be more people than average who, when placed in this room, took an unexpected turn for the worse, or died unhappily (or both).

It was then suggested by a member of staff who had been there at the time that this could be connected with a woman who had been in that room and had died there – her death having been a particular struggle. It further came out (though later) that this same woman had been much feared and disliked and had been involved in some sort of occult activities. She used to dress up in some sort of robes and was always particularly unpleasant afterwards. In the end her robes had been confiscated.

On the assumption that the influence of the woman needed help to be moved on, a Communion service was celebrated in the room and the immediate results seemed positive – though several of those present (mature Christians) reported that it had been quite bumpy. (This, I would say, is very unusual – mostly such services are very peaceful.) I was not present, but those there felt it had been successful in the end. One man I talked to later described how he had been physically and quite violently pushed.

However, within a day or two, the patient, now in this room, reported a companion. The patient was elderly and not entirely with it, so we relied on how she was affected rather than her witness to what was happening. She said there was someone in the room with her, *but it was nice because they were friendly.* The staff was pleased to hear that, but when this was reported to the team involved in the service it was not heard as good news.

Within a few days the "nice companion" had turned very nasty indeed and the patient had to be removed from the room. Once outside she was perfectly calm. One of the team who has considerable gifts of discernment suggested that we now had not a lost soul but an evil spirit to deal with.

Consequently, we had a second Communion service in the room (at which I was president) and the intention was to deliver the place from this evil. The service included an exorcism. The member of the team with the discernment felt a considerable resistance, but that the situation was resolved and certainly the staff seemed happy that the room was cleared and that for the last six months no more trouble was reported.

The Deliverance Ministry is not an exact science and we sometimes can do no more than thank God that he has acted, without our knowing precisely what the problem was. Different interpretations may be placed on what happened here. My own belief is that as a result of the first Eucharist the spirit of the woman who had been stuck in her room after death was released.

However, because of her occult activities, she had attached to her an evil spirit, which now had become much more dangerous and was looking for a new attachment – by seduction or fear. In the first service a human soul was released from its earthly shackles and presumably from evil spiritual ones too. In the second service an evil entity was expelled and the place delivered.

Other interpretations may, of course, be possible.

The final sentence is important. These are difficult situations to interpret. What is clear is that the idea that the "spiritual companion" was beneficial to the frail old lady was *quite false*. People involved in occult activities often leave an unwelcome presence in places where they used to live. They can also affect their descendants in a negative way.[8]

Stratagem (3) Infiltrate Christian organisations

Some years ago, we were concluding a Parish Weekend with a time of ministry. A small team, unused to such matters, prepared to pray for the Holy Spirit to bless individuals. We had just started to pray – there were about a dozen people present – when one lady started to sing. She was singing "spiritual songs", but something seemed to be wrong. St Paul may have had the grace to put up with this for several days, but I had had enough after a few minutes. Quietly, but firmly, I told her to "shut up in the Name of the Lord". Graciously, she left the room. Back home, she was released from an evil spirit connected with her religious background, and afterwards, I believe, grew strongly in the Lord. This became a particularly significant evening which resulted, amongst other things, in three people becoming involved in full-time Christian ministry. Satan, with subtle soothing singing, was trying to prevent such an outcome.

A much more significant example comes from the church in Finland, told to me by the Revd. Dr Mark Stibbe:

Deception in Finland

One of the most disturbing and destructive cases of deception I've ever come across occurred in the late 90s in Scandinavia. It still pains me to write or speak about these events today.

One of the biggest Charismatic churches in Northern Europe was split by a man who appeared to have been dramatically converted from a New Age background. We will call him Hans.

The senior pastor of the large church in question (let's call him Eric) had been praying for revival for a long time and felt that this was it. Certainly the stories of people being saved and healed were very dramatic. The numbers of those reported to be coming to faith were also very impressive. The fact that the new converts were from a New Age background also aroused interest. Furthermore, the person at the epicentre of this movement had an extraordinary ability to see into people's lives and to speak about hidden things.

Eric became intimately involved with the inner core of this group. However, over a period of time, disturbing views started to emerge. The leaders began to teach that the Bible was not necessary because you could receive revelation directly from the Father – revelation that was 100% accurate. This knowledge was received during trances, experienced by those who led the movement, especially by Hans.

Not surprisingly, having left Scripture behind, unbiblical practices started to appear. The most blatant of these was the view that men could have two wives – one by legal marriage and a "soul wife" from within the movement. Needless to say, Eric's marriage subsequently broke up. This was tragic not only because of the dreadful unhappiness it caused to his wife and children; but also because Eric's wife who had also been converted out of a New Age background, had discerned all along that there were very mixed spirits at work here.

I was somewhat involved in the assessment of this situation. Initially, when I met Hans, I was ambivalent. On the one hand, he was clearly able to see things by virtue of some kind of supernatural insight. On the other, there was something in my spirit that was uneasy. While he was saying the right things doctrinally (at this stage), something did not ring true. Yet he was so credible and persuasive, I felt led to be generally positive. I did not see that he was possessed by a spirit of divination.

How easy it is to be deceived! Looking back on it, I can see the symptoms of deception and I shall be a lot more cautious next time the spectacular hits my radar. The effects of this movement have been devastating. Marriages have been wrecked, a church almost destroyed (though now, thankfully being restored), and the prophetic discredited in a whole nation. We should all be careful not to become complacent. If that senior pastor could be deceived, anyone can be.

An interesting example came from the early church (c. AD600).

Deception in a monastery

Deceptions come in many forms. Brother Yun (see Chapter 4 p 103) tells of the infiltration of the Chinese house churches by government spies posing as new converts. Gregory the Great, writing c. AD600, tells of an incident in the province of Valeria which caused a devout abbot, called Equitius, some trouble.

As a young man, Equitius, like many others, had suffered from violent temptations of a sexual nature. He had prayed fervently for help. One night, he had received a vision. He saw himself being made a eunuch, while an angel watched over him (see Matthew 19:11–12). From then on, he was completely freed from all temptations of this sort.

Gradually, he became a leader of various communities, both for men and women. He was renowned for his holiness, and pastoral insight. On one occasion, the local Bishop brought him a man called Basil who said that he was a monk, and who wanted to join a monastery under the direction of Abbot Equitius. Equitius took one look at the man and said to the Bishop, "Father, the man who you recommend looks to me like a devil and not a monk."

The Bishop insisted that Basil was accepted, and Equitius took him into his community. Soon afterwards, Equitius was called away on an evangelistic mission, some distance from his monastery. While he was absent, a nun in one of the convents which was also under his care, fell ill. She had a high fever. In this state she kept shouting "I am going to die, unless the monk Basil comes to cure me!"

When they heard about this, the monks were very unwilling to let anyone visit the convent, least of all Basil who was so new to their community. They sent a messenger to their abbot. Equitius, when he heard the news, smiled and said, "The nun who is sick is hysterical. The fever has now left her, and she is no longer asking for Basil. As to Basil, he is a devil – tell him to leave the monastery!"

On investigation, it turned out that Equitius was correct. A number of magicians had recently been arrested in Rome. Basil, who was unsurpassed in his skills in the magic arts, had managed to escape – disguised as a monk. The Abbot returned, and discovered that the nun had indeed been cured exactly when the words of healing had been spoken.[9]

Christians are remarkably gullible! At least twice I have been deceived, once by a wandering "charismatic friar" who claimed to have gifts of prophecy and healing. For a short time, he seemed like a gift to a parish that was just awakening to such matters. Fortunately, before he could do much harm, and just as we were realising that we had been deceived, he disappeared as suddenly as he had come.

Guarding against such deceptions is never easy. Some people, like the abbot in my previous story, have the gift of discernment. Mark Stibbe's account of the trouble caused by Hans has a number of classic features, notably the persuasive power of the apparently gifted prophet counterbalanced by the misuse of Scripture and a general feeling of unease. We must learn to test such people.

Those who are genuine, are always willing to have their ideas and their prophetic guidance tested (see 1 Thessalonians 5:21), are quite humble, and open to correction. Those who are not genuine usually resent any sort of testing and assume an air of self-righteous infallibility.

Satan is at his most dangerous when he infiltrates in this sort of way. The result, unless the deception is quickly discerned, is invariably disunity and spiritual disaster.

Stratagem (4) Develop your psychic gifts

There are many warnings in Scripture about the 'signs' that Satan can perform.

The Lord said to Moses and Aaron, "When Pharaoh says to you 'Perform a miracle,' then say to Aaron, 'Take your staff and throw it down before Pharaoh,' and it will become a snake." So Moses and Aaron went to Pharaoh and did just as the Lord commanded. Aaron threw his staff down in front of Pharaoh and his officials, and it became a snake. Pharaoh then summoned the wise men and sorcerers, and the Egyptian magicians also did the same things by their secret arts. Each one threw down his staff and it became a snake. But Aaron's staff swallowed up their staffs. Yet Pharaoh's heart became hard and he would not listen to them, just as the Lord had said. (Exodus 7:8–13)

For false Christs and false prophets will appear and perform signs and miracles to deceive the elect – if that were possible. So be on your guard; I have told you everything ahead of time. But in those days, following that distress, "the sun will be darkened, and the moon will not give its light; . . ." (Mark 13:22–24)

The coming of the lawless one will be in accordance with the work of Satan displayed in all kinds of counterfeit miracles, signs and wonders, and in every sort of evil that deceives those who are perishing. They perish because they refused to love the truth and so be saved. (2 Thessalonians 2:9–10)

And he performed great and miraculous signs, even causing fire to come down from heaven to earth in full view of men. Because of the signs he was given power to do on behalf of the first beast, he deceived the inhabitants of the earth. He ordered them to set up an image in honour of the beast. (Revelation 13:13–14a)

I have received a substantial testimony on this subject, and it will form the basis of the next chapter. At this stage, I would reiterate that the fruit of all such "signs" must be tested. Are the people who perform signs basing their lives upon the teach-ings of Jesus? Are their lives built on his words, and their deeds done in his name, and at the "will of my Father who is in heaven"? (Matthew 7:21)

Elsewhere Jesus said, of the Holy Spirit,

> "But when he, the Spirit of truth, comes, he will guide you into all truth. He will not speak on his own; he will speak only what he hears, and he will tell you what is yet to come. He will bring glory to me by taking from what is mine and making it known to you."(John 16:13–14)

True signs bring glory to Jesus, false signs bring glory (and often financial gain!) to man.

Stratagem (5) False appearances and false prophecies

St Anthony (c. 251–356) was a great Saint, and much sought after for advice, prayer and healing. His ministry was effective. A number of testimonies are given in *Vie d'Antoine*, written by Athanasius (c. 296-373).[10] Here is a general comment:

> This is what he prescribed to his visitors. He had compassion on the sick and would pray with them. Often, and for many things, the Lord would grant his request. When this happened, he would never boast, and when it didn't he would not complain, always giving thanks to the Lord and encouraging the sick to be patient and to recollect that to bring healing belonged neither to him nor to any man, but to God alone, who heals when and whom he wants.
>
> The sick would accept the old man's words as a healing in them-selves, for they learned to not be discouraged, but rather to be patient. And those who were healed learned to give thanks not to Anthony but to the Lord alone.

He was frequently attended by evil powers, often pretending to be from God. Here are two sections from the book which illus-trate Satan's tricks, and Anthony's defence.

Once a demon appeared, seeming to be of great size, and dared to say: "I am the power of God and I am Providence. What would you like me to grant you?" So I breathed on him even harder, whilst naming Christ and forced myself to hit him, and I think I did succeed in doing this. Immediately, this enormous demon disappeared with all his minions at the name of Christ.

Once, whilst I was fasting, the Deceiver himself came in the guise of a monk. He seemed to be carrying bread, and he gave me advice, saying, "Eat, give up all these efforts; you're only a man like me, and you'll make yourself ill."

But I spotted his tactic and got up to pray. He didn't like this; he disappeared and seemed to go out of the window like a puff of smoke. How often, in the desert, did he show me gold, apparently, with the sole aim of getting me to touch it and look at it.

But I would say a psalm against him, and he would disappear. Often they would strike me, and I would say *"Nothing can separate me from the love of Christ."* And after that they would strike one another even more forcibly.

But it wasn't me who would make them stop and cause them to become powerless, it was the Lord who said, *"I saw Satan fall like lightning."* So, my children, remembering the word of the Apostle, I offer myself as an example, so that you would learn not to become discouraged in your ascetic life, and not to be afraid of the appearances of the devil and his demons.

So as not to fear this, you also have this criterion at your disposal. When an apparition comes, in order not to succumb to fear you must begin by interrogating him on his nature. *"Who are you, where do you come from?"*

If it is a vision of saints, they will reassure you and change your fear into joy. But if it is a demonic vision, it will immediately weaken on seeing a bold spirit. In effect the simple act of asking, *"Who are you, where do you come from?"* is a sign of imperturbability. So Jesus learnt by interrogating.

St Anthony had a great influence in his generation. His holy life led many to seek his spiritual wisdom, and prayer. The ferocious, yet subtle, attacks from evil powers show how important his witness was.

Spiritualist attack

Much more difficult is the deception caused by spiritism, spirit guides, and the like. It is a particular problem in the healing ministry.[11] Many "healers" call themselves Christians, yet act completely independently of the Body of Christ and of the guidelines of Scripture. I well remember going to a meeting in a house on the edge of a Cathedral close. About 50 people were packed into the living room. The visiting speaker was an itinerant Pentecostal preacher. He gave a lengthy exposition of the connection between the prophecy of Isaiah 53 and the Healing Ministry of Jesus.[12] People were getting restless. "Why doesn't he get on with the healing?" was a fairly frequent comment. When he did start to pray two very different things happened. Some people were healed, at least one very dramatically. One lady took off some bandages for her leg, and some skin ulcers had completely disappeared. Then other people started to queue up for prayer. I joined the queue. I was just beginning to suffer from a very bad hip problem. The lady in front of me asked for prayer. The visitor declined to pray for her. "I can't pray for you, you are a spiritualist." "What does that matter?" she replied. There was a considerable argument, and the meeting descended into chaos. The visiting preacher had uncovered a nest of spiritualism, led by a local canon's wife. Years later, I met the preacher. I asked about his memories of that evening in a Cathedral city. He told me that it had caused him great distress and that he had even been accused of stealing some of his hostess' jewels!

Sacred texts

Many sacred texts claim implicitly, or explicitly, to be inspired by angels. The problem for Christians is that these claims invariably cut across fundamental Christian beliefs. Christians have two alternatives, either to deny the inspiration of Scripture, or to challenge other religious texts where they oppose what is written in the Bible.

The Koran is very relevant to this debate. To Muslims, it is *the* Holy Book, to be trusted as infallible, and in one sense untranslatable from the original Arabic. It is generally believed (although this is not specifically claimed in the text) to have been dictated by Jabrail (the angel Gabriel), the angel of Revelation, to the Prophet Mohammed.

The Koran presents a very different view of angels to that given in the Bible. Sura II tells of the angels being presented to Adam. The angels bow down to Adam, acknowledging him as the Lord's viceroy on earth.[13] One of their number, named Iblis, rebels and becomes the leader of the opposition.

Later, in Sura XXXVIII, Iblis asks for respite from his curse, given as a result of his earlier disobedience; this is granted and he is given permission to pervert all except the sincere servants of Allah.

Sura XIII tells of God's attendant angels who can bring protection, and destruction; Sura XLII speaks of angels praising God in the heavens, and asking forgiveness for those on earth. For the most part, their role is destructive and concerned with the judgment and doom of unbelievers.

The cycle of stories concerning Abraham and Sarah, the promise of the birth of Isaac, and the destruction of Sodom (Genesis 18 and 19) are told in several Suras (XI, XV, XXIX, and LI) with significant differences from the texts of the Bible. Abraham is suspicious and afraid of the angels when they fail to eat his food, Sarah is present (not an eavesdropper) when Isaac's birth is promised, and Lot's wife is doomed to stay in Sodom.

Angels (Sura III) and God's Spirit (Sura XIX) come to tell Mary of the forthcoming birth of Jesus. The birth is portrayed as miraculous, Mary is suitably puzzled (as in Luke 1:34), but the birth takes place under a palm tree. Her family reject her, telling her she has committed a monstrous thing. At the end of the second account, the prophet is told that it "is not for God to take a son".

Although Jesus is acknowledged as a great prophet, there are no angels at his Resurrection – for the simple reason that there is no Resurrection in the Koran. Sura IV, in a crucial divergence from Scripture, states that the Jews were unbelieving, uttered a mighty calumny against Mary, and did not slay Jesus, Son of Mary, the Messenger of God. "They did not slay him, neither crucified him, only a likeness of that was shown to them."

Thus Jesus and Mary are to be honoured, Jesus' teachings (when correctly interpreted) are to be listened to, but the Atonement is negated, the Resurrection bypassed, and the Gift of the Spirit ignored. By contrast, Sura LXI tells of a messenger called Ahmad, whose coming Jesus prophesied.

Christians will obviously treat the Koran with respect; they will agree with some of its moral teaching, but they will inevitably regard parts of it as false – *otherwise they end up denying many of the central beliefs of their own faith.*

While such a statement obviously creates huge difficulties for interfaith worship; it doesn't rule out sensible dialogue. Many Muslims seem much to prefer Christians to remain true to their scriptures, rather than search for a compromise which ultimately denies the truth of either faith. Good relationships between people of widely different beliefs depend on integrity, and respect for one another as people, however much we may differ in our understanding of God's Revelation.

The Book of Mormon

The Book of Mormon, and the strange story of the Angel Mormon's approach to Joseph Smith, presents us with similar choices. Many of the Mormon doctrines, and the dictated golden plates (hidden, found, and then lost), are contrary to Christianity. Many Mormons seem charming and hard working, and they are faithful and dedicated in propagating their faith. But once again, we have the dilemma. The Bible and the Book of Mormon cannot both be true. From a biblical perspective, we are forced to challenge Joseph Smith's account, and face the consequences.[14]

There are also "Christian" doctrines, which appear to have been promulgated by deceiving spirits. A particular example is the so-called "prosperity" Gospel which, at its worst, implies that if you tithe your wealth (to a particular preacher), you will be blessed with material prosperity (viz. Malachi 3:6–12 is an example). This teaching, which is completely at variance with Jesus' teaching (Luke 12:32–34), has stimulated greed in the rich West, and chaos in poor Third World countries.

Stratagem (6) Lure people into dark arts

This is really outside the scope of this book. It is difficult to know how successful Satan has been in acquiring active soldiers. Rare books like *From Witchcraft to Christ*[15] tell us about the active work of covens. The Transformations Videos[16] tell of spiritual battles which preceded spiritual revival. Often one key person had to be spiritually discerned – rather as Paul discerned and disarmed Elymas in Cyprus (Acts 13:10).

Recently at a conference[17] I met Peterson Sozi, a Ugandan pastor. He told me this remarkable story. It seems very significant that Mwera was a place well known for demon worship, and also the scene of the martyrdom of some of the first Christian converts in the 1880s. Soon after the gospel came to Uganda, the King of Buganda killed 21 Christians by fire. His chief executioner, called Malajanga, came from this village, and is buried there.

Mwera Community Transformation

Patrick Kigozi was a powerful witchdoctor. He was based in Mwera, where he had three simple aids – a gourd, through which he used to speak to his wife as though it was a mobile phone, a small drum, and a shrine at his ancestral village. The shrine was a "ground station" dedicated to the devil. From there, he co-ordinated his considerable powers. Unusually for Uganda, there was no church in the village. One day he had a duel with another witchdoctor to see who had the most Satanic power. They gave each other 30 minutes to kill the other, each using his power. The other witchdoctor failed. Then, with most of the villagers watching,

Patrick exercised his powers. The other man was killed. The police came to investigate how and why the other man had died. They arrested many villagers, and they were taken to the police headquarters at Mpigi, and locked up. Patrick was not arrested. The next day, he went to the police, and told them that the villagers were innocent – adding that they were free to lock him up instead of the innocent villagers. The villagers were released, and Patrick was locked up in a secure police cell. Soon afterwards, Patrick escaped without opening the door. (A sort of demonic equivalent of Acts 12?)

In early 1990, Pastor Sozi was leading a "Back to God" evangelistic mission in Katwe, a suburb of Kampala. The outreach included gospel singing, testimonies, teaching about HIV/AIDS awareness, showing Christian films, and evangelistic preaching and counselling. The message, as often in Africa, was well amplified! On the final night, Patrick Kigozi heard the message, and the Word of God touched him deeply.

The next day, he made his way back to the Crusade ground looking for the preacher. The locals directed him to the First Presbyterian Church, and someone from the church directed him to Pastor Sozi's house in Kasubi.

When he found Pastor Sozi, Patrick related how he had been convicted by the message, and indicated that he wanted to surrender his life to Jesus. Pastor Sozi encouraged him to repent of his sins, and accept Jesus as his Saviour. Patrick interrupted – saying that he did not think that he could be saved because he was a powerful witch doctor, a member of the national executive of witch doctors in Uganda. He added that the demons that he worshipped were very powerful, and were capable of killing the pastor and himself! The pastor assured him that Jesus had enough power to destroy all satanic powers, and that nothing would happen to him if he gave his life to Jesus. The witch doctor gained some faith, and prayed to receive Jesus into his life (see John 1:12).

After the prayer, Pastor Sozi asked Patrick about the fetishes which he had been using, and said that they should immediately be destroyed by fire. Patrick said that he used few fetishes – just the gourd, the drum, and the shrine.

Pastor Sozi realised that Patrick was not a simple witch doctor, and mobilised a team for action. He went to the National Television Studio, and obtained a camera crew who could film all that was going to happen. Patrick had several shrines, in the Kampala area, where he used to meet his clients. The gourd and the drum were duly collected, and they drove to Mwera. Their vehicle was mounted with a megaphone, and they drove around the village informing them that Patrick Kigozi now believed in Jesus, and that at 2 p.m. his shrine and fetishes were going to be publicly burnt!

Many of the villagers ran to Patrick's house to see what would happen. They couldn't believe that he could be saved, and expected the demons to destroy Patrick, and/or, the evangelists.

At 2 p.m., Pastor Sozi, with a small group of born-again Christians, started to worship God. They continued in prayer while Pastor Sozi and Patrick set fire to the drum and the gourd. When these were reduced to ashes, the shrine was burnt to the ground. Near the shrine, the ground station, full of rare plants, which had been planted after nine days of satanic ritual and animal sacrifices, was dug up and cleansed in the name of Jesus!

Patrick Kigozi and Peterson Sozi were unharmed. The villagers were amazed and impressed. They met together, destroyed their own satanic shrines, and unanimously agreed to give ten acres of land to "Back to God" ministry so that a school could be built. They wanted their children taught about Jesus!

The American Embassy in Kampala helped to construct a four-classroom block for over four hundred children. The Ambassador himself came to open the school. Of course, there are still many needs. Most of the children who attend the school are orphans, having lost their parents either to AIDS, or in the civil wars. Pastor Sozi is looking for more partners to establish this school for the glory of God![18]

These sorts of stories seem very strange to most Western Christians. It is important to understand that these are places where Satan wields immense and obvious power. For the most part, Satan is content to have people innocently pursuing "harmless" practices – practices that will make it much harder for them to turn to Christ.

> The god of this age has blinded the minds of unbelievers, so that they cannot see the light of the gospel of the glory of Christ, who is the image of God. (2 Corinthians 4:4)

The veil, which is naturally over all our eyes, seems *more firmly* fixed over those who have strayed into these matters. The next chapter is a testimony to God's grace in delivering one person from the clutches of these sorts of things.

My own limited experience suggests that there are places where the witch doctors have unusual power (see p 21f). There also seem to be places where Satanists have chosen to meet for whatever purpose. I have visited quarries, disused railway tunnels and the like, where to the discerning eye there were clear signs of Satanic activity. Once in a tunnel, I felt a very evil presence. An experienced exorcist had the same experience. As I put out my hand to touch a niche in the tunnel, I felt a sort of spiritual shock, which was profoundly unpleasant. The exorcist was certain that this was a place where senior members of a local coven were empowered for leadership. Another exorcist discerned that a disused railway bridge evoked very dark spiritual feelings. He was convinced that very unpleasant things had taken place there. A few years later, independently, another experienced woman of prayer felt something very similar in the same place.

The strangler fig

Occasionally, people are trapped by powerful experiences,

without even realising what has happened to them. Recently I had the privilege of praying with a woman, who it is best not to name (I write with her permission), a refugee from an African country. Her heartbreaking story, in summary, was this:

> My parents had difficulty in conceiving. After fifteen years, they went to a witch doctor. His spells were efficacious and I was born. Aged fourteen, I was sent to my future mother-in-law's house. She, knowing my parent's difficulties, took me to a witch doctor so that I would conceive. My husband was a successful businessman. I was so ill after the birth of my first child that I ran home to my parents. They sent me back. My husband went into politics. He was on the side of the government, and had quite a prominent position. He accompanied me to the hospital when I was pregnant with my second child. He was disgusted by the state of the hospital, and tried to get something done politically. When my third child was born, he found there had been no improvement. He joined the opposition.
>
> On New Year's Day 1997, we were arrested. He was effectively told to keep out of politics or be killed. He was very determined and wouldn't be silenced. In May 1997, he was murdered in police custody. I, and my youngest two children, were helped to escape to England. My eldest is still in hiding in the African country.

For five years, she has struggled to make a new life in England. She has been helped by good Christian friends. She made much progress, but was locked into grief, self-pity and anger.

When we began to pray, it appeared to be a problem of unforgiveness – she needed to forgive the President, the police, her husband ("if he hadn't been so obstinate this needn't have happened"), her mother-in-law, and her parents. We made little progress until, by the Holy Spirit, a word which was the name of the witch doctor's controlling spirit (the one her parents went to) was revealed. As soon as that happened, she was transformed. "That's it!" she screamed, and behaved for a few minutes like a powerful witch doctor – screaming, chanting, and displaying blazing eyes. After some quiet prayer, the spirit was released. She slept for the next week, and soon afterwards was able to pray to forgive all those who had hurt her. We made the important distinction between forgiveness and justice – we could pray for justice, but still pray for forgiveness for those who had murdered her husband.

This story illustrates my point that occult problems cling very deeply to people, and make it hard for them to receive Christ in the first place, and to forgive others. My friend had received Christ, but couldn't make any real spiritual progress because of her grief and understandable anger.

Her experience reminds me of the strangler figs in Africa. A large bird, often a hornbill, drops the seed of a fig in the crown of a growing tree. The fig takes root and slowly grows *downwards*. It is not particularly dangerous, just unsightly, until years later it reaches the ground and takes root. At this stage, the host tree is in real danger of destruction.[19]

For the most part, Satan is content to have people innocently pursuing "harmless" practices – practices that will make it much harder for them to turn to Christ.

A Christian response

Faced with this plethora of subtle, and sometimes open, stratagems, it is easy for the Christian to despair. We would be wise to remember the words of Elisha to his frightened servant "those who are with us are more than those who are with them" (2 Kings 6:16). We need to remember that the victory has been won.

> And having disarmed the powers and authorities, he made a public spectacle of them, triumphing over them by the cross. (Colossians 2:15)

Oscar Cullmann,[20] in 1944 in the midst of the war, *working in Germany*, used a prophetic image about the outcome of the war. "The decisive battle has been fought, victory has been

secured (through the Normandy landings), but the cease-fire –
Victory Day, has not yet come."

Victory Day for Christians will come. Isaiah puts it very
powerfully. Read these two contrasting prophecies and take
heart!

> Keep on, then, with your magic spells and with your many
>   sorceries,
> which you have laboured at since childhood.
> Perhaps you will succeed, perhaps you will cause terror.
> All the counsel you have received has only worn you out!
> Let your astrologers come forward,
> those stargazers who make predictions month by month,
> let them save you from what is coming upon you.
> Surely they are like stubble, the fire will burn them up.
> They cannot even save themselves from the power of the flame.
> Here are no coals to warm anyone; here is no fire to sit by.
> That is all they can do for you – these you have laboured with
> and trafficked with since childhood.
> Each of them goes on in his error; there is not one that can save
>   you. (Isaiah 47:12–15)

> How beautiful on the mountains are the feet of those who bring
>   good news,
> who proclaim peace, who bring good tidings,
> who proclaim salvation, who say to Zion, "Your God reigns!"
> Listen! Your watchmen lift up their voices; together they shout for
>   joy.
> When the Lord returns to Zion, they will see it with their own eyes.
> Burst into songs together, you ruins of Jerusalem,
> for the Lord has comforted his people, he has redeemed Jerusalem.
> The Lord will lay bare his holy arm, in the sight of all the nations,
> and all the ends of the earth will see the salvation of our God.
> (Isaiah 52:7–10)

That is the Christian hope. Every time we see a small victory
against the dark powers, we are reminded of the far greater
victory won on the first Easter Day, and the final victory to be

won when "The Son of Man is going to come in his Father's glory with his angels" (see Matthew 16:27).

Notes

(1) Philip Pullman's *His Dark Materials* trilogy, Point, London, 1995, is a very readable recent example of this genre.

(2) Laeh Maggie Garfield and Jack Grant, *Angels and Companions in Spirit,* Celestial Arts, 1984, pp. 90–99.

(3) Richard Webster, *Spirit Guides and Angel Guardians,* Llewellyn Publications, 2001.

(4) Hope Price, *Angels*, Macmillan, 1993, p. 5.

(5) Richard Webster, *op. cit*, pp. 152–3.

(6) See Chapter 7, pp. 170ff. The quotation is from Section 16 of De Cura Pro Mortius. Included in *Nicene and Post Nicene Fathers* 1st series. Hendricksen, 1995, Vol.3. I have somewhat modernised the English translation (the italics are mine).

(7) See John Woolmer, *Thinking Clearly about Healing and Deliverance*, Monarch, 1999.

(8) See John Woolmer, *op. cit*, pp. 261–4 and elsewhere.

(9) *St Gregory the Great – Dialogues* – translated by O J Zimmerman, New York, 1959, p. 16.

(10) From *Vie d'Antoine* by Athanasius, translated into French by G J M Bartelink in the series Sources Chrétiennes No. 400, sections 40, 43, 56, translated here by Dr Alison Morgan. Athanasius wrote as a contemporary, and as someone who had first hand knowledge of Anthony. His own theological struggles against the Arian heresy were vital in preserving the historic faith in the fourth century.

(11) See John Woolmer, *op. cit,* pp. 275–284.

(12) See John Woolmer, *op. cit,* p. 96ff and 293ff for a different viewpoint.

(13) *The Koran*, translated by A. Arberry, Oxford World Classics, 1998, is an excellent English translation. Strictly

speaking, the Koran is untranslatable and only available to those who read Arabic.

(14) See, for instance, Francis J. Beckwith, *The New Mormon Challenge*, Grand Rapids, Zondervan, 2002.

(15) Doreen Irvine, *From Witchcraft to Christ,* Concordia, 1973.

(16) Transformations Videos are distributed by Gateway Christian Media, PO 11905 London NW10 4ZQ.

(17) "Transforming Communities" at Swanwick, UK, December 2002, hosted by ARM (Anglican Renewal Ministries), SOMA, (Sharing of Ministries abroad), and Springboard (the Archbishops' initiative for evangelism).

(18) For more information about "Back to God Ministry" visit their website www.gobacktogod.com

(19) The Fig Tree Arch in the Arusha National Park in Tanzania is a classic example. The fig tree has grown so large that you can drive a vehicle beneath where it has divided. The host tree disappeared many years ago.

(20) Oscar Cullmann, *Prayer in the New Testament,* SCM, 1995, p. 46ff.

10

Jesus Spells Freedom

This chapter is substantially a testimony from someone who came out from an active involvement in shamanism into a radiant Christian discipleship. We shall see the subtle attraction of "apparently harmless" contact with the "spirit" world, and how Jesus can come to set people free.

Jesus Spells Freedom

I first met Deborah at a prayer day that I was taking for J. John's Just Ten Mission in Bath. I was impressed by her sincerity, her stability, and her positive desire to warn others of the dangers of the things she had practised.

She gave a powerful testimony during the Mission and helped me with the Channel 4 programme *The Good, the Bad, and the Pagans* which was transmitted in the Spring of 2001. Her clear testimony is both a warning and an encouragement. Most Christians know little about these matters. Deborah's journey, which involved much suffering, is a very post-modern one. She had little understanding of Christianity, a gentle drift into the world of spirit guides, and the likelihood of a life clouded by a parasol of strange spiritual experiences and personal chaos. In this situation, through a concerned Christian friend, Deborah sought advice and heard the very voice of God, the angel of light was exposed, and the world of shamanism collapsed at the "sound of rushing waters" (Revelation 1:15). Deborah has written here in great detail about shamanism, which clearly has an *attractive* side to it. Deborah's experience was of people who were often kind, well meaning, wanting to bring healing to others. They have discovered a different supernatural world, and would often not know that the church, too, was in touch with the supernatual – albeit from a very different perspective. The people who practise it are neither obviously evil, nor particularly weird. They *genuinely* believe they are discovering God, and channelling his light and energy to others. Satan sells his wares with great subtlety. Why promote black magic when something gentler, and far more beguiling, can achieve the same result? Religious language and Christian terminology, are used to couch dubious activities.

"Tarot, astrology, and other divinatory procedures are under the protection of archangels, who keep the unready from access to more than they can handle" is a typical quotation.[1]

This story is a warning about the subtlety of Satan's deception, and an encouragement for us to pray for others to experience the freedom and salvation that God gave to her.

Deborah's testimony

I was born a Jew, into a humanist, Labour Party, agnostic and very loving household. School RE was no more to me than ancient literature, maybe history. At University, I sang in chapel choirs as a means of accessing colleges with better dinners. The psalms were an exercise in elegant phrasing and breath control. The bells of Durham Cathedral cut into my work next door in the music faculty every quarter of an hour; I used the sound in an electronic composition. The only time I entered the Cathedral for other than musical reasons, after the death of a beloved aunt, I found solace in a shaft of dusty sunlight by Norman pillars.

I heard much more sacred music when I married a conductor who specialised in Renaissance liturgical reconstructions. I especially recall his performance of Lassus' Lamentations for Good Friday: Clive brought the music to an utter hush – emptiness and fullness met at the moment Jesus gave up the ghost. But I was only aware of art, the human heart, and some unfathomable sense of something other I could not name. I thought Jesus was a nice man who had died.

Eighteen months into our marriage, Clive fell ill with encephalitis. It destroyed large areas of his brain that have to do with memory.

The ambulance dropped him at the hospital 17 years ago and he has not come home yet. He lives in care. Some people wrote to me of healing and miracles, others of the benefits of aloe vera or other herbal preparations. One doctor described my husband as a deceptive proxy – a corpse the undertaker has forgotten to take away. Virtually everyone told me to move on, live again, marry elsewhere. But we still loved each other, we still do. The Cliveness of Clive was undiminished and, though the scientists wrote reams about his amnesia, enumerating norms and deficits, none of their tests could measure the most essential of qualities – love and identity and consciousness – his capacity to still be absolutely himself.

My need to try to elucidate what my heart knew all along led to a compulsion to write. I attempted to track truth with a pen – but it was slippery and I could never seem to find a name for the treasures I knew deep in my heart. The fault, I reckoned, must lie with my writing skills. At a point where I could not bear to live in the same country as Clive and not visit him – and after eight years solid campaigning for brain-injured people in similar predicaments – I sold everything and apprenticed myself to writers and poets in New York.

The creative artist is often aware of tapping into a higher consciousness. You write things you couldn't have known, paint images before you see them. Identical myths sprang up in different cultures before man could travel. I was curious to know, where did the writing come from? I read Jung and Joseph Campbell, philosophers and psychologists. I had long been intrigued by the phenomena of brain and mind and aware of some other part of us I called spirit, which seemed to connect to a universal spirit or nature. I was especially struck by coincidences and would often marvel at the abundance of these in my life.

In New York I found what appeared to be the answer to my quest. Here I came across a live tradition of shamanism, not only among the indigenous people, but taught by anthropologists who had put down their notebooks and joined in. There were workshops on every street corner. Using the simple techniques of "medicine men", anyone could send their spirit journeying to spirit guides and thereby appear to accomplish many useful tasks: they claimed to find lost children, know where to hunt buffalo or heal disease. More usually in modern society, people used shamanism as a short-cut to personal revelation, obviating the protracted and tedious processes of psycho-therapy and psycho-analysis which so many New Yorkers had come to rely on. This sounded like a route to the place where the writing happened and, possibly, to an appropriate miracle for my husband.

One spring Saturday I enrolled for a workshop in Greenwich Village. My fellow students were pleasant and interesting, many from the caring professions – nurses, teachers, social workers, the odd police officer feeling the need to develop a sixth sense, people from every walk of life. I heard that the American military were quietly calling in shamans where their surgeons had failed. The word "occult" was never mentioned, and I do not believe those practising shamanism had any idea they were practising a dark art.

So, what is shamanism? To the casual observer or anthropologist, there may not be much to see – perhaps just someone lying on the floor with their eyes closed. However, it is a supernatural experience. Most people, having not had the benefit of seeing the Holy Spirit at work in churches, are amazed in the first place to discover incontrovertible evidence of the supernatural. Such is the deception, that they do not stop to wonder if it is safe, and are only satisfied that it is real. The teachers and practitioners work with care and integrity. It appears to be harmless and helpful.

At this point I wonder whether a description of the experience could seem attractive to any Christian who may not enjoy a rich prayer life, or who is not deeply rooted in Jesus, in the Word. Pray now that if what you read next sounds too interesting, then the LORD will reveal that all of the visions, miracles, signs and wonders in His Word are also literally true and that His infinite power is accessible to you today. Remember that Pharaoh's magicians matched most of the signs and wonders Moses and Aaron performed, and if you do not feel your own ministry is as powerful as what I am about to describe, then ask the Holy Spirit and the church to teach you more. Like the messenger reporting to Job after Satan's first attack – "the fire of God fell from the sky" (Job 1:16), – a miraculous sign also prophesied for one of the satanic trinity, (Revelation 13:13) – shamanic practitioners assume, as I did, that the signs and wonders they witness are from God. I saw no difference between myself and Christians. I thought we both had different routes to the same God, only mine was more interesting. Conversely, I have come across people calling themselves Christians who see signs and wonders performed by the Holy Spirit in the name of Jesus, and think it must be black magic, as if they doubted God's power as attested throughout the Holy Scriptures.

Some may advise that you can discern deception by the lack of "fruit". But many are convinced that their lives are enhanced by "alternative" spiritual practices, from feng shui and reiki to chanting and yoga; they will witness to the beneficial effects on their finances, health and relationships. Equally, someone who follows Jesus might be in wilderness time as a potter works on clay. Jesus told us that people would hate us because of Him. He tells us "the kingdom of heaven is like a merchant looking for fine pearls. When he found one of great value, he went away and sold everything he had and bought it" (Matthew 13:45–46). We are asked to lay down our lives, give everything, for Jesus, and we gladly do so for love of Him. But the world may not always see measurable fruit, and neither perhaps may we until we get to heaven. But we will get there. If the LORD had not plucked me from this dangerous path, I would have ended up in the Lake of Fire for eternity. Think of that and praise God. And pray that the LORD will lead you to others so deceived and use you to lead them straight into the arms of Jesus.

(It is interesting that I had not thought about shamanism, and indeed had forgotten it, in the three years since being saved: the LORD is gracious. I am now recalling it for the purposes of this piece, and only after He has rooted me firmly in my life with Him and in the Word.)

This, then, is a brief description of shamanism, which is hugely popular in the US and, last time I looked (1999) on the rise in the UK. The Foundation for Shamanic Studies in the USA promotes and protects shamanism in cultures around the world. It is largely practised by ordinary educated well-meaning people.

No-one calls themselves a "shaman" or "medicine man" but the name is earned through others acknowledging a person's verifiable and sustained authority in the spirit world. Most call themselves "shamanic practitioners". The individual journeys in the spirit to one of three other realities – lower world, middle world or upper world. The process is called a "shamanic journey". Instead of praying about something, they "journey on it". People visiting any of these worlds for the first time will have classic experiences, "seeing" similar landscapes and meeting similar spirit guides, thus confirming to them that this is a real, rather than an imagined, experience. Practitioners journeying at the same time may arrive at the same place, and come back with similar guidance, further confirming the reality of these experiences. When I journeyed for a complete stranger about the source of her pain (not knowing the nature of her pain), the spirit took me up and flew me to an island glittering in the sea. I drew the shape of the island and the peninsular next to it afterwards; she gasped and said that it was the island off the coast of Florida where she grew up. From the first workshop, most students go home with access to the world of spirit and a personal relationship with a guide.

The spirits of the lower world tend to be animals. On the first journey, practitioners meet a power animal who acts as key guide and protector. It is said to be unsafe to venture forward without one's power animal leading the way. A person can have more than one power animal; they present themselves according to the nature of the mission. The guide to the middle world is usually an animal too, but spirit guides to the upper world mostly appear in human form. In my case it manifested as a writer from another century I much admired. "He" looked at me with loving eyes and appeared to be helping me with my writing.

Landscapes of the lower world start rocky and dark but open out into lush green meadows or desert rock or caves or jungle or surreal places. The middle world is just this world and one skirts the globe, crossing seas quickly or moving through a city like superman, flying to a particular street. Most people know something of this experience from flying dreams. The upper world is reached through about seven layers of cloud, sometimes a sea of flowers and then one pushes through a membrane around the earth and arrives in space before going onto some surreal and peculiar landscape perhaps on a planet. Watching TV, I have seen a rise in the incidence of shamanic-looking landscapes, especially in advertisements. This is not a pastime for the kooky few, but has penetrated right through society.

A journey goes like this. One chooses which of the three worlds seems appropriate for the mission. Every practitioner has his or her own points of departure – usually a real place. You see it in your mind's eye while preparing to journey. A tree hollow, well, spring or animal burrow goes to the lower world; from a looking-glass, cleft rock or the room where one is, are the entrances to the middle world; and the upper world is reached from a chimney, tree, tall plant or tornado. Such shamanic imagery is rife in folklore – Alice's looking glass and rabbit burrow, Santa Claus' chimney, Jack and the Beanstalk and the tornado in the Wizard of Oz to name but a few. Fairy stories seem harmless. So did shamanism. My apartment looked out on the World Trade Center so I imagined leaving from the twin towers.

The first part is, then, imagination – a way of focusing. This point-of-departure work is to get you to where you are going. It's like taking a plane: you buy the ticket, show up at the airport and check in. Then others take over the journey.

The "altered state of consciousness" necessary to the journey is known as "shamanic consciousness". Achieving this is easy (one is always in control and simultaneously aware of the physical world, but attuned to the spirit world). An aid to shamanic consciousness is a regular drumbeat (either live drumming or a tape – the tapes come in durations of 15, 20 or 30 minutes). It goes at a moderate pulse for the journey itself, then switches to a fast pulse to signal it is time to come back to the room and during the return journey. It concludes with a punctuation drumming to signal the journey is at an end. There is said to be a danger in coming back too fast as one might leave a part of one's soul in another world, a case of the shamanic "bends"! This would require a soul retrieval journey. Not everyone uses a drum. The Tibetans use a "singing" bowl or bells and some tribes use drugs, such as the peyote mushroom.

The journeyer goes with a question for the spirit guides, or with a mission, which might be healing a person or some land, soul retrieval, or assisting a soul after death. Shamanic practitioners believe that people become fragmented through the traumas or sadnesses of life and leave soul parts behind. Soul retrieval is their means of finding and returning lost soul parts. When the journeyer is able to tell the journeyed-for (perhaps with no prior knowledge of that person) that they went back to the Californian adobe house where they grew up and witnessed an event that took place there, the journeyed-for is naturally moved and convinced. The soul-retriever calls the split-off soul to come back. The power animal assists (if it is a horse or a bird, the lost part may ride on its back). Then, when the journeyer has returned to the room, he or she will sit up and blow the soul part into the person's chest with three big blows of breath. The person then may spend several days "re-inte-grating" the "lost soul part", perhaps going through a grieving process staved off before. I had several "lost soul parts" "restored" to me, and was sure that the nice lady in Brooklyn performing this task could really "see" my teenage self in Bushy Park, Teddington, England.

The shaman assisting souls after death is known as a "psycho-pomp". A restricted few undertake this because of the perceived dangers. The shaman may "find" a dead person holding onto a soul part of someone living, and the shaman then persuades the deceased to surrender their loved one for the good of both. The psycho-pomp, assisted by sundry power animals would then guide the deceased to its eternal home, and restore the released soul part. No-one ever mentioned hell, although there appeared to be some-thing called "the void" where soul parts might get lost.

The psycho-pomp and other shamans tend to have difficult lives. They see this as an occupational hazard but worth the risks in order to perform what they believe to be an important service to land and people. Often before someone is "called" to become a shaman, they have what is termed a "shamanic illness"; there is typically a period of severe ill health before the onset of an awakened spiritual life. They have no idea that the whole thing is communing with Satan. They do not know that all the visions are deceptions from Hell. They could never imagine that their trusted power animals were really demons.

Any session generally began with "shamanic dancing". We would ask our power animals to dance through us and the dance itself might bring visions that would be helpful later. The church seems to dance very little now, yet there used to be a tradition of calling the Rabbi to dance when someone was sick. Christians today are finding that dancing is a great way to open to the Holy Spirit, who may give dance for healing, prophesy and for anointing or ministering to others (cf. The International Christian Dance

Fellowship). Dance as you worship the LORD and see what happens. Look at David. (See 2 Samuel 6:12–17; Psalm 30:11, Psalm 149:3.)

"Healing" was sometimes done by a team of shamanic practitioners. Some will form a "canoe" pretending to row, while the main shaman does the business, often comprising a dance journey and collecting spirit items to bring to the sick person.

I myself was saved on 10th March 1999 at 7.15p.m. Content with my shamanic route to "God" but not at all content with my life, which was in some considerable chaos, I was on the phone to a Christian friend and asked her to pray for me. As she did so, she broke out into a beautiful language, which I knew to be "tongues". As she prayed, I felt a force come down the telephone and start to fill me up. I dared not move. When the prayer subsided I opened my eyes and saw that my whole room (covered in boxes from a recent move) was sparkling like the countryside in summer after rain. I myself felt utterly clean (though I hadn't realised I was dirty). Then my friend said that God wanted her to tell me something about the shamanism.

"What, no good?" I asked.

"No," she said.

"Oh! Sorry God!" I said.

Then my friend began to pray again, and I felt the force coming into me, this time from above, and filling me up more so that I felt full of new substance, whereas I had previously felt shapeless and disoriented. Then I heard a voice. It was like the whole sky full of thunder, but it was also very intimate, close to my right ear. It was loud with love, and it thundered, "BREAK FREE!" three times. It was only afterwards I remembered that the movies tell you, God speaks with a voice of thunder. At that stage I was not familiar with the Bible (viz. John 12:29).

After the prayer, my friend wanted to check what had actually happened. She asked if I now knew that Jesus was the Son of God and that He had risen from the dead. I did. She asked me, did I believe in re-incarnation. Twenty minutes before I did, but now I did not. She was very happy. I knew for certain that I had met God, maker of all things, right there in my room, and I knew I was changed forever. I knew that all the earlier part of my life had been a lie. These were things I could not have accepted from another person, but I had been given a new heart by God (see Ezekiel 36:25-27).[2]

Having encountered God, Maker of All Things, and heard His voice, I felt rather as if I had seen a UFO – that I should report it to someone official. Whom could I tell? The police? The council? Someone had to know. I looked out of the window and saw a church tower. Perhaps a vicar would be a good place to start. When I reached the church, the door was open, and a "ploughman's lunch" was in full swing. I wandered past the assembled company down the nave and sank tearfully to my knees, thanking God for what He had done for me. When I was done thanking Him, and was heading back past the "ploughman's", a lady caught up with me, welcomed me and gave me a yellow card to fill up. She turned out to be the oldest member of the church, baptised there over 80 years before, and I was the youngest, a member for about five minutes. I was later baptised and confirmed in this church to the bemusement of family and friends, and to my great joy.

Before the baptism I had a bonfire of all the books, drums, rattles, tapes and other new age paraphernalia. This is essential (see Acts 19:19). Make sure there are no animals or small children near the bonfire as spirits can attach themselves (in the same way you can pick up "slime" when laying on hands or doing deliverance if you are working without authority and prayer cover). Don't feel inhibited about praising God, just because you are in the garden. Two or three people there in agreement (see Matthew 18:18–20) would be helpful. Watch the fire until all is burned.

The power of new age symbols and curses appears not always to be understood. I have been horrified to come across churches and synagogues where yoga or the Kabbalah or other new age trash is taught, and have found a Christian choir singing blindly of shamanic symbols from a "Christian" worship book. We know the power of the cross, and the handkerchiefs and aprons touched by Paul (Acts 19:12). So we should concede that objects, songs and signs from wrong sources might by the same principle have satanic power attached, or at the least be dishonouring and painful to our Father. Be very discerning. Ask, is it profane? If dubious, destroy it (in a way that no-one else can retrieve it; burn if possible), whatever its worldly value. God will honour that.

Many people who turn to Jesus from these sorts of experiences, have a difficult spiritual journey. It is as though the ivy of the past continues to try to wound and hamper the growth of the new spiritual being. They seem to be particularly vulnerable to spiritual counter-attack. The church needs to disciple such people with particular care. Often, they are open to the Holy Spirit and understand the real nature of the spiritual battle in a way which others seem to lack.

Deborah was blessed with a wise church, loving friends, and the guidance of the Holy Spirit. She was encouraged to start each day with worship and prayer, to turn to God frequently, committing everything to Him, and to become deeply rooted in His Word. She has been given much insight, both into the subtle folly of her previous path, and also to the need for the church to understand much more fully the reality of these matters.

On Easter Sunday 2002, Clive and Deborah renewed their marriage vows.[3] The pastor wrapped their hands in a gold stole, and Deborah felt that they were experiencing something of eternal quality. The world might regard their marriage as devoid of most essentials, but they are convinced that it is a marriage made in heaven, and are delighted in it. With the angels, they too, we may hope, will worship together "in spirit and in truth".

Notes

(1) The amazing statement came from *Angels and Companions in Spirit*, p. 79, Laeh Maggie Garfield & Jack Grant, Celestial Arts Publishing, 1984. One of the authors claims to be a practising Quaker (see Ch. 7, p. 219).

Another similar book *Spirit Guides and Angel Guardians*, Richard Webster, Llewellyn, 2001, has a chapter with the revealing title "Creating your guardian angel".

(2) This text is often read at Anglican Confirmation Services, and is particularly appropriate. Deborah had felt this

cleansing, she had put away her idols, and, by grace, been given a new heart.

(3) Deborah Wearing is currently writing a book due to be published by Doubleday in 2004, about her husband Clive, his amnesia, and their life together and apart.

11

Of Men and Angels

In this final chapter, we return to the fundamental theological questions raised in the opening chapter which concern the basic truth of the stories cited, the biblical parallels, the fruit, and the dangers of these sorts of spiritual encounters. Finally, we look at some theological issues, and consider why we need a theology of angels in today's world.

Of Men and Angels

O Lord our Governor, how excellent is thy Name in all the world:
thou that hast set thy glory above the heavens!

Out of the mouth of very babes and sucklings hast thou ordained
strength, because of thine enemies: that thou mightest still the
enemy, and the avenger.

For I will consider thy heavens, even the works of thy fingers: the
moon and the stars, which thou hast ordained.

What is man, that thou art mindful of him: and the son of man, that
thou visitest him?

Thou madest him lower than the angels: to crown him with glory
and worship.

Thou makest him to have dominion of the works of thy hands: and
thou hast put all things in subjection under his feet;

All sheep and oxen: yea, and the beasts of the field;

The fowls of the air, and the fishes of the sea: and whatsoever
walketh through the paths of the seas.

O Lord our Governor: how excellent is thy Name in all the world!

(Psalm 8, Book of Common Prayer)

The NIV translates v. 5 "You have made him a *little lower* than
the heavenly beings and crowned him with glory and honour"
(my italics).

This wonderful psalm places man at the centre of God's

260

creative purposes. It outlines both the destiny, and the responsibility of man. Bishop John Taylor, in his prophetic book[1] about the Third World *Enough is Enough* uses the evocative phrase 'non-violent dominion' to describe man's ideal relationship with Creation. This psalm also highlights our spiritual destiny. What does the Psalmist mean by "Thou madest him lower than the angels: to crown him with glory and worship"?

We cannot really compare the role of men and angels – they are manifestly different, both in quality and in scope. Angels, as we have seen, have great limitations; but they act (leaving aside the role of the hostile fallen angels) as God's perfect messengers and agents. There is a sublime mystery about their availability, and about our ability to see them. Man has a different role, and ultimately, according to Scripture, an even more important one. Meanwhile, in our humble, fallen state, we need to learn what God's purposes for us are, and the role of the orders of angels within these purposes. The writer of Hebrews puts it sublimely with his great vision of the future:

> But you have come to Mount Zion, to the heavenly Jerusalem, the city of the living God. You have come to thousands upon thousands of angels in joyful assembly, to the church of the firstborn, whose names are written in heaven. You have come to God, the judge of all men, to the spirits of righteous men made perfect, to Jesus the mediator of a new covenant, and to the sprinkled blood that speaks a better word than the blood of Abel. (Hebrews 12:22–24)

At the end of the first chapter, I raised seven fundamental questions, and it is to these that I now want to return.

1. Are the accounts true?
2. Has the Bible got any similar stories or relevant texts?
3. What fruit came from these events and did they glorify the name of Jesus?
4. What are the dangers of these sorts of experiences?

5. What are the theological issues raised by them?
6. Why is it important to have a theology of angels in today's world?
7. Why do angelic appearances seem so much more common in today's world?

Are the accounts (the eight postcards) true?

I have answered this in more detail at the end of Chapter 1. Obviously they, and the other testimonies in the book, are open to different interpretations. But, as a mathematician, I would maintain that the simplest explanation, the literal one, is most likely to be correct.

Has the Bible got any similar stories or relevant texts?

All the stories in Chapter 1 have scriptural parallels. Peter (Acts 12:1–18) had a miraculous escape from prison. On that occasion, his life was saved by an angel; ultimately, as we know with reasonable certainty, he was imprisoned and executed in Rome.[2] God, sovereignly, protects people; but that protection is not a blanket cover for the rest of their lives. Kenneth had his life saved in China, but he and his wife still suffered imprisonment and danger for many years.[3]

Paul, in Corinth (Acts 18:9–11), and at sea (Acts 27:23), was strengthened by a vision and an angel. Mark Stibbe's experience helped to confirm his calling and to shape his influential ministry.

Stephen's face "was like the face of an angel" (Acts 6:15). Paul wrote that just as Moses' face reflected something of the glory of God (see 2 Corinthians 3:7), so Christians "who with unveiled faces all reflect the Lord's glory, are being transformed into his likeness with ever-increasing glory, which comes from the Lord, who is the Spirit" (2 Corinthians 3:18). Theo's face on St Luke's Day 1990, looked like that to me, as did the Zambian grandmother's face 19 months later. Her sighting of a figure clothed in white is typical of many scriptural experiences where angels are involved (see Acts 1:10, Mark 16:5, John 20:12, etc.).

Martin Cavender's prayer partner was aware of angelic protection in a potentially violent situation. Elisha's servant similarly had his eyes opened (2 Kings 6:8–23). The scale of protection, and the quantity of angels, was obviously much greater in the biblical incident, nevertheless there are similarities.

Henry's dream is an echo of many scriptural stories. Some like Nebuchadnezzar (Daniel 4) apparently experienced repentance and new life through profound dreams.

Rosemary Gooden's protection on the A303, and Clare's experience with her children would seem to be straightforward examples which illustrate Jesus' teaching about guardian angels.

Most of the examples in the rest of the book have clear Scriptural parallels. The obvious exceptions are in the New Age material, which invariably deviates from Scripture, and the "near-death" experiences. I believe the experiences of Curma, baptised by the great Augustine; Dorothy Kerin, Ian McCormack, and the Nigerian Pastor, need to be judged by the next test.

What fruit came from these events and did they glorify the name of Jesus?

As I indicated in Chapter 7, the experiences granted to Curma, Dorothy Kerin, Ian McCormack, and the Nigerian Pastor all seem to have borne great fruit. To hear Reinhard Bonnke talking with such reverence about the Nigerian incident is deeply moving. No triumphalism, no great claims for his ministry, just sheer delight at God's sovereign power.

Similarly, I believe that in all the cases I've cited in the first chapter, and as far as I can tell in others in later chapters, there has been considerable fruit in the people's lives – fruit that has affected others who have been influenced by their testimonies. For example, it was wonderful in August 1999 (and again in May 2002) to hear Father James, priest of the Zambian village which we had visited in 1992 (p 21f) testifying to the great encouragement that visit had been. It was a great privilege to share prayer with him, in circumstances which included dealing with a woman with a powerful evil spirit which spoke to him in fluent French, and a young man who grunted like a pig for about an hour during and after a period of worship. His gentle discernment enabled the young man to be set free later in the evening. Father James confronted a "pig spirit" (which I found very strange until reading Acts 16:16 in Greek, when I realised that the slave girl in Philippi literally was described as having a "python spirit"). As a result, a very disturbed young man was set free. The young man had had a tragic history, which included abduction and near murder from his home in Lusaka, and then being taken many miles north to Chipili in the Luapula province. Here he stayed with relatives who seemed to be deep into witchcraft, and he felt himself taken over in the middle of the night by evil powers. Somehow he had joined the local church choir, and on this occasion, had walked 50 km to take part in our services in the neighbouring parish of Mwenda.

I believe, that all the encounters cited in Chapter 1, helped people grow in faith and expectation. In all cases, the name of Jesus was honoured, and the glory given to him (see John 16:14). I believe that Jesus has been glorified by the ministry of Ken, which has helped set so many troubled people free;[4] by the ministry and writing of Mark;[5] Theo's quiet and holy death was a gentle sign to his family; Martin and Henry have both been greatly used by God;[6] Rosemary's gentle faith is a constant encouragement to others; and Clare's willingness, at some personal cost[7] to minister in Zambia and at home, was greatly influenced by a number of spiritual experiences of which the protection of her youngest child was one of the most significant.

All these people are working in Jesus' vineyard, all bear

witness to his glory, none of them see these experiences as an end in themselves. God's grace has produced fruit; just as it does when revealed in more normal ways!

Another important observation is that all these experiences were *unsought and unexpected.* I am a singularly unobservant person, particularly when engaged in leading a service. Theo's face would have had to shine very dramatically for me to notice. In Muto, we were facing a great deal of spiritual opposition, but God's intervention came in a way that was a complete surprise. He used a local person of no particular spiritual standing, and in a way which superseded our most optimistic prayers.

What are the dangers of these sorts of experience?

The classic warning text is:

> Therefore do not let anyone judge you by what you eat or drink, or with regard to a religious festival, a New Moon celebration, or a Sabbath day. These are a shadow of the things that were to come; the reality, however, is found in Christ. Do not let anyone who delights in false humility and the *worship of angels disqualify you* for the prize. Such a person goes into great detail about what he has seen, and his unspiritual mind puffs him up with idle notions. He has lost connection with the Head, from whom the whole body, supported and held together by its ligaments and sinews, grows as God causes it to grow. (Colossians 2:16–19) (My italics)

This is a solemn warning. Quite simply, it is unacceptable either to worship angels, or to glorify in angelic experiences. If God chooses to give people these sorts of experiences, they can only respond in humble gratitude and holy fear. There is no room for pride, or spiritual one-upmanship. There is no place for setting these experiences over or against Scripture. Such experiences need to be tested. Matthew 24:24 – "For false Christs and false prophets will appear and perform great signs

and miracles to deceive even the elect – if that were possible"
warns us that there will be many false signs in the end times,
and 2 Thessalonians 2:9–11: "The coming of the lawless one
will be in accordance with the work of Satan displayed in all
kinds of counterfeit miracles, signs and wonders, and in every
sort of evil that deceives those who are perishing. They perish
because they refused to love the truth and so be saved. For this
reason God sends them a powerful delusion so that they will
believe the lie" is even more explicit. Deborah's testimony
(Chapter 10) gives a recent example as to why these warnings
are so necessary. There is a danger, too, that practising Christians will cross the boundary set by Scripture, and start to spec-
ulate on what they call "higher things".

Unusual spiritual experience can make for light heads, and
poor theological judgment. Either we will stay close to Jesus,
listening carefully to his word and obeying his voice, or we will
face spiritual shipwreck. Based on his word, we can only rely
on our relationship with Jesus – which is given to us by God's
grace. Good works, and spiritual experiences will follow, not
precede, God's grace. "For it is by grace you have been saved,
through faith – and this not from yourselves, it is the gift of
God – not by works, so that no-one can boast. For we are God's
workmanship, created in Christ Jesus to do good works, which
God prepared in advance for us to do." (Ephesians 2:8–10)

What are the theological issues raised?

At this late stage, I would mention two. First there is a sharp
question about the unfairness of such intervention and protection. Secondly, there is a serious question about the theological
world-view, which these experiences support and encourage.

An unfair world

I wrote, originally, a few days after a horrific train crash caused
by a Landrover leaving a motorway and falling down a railway
embankment. The driver, desperately aware of an oncoming

train, was able to use his mobile phone and dial for help. The emergency services did not have time to alert the train, which was approaching at 120 mph. A week earlier, the train would have been going far slower because of speed restrictions imposed just before as a result of an earlier crash. The passenger train more or less survived the crash, but didn't stay completely on the track. Part of the train lurched to the right just when an incredibly heavily loaded goods train approached in the opposite direction. In the resulting carnage, ten people were killed instantly, many others critically injured, and the driver of the Landrover will have to live with the devastating consequences of a freak accident.

This raises a serious question. If angels could save two lives on the A303, why didn't they prevent this disaster? Behind it lurks a far more sinister question. If angels could save one missionary's life in N.W. China in 1938, where were they at Auschwitz? Where were they on September 11th 2001? A few people may testify to miraculous escapes from the Twin Towers disaster, thousands cannot.

These are sharp questions. Those of us who believe that God intervenes in human affairs cannot avoid them. Oscar Cullmann writes brilliantly with these issues at the centre of his thinking, in his *Prayer in the New Testament*.[8] He faces up to the frequently asked question "How can we pray after Auschwitz?" (see also p 111).

The infant church saw James executed (presumably prayed for) just before Peter's miraculous escape (Acts 12:1–4). Later, second-generation Christians had to face up to the imprisonment, probably caused by betrayal,[9] and then the martyrdom of Peter and Paul under the insane Emperor Nero. Jesus commented on a tragedy when a tower fell (Luke 13:1–5) concluding with an astringent warning implying that life could be short and, "I tell you, no! But unless you repent, you too will all perish." Considering these experiences may cause intellectual and theological pain – but what alternative is there? We live in a world increasingly dominated by materialism and commercial greed, and potential environmental disasters on the one hand; and by superstition, white witchcraft, and non-Christian "spiritualities" on the other. Scripture bears witness to a supernatural God whose grace affects Christians and others in numerous ways.

The driver of the Landrover has been found guilty of causing the accident. If we drive when overtired, or otherwise distracted, we can hardly expect angelic protection from the consequences of our selfishness. Sometimes huge consequences come from relatively small mistakes.

A dangerous world-view

Throughout Christian history, men and women have had extraordinary experiences of guidance, protection and visions. These have been used by the Holy Spirit to encourage and strengthen the faithful, and also as challenges, or warnings to those outside the Kingdom. Our Task is to bear unstinting witness to what God is doing in his world, and to be open to all that he is offering. We should follow the wise advice of St Paul and St John:

> Be joyful always; pray continually; give thanks in all circumstances, for this is God's will for you in Christ Jesus. Do not put out the Spirit's fire; do not treat prophecies with contempt. Test everything. Hold on to the good. Avoid every kind of evil. (1 Thessalonians 5:16–22)

> Dear friends, do not believe every spirit, but test the spirits to see whether they are from God, because many false prophets have gone out into the world. This is how you can recognise the Spirit of God: Every spirit that acknowledges that Jesus Christ has come in the flesh is from God, but every spirit that does not acknowledge Jesus is not from God. This is the spirit of the antichrist, which you have heard is coming and even now is already in the world. (1 John 4:1–3)

With these texts, we may be open to the work of angels –

always remembering that, if genuine, they are simply God's messengers: messengers both of comfort, *and of judgment*.

The modern assumption, particularly by writers from within the New Age movement, that angelic experiences are part of a convenient theological trip has no warrant from Scripture.

> Therefore, since we are receiving a kingdom that cannot be shaken, let us be thankful, and so worship God acceptably with reverence and awe, for our "God is a consuming fire". (Hebrews 12:28)

Scripture gives many examples, and includes many texts, of angelic protection; but we will also find that angels are also used as messengers of God's judgment and wrath (see also Chapter 7, throughout).

Is it important to have a theology of angels in today's world?

A very natural answer, particularly taking account of St Paul's warning to the Colossians would be that angels are at best a very speculative part of theology, and that we would be better to concentrate on the fundamentals of the faith.

There are, however, good reasons to take a different view. First, angels feature considerably in the life and teaching of Jesus. Secondly, they appear at many key moments in both the Old and New Testaments. They are an indispensable part of both spiritual warfare and heavenly worship. Thirdly, the Scriptures warn us about the possibility of deception. The pages of Scripture are full of those who have great spiritual gifts, and yet fail to fulfil their spiritual potential. King Saul, King Solomon, Judas Iscariot, Ananias and Sapphira, Demas, all spring to mind. Their stories are both great puzzles, and great warnings. Today when "spirituality" is a great theological buzzword, we need to be especially careful to check spiritual experiences against the gold standard of Scripture. There is a desperate need for spiritual discernment. If someone is "healed" or has a "vision", this is usually thought to be a good thing, yet Jesus clearly warned of the possibility of deception. Nowhere did he advocate a safe, dry religion – far, far from it! – but equally he never taught that everything that claims to be spiritual is from God. All angelic experiences need to be tested. There is one test that above all others helps to distinguish wheat from chaff.

> And having disarmed the powers and authorities, he made a public spectacle of them, triumphing over them by the cross. (Colossians 2:15)

At Calvary, the dark powers were defeated. The Cross was and is the ultimate dividing line between darkness and light. The Cross which separated the penitent thief from his apparently impenitent colleague, separates holy angels from false ones. The holy angels are struck with awe and wonder by the mystery of the Cross; false ones turn away in dismay, and deny that it ever took place, or seek to nullify its cleansing power.

Why do angelic experiences seem so much more common in today's world?

Many different explanations are currently on offer. New-agers like to tell us that angels are appearing to give mankind a last chance to love one another before they destroy the world through pollution, and war. The Age of Aquarius is the world's last chance to sort itself out. They certainly have a point, and rightly tell us to treat the environment with much greater care. The problem is that even the most cursory reading of their literature, which is, of course, very varied, tells us of angels, often called Gabriel and Michael, instructing people to do things that are completely contrary to Scripture. Most of their angels, or spirit guides, are summoned to serve their own ends, whereas in Scripture angels so clearly come as messengers of God.

From a very different perspective, many will doubt the reality of such experiences. Neither angels nor demons fit a rational world-view, and such experiences will be discredited as naïve, medieval, or simply unbelievable. The apparent increase in such experiences can be explained as a curious post-modern phenomena whereby an increasingly confused and desperate world clutches at supernatural straws to try and convince itself that there might, after all, be a meaning, or purpose to life.

For those for whom the teaching and authority of Scripture is normative, there is a natural desire to accept and believe in the existence of angels, and their place in the Divine Order and purpose of the universe and of our world. Some will be very cautious, citing Paul's warning about false miracles, signs and wonders (see 2 Thessalonians 2:9–11), and Jesus' clear teaching that near the end "false Christs and false prophets will appear and perform great signs and miracles to deceive even the elect – if that were possible" (Matthew 24:24). Others will be wildly optimistic, seeing evidence of increased angelic authority as a sign of the nearness of the Parousia, the return of Jesus. They will cite Jesus' words, "Learn this lesson from the fig-tree: As soon as its twigs get tender and its leaves come out, you will know that summer is near. Even so, when you see all these things, you know that it is near, right at the door." (Matthew 24:32–33)

Another, rather simpler, explanation, is that we are living in an age which is far less rational and more open to these sorts of experiences, consequently far more people experience them, and are prepared to talk about them. Also, in the age of the Internet, far more people exchange information about angels. What, in days of the past, would have been very private experiences, now are often in the public domain. It could also be said that books like this one are adding to the exchange of information, and helping some people to be far more open to this aspect of Divine communication.

My own view inclines strongly towards this last explanation. I remain very sceptical about any angelic messages purporting to tell us that the Second Coming is imminent. Such teaching is contrary to the main thrust of Scripture (see earlier, p 54 and elsewhere).

Conclusion

In Europe, at the beginning of the 21st century, we seem to be living in an arid spiritual desert. Jesus deliberately chose the desert (Mark 1:12–13, etc.), so did St Anthony (p 230f) who withdrew from the world into the desert and did mighty battle with the principalities and powers. His ministry bore great fruit and his biographer, St Athanasius[10] (c. 296–373) helped to keep the orthodox Faith at a time of great peril. Anthony's wilderness became a mighty outpost for the Kingdom of God. Our desert, too, could be transformed into a place of crocuses (see Isaiah's great vision in Chapter 35); if we, by faith, are open to the many and varied experiences that our gracious God offers us. For those who, like me, have not experienced direct angelic encounters, there is the wonderful encouragement of Jesus' famous words to Thomas:

> Because you have seen me, you have believed; blessed are those who have not seen and yet have believed. (John 20:29)

Scripture teaches that it is only by grace that we are saved; Scripture (especially at the end of the Sermon on the Mount – Matthew 7:21–23) reminds us that performing and experiencing signs and wonders is no guarantee of having Jesus' approval and acceptance. Angels, and other spiritual beings, should neither be sought or worshipped (Colossians 2:18). However, sometimes, by grace, God's people will experience their help, receive their guidance, or even hear them at worship.[11]

Our arid, rationalistic, post-modern culture needs the refreshment that genuine spiritual encounters always provide.

The Book of Common Prayer[12] has a majestic collect for St Michael and All Angels Day:

O everlasting God, who has ordered and constituted the services of Angels and men in a wonderful order; mercifully grant, that as Thy holy Angels always do thee service in heaven, so by thy appointment they may succour and defend us on earth; through Jesus Christ our Lord.

We, frail, sinful human beings need the service, succour, and defence of angels under the gracious providence of God.

The angels who "long to look into these things" (1 Peter 1:12) understand more fully the purposes of their Creator as they see "how wide and long and high and deep is the love of Christ" (Ephesians 3:18) and begin to understand that this love is given so that fallen man may "know this love that surpasses knowledge" and "be filled to the measure of all the fullness of God".

Now to him who is able to do immeasurably more than all we ask or imagine, according to his power that is at work within us, to him be glory in the church and in Christ Jesus throughout all generations, for ever and ever! Amen. (Ephesians 3:20–21)

The glory of the church depends on the grace of God and the true experience of its people. Angels are a small, but significant, part of that many-splendoured experience.

Praise the Lord, you his angels, you mighty ones who do his bidding, who obey his word. (Psalm 103:20)

Most of the work and worship by angels is confined to the heavenly realms. Their work on earth is largely unseen. If we believe, by faith, in their existence we do well; if, by grace, we are occasionally aware of angels as "ministering spirits sent to serve those who will inherit salvation" (Hebrews 1:14) we are very privileged.

Evidence for the existence of angels, duly tested and weighed, should be welcomed by those who want to defend the truth of the Christian Gospel. Such evidence should give us both a glimpse of future glory, and a solemn warning about the dangers of deception.

I hope that the accounts given in this book are consistent with the experiences and teaching of Scripture, both to its encouragements and its warnings. Without a belief in the existence of angels, we take another dangerous step towards a man-centred rational gospel; with a belief in their existence, we remain faithful to the experience and teaching of Jesus of Nazareth and his Apostles.

In Chaos Theory,[13] it is said, a little flippantly, that one butterfly flapping its wings in South America can trigger a hurricane in Africa. Tiny actions can have dramatic consequences.

In today's post-modern world, it could be said, rather more seriously, that the sight or sense of an angel, winged or not, could so deepen someone's faith that they will be inspired to attempt "something beautiful for God".[14] True spiritual experiences can, and should, have *profound* consequences.

Notes

(1) John V. Taylor, *Enough is Enough*, SCM. A prophetic book written in the 1960s about follies of the current policies of international aid.

(2) For more details, see note 21 to chapter 4 on page 117.

(3) Frances and Kenneth McAll, *The Moon Looks Down,* Darley Anderson, 1987.

(4) Kenneth McAll, *The Healing of the Family Tree,* SPCK, 1982.

(5) Dr Mark Stibbe, *Thinking Clearly about Revival,* Monarch, 1998.

(6) Martin Cavender is national director of Springboard, the Archbishop's initiative for evangelism.

(7) At the time of writing, Clare had returned from a mission trip to Zambia with great exhaustion and a severe bout of malaria.

(8) Oscar Cullmann, *Prayer in the New Testament*, SCM, 1995, p. 3 and throughout this marvellous little book.

(9) See First Epistle of Clement to the Corinthians, Section 5. 1 Clement was written c. AD96.

(10) Athanasius (c. 296 – 373) wrote in the lifetime of the Saint the magnificent biography of St Anthony quoted extensively in Chapter 9.

(11) See Hope Price, *Angels*, Macmillan, 1993, Chapter 7, 'Unseen angels'. There are numerous other examples of people hearing angels singing and also of supernatural sounds in the Revivals in North West Canada and in the Hebrides. See Transformations II Video, and Chapter 5, p. 125.

(12) Book of Common Prayer, p. 283. Collect for St Michael and All Angels (September 29).

(13) This elegant recent mathematical theory deals with cases where classic Newtonian equations break down, and provides a model for wonderfully diverse pieces of mathematics in numerous physical fields. Despite its name, the theory leads to beautiful designs, and almost mystical patterns in apparently chaotic situations. See for instance any popular text on Chaos Theory which can give even non-mathematicians a glimpse of the beauty and design in unlikely scenarios.

(14) The title of Malcolm Muggeridge's book about the work of Mother Teresa of Calcutta.

Select Bibliography

Muthena Paul Alkazraji, *Christ and the Kalashnikov*, Marshall Pickering, 2001 (An interesting account of mission work in Albania, including a number of supernatural incidents).

Bede, *Ecclesiastical History of the English People*, translated by Leo Sherley-Price, Penguin, 1955 (Bede is essential reading for those interested in early English church history – its miracles, failures, and triumphs).

Wallace and Mary Brown, *Angels on the Walls*, Kingsway, 2000 (An inspirational book especially for those struggling with presenting the Gospel in difficult inner-city areas).

Michael Cassidy, *A Witness for Ever*, Hodder and Stoughton, 1995 (The defeat of apartheid in South Africa by prayer, working across racial and political barriers, and signs of God's presence).

Oscar Cullmann, *Prayer in the New Testament*, SCM, 1995 (An intellectual masterpiece completed at the age of 90 by a great theologian).

John Drane, *What is the New Age Still Saying to the Church?* Marshall Pickering, 1999 (Essential reading on the New Age Movement).

Billy Graham, *Angels, God's Secret Agents*, Hodder and Stoughton, 1977 (An old classic, often reprinted).

Michael Green, *I Believe in Satan's Downfall*, Hodder and Stoughton, 1981 (A clear understanding of the nature of the spiritual battle).

Rosemary Guiley, *Encyclopaedia of Angels*, Facts on File, 1996 (A very useful reference book written from no discernible religious standpoint).

John Knight, *Rain in a Dry Land*, Hodder and Stoughton, 1987 (A powerful account of how God changed John's ministry through the power of the Holy Spirit).

Ramsay Macmullen, *Christianising the Roman Empire AD 100–400,* Yale 1984 (An inspirational book about evangelism, accompanied by signs, in the early church).

Michael Mitton, *Restoring the Woven Cord*, Darton, Longman and Todd 1995 (A good introduction to Celtic spirituality).

Dr H. C. Moolenburgh, *Meetings with Angels*, C. W. Daniel, 1992 (Many case histories).

Dr Alison Morgan, *What Happens When We Die?*, Kingsway, 1995 (A very comprehensive view of a difficult subject – obtainable now via Holy Trinity Church Office, Turner St, Leicester LE1 6WY).

Dr Victor Pearce, *Miracles and Angels*, Eagle, 1999 (Much original and unusual documentation of wartime and other incidents).

Hope Price, *Angels*, Macmillan, 1993 (Many case histories).

Mark Stibbe, *Thinking Clearly about Revival*, Monarch, 1998 (Essential reading on an important and neglected subject).

Peter Wagner, *Territorial Spirits*, Sovereign World, 1991 (This and other titles by Wagner form a good introduction to spiritual warfare).

Peter S. Williams, *The Case for Angels*, Paternoster, 2002 (A useful intellectual study).

Brother Yun, *The Heavenly Man*, Monarch, 2002 (The most inspirational book that I've read for many years).

Transformations Videos are distributed by Gateway Christian Media, PO 11905, London NW10 4ZQ and give a good visual account of many deep spiritual matters.

Kingdom Power Trust, via St Andrew's Church, Quickley Lane, Chorleywood, WD3 5AE, distribute *A Glimpse of Eternity – the Story of Ian McCormack*.

Biblical Index